HILLARY RISING

THE POLITICS, PERSONA AND POLICIES OF A NEW AMERICAN DYNASTY

JAMES D. BOYS

Biteback Publishing

First published in Great Britain in 2016 by
Biteback Publishing Ltd
Westminster Tower
3 Albert Embankment
London SE1 7SP
Copyright © James D. Boys 2016

ISBN 978-1-84954-964-6

10 9 8 7 6 5 4 3 2 1

A CIP catalogue record for this book is available from the British Library.

Set in Adobe Caslon and Avenir by Adrian McLaughlin

Printed and bound in Great Britain by
CPI Group (UK) Ltd, Croydon CR0 4YY

CONTENTS

DRAMATIS PERSONAE

Democratic Candidates for President 2016

Hillary Rodham Clinton	US Secretary of State (2009–13)
Lincoln Chafee	Governor of Rhode Island (2011–15)
Martin O'Malley	Governor of Maryland (2007–15)
Bernie Sanders	US Senator from Vermont (2007–)
Jim Webb	US Senator from Virginia (2007–13)

Republican Candidates for President 2016

Jeb Bush	Governor of Florida (1999–2007)
Ben Carson	Director of Paediatric Neurosurgery, Johns Hopkins University Hospital (1984–2013)
Chris Christie	Governor of New Jersey (2010–)
Ted Cruz	US Senator from Texas (2013–)
Carly Fiorina	CEO of Hewlett-Packard (1999–2005)
Jim Gilmore	Governor of Virginia (1998–2002)
Lindsey Graham	US Senator from South Carolina (2003–)
Mike Huckabee	Governor of Arkansas (1996–2007)
Bobby Jindal	Governor of Louisiana (2008–)
John Kasich	Governor of Ohio (2011–)
George Pataki	Governor of New York (1995–2006)
Rand Paul	US Senator from Kentucky (2011–)
Marco Rubio	US Senator from Florida (2011–)

Rick Santorum   US Senator from Pennsylvania (1995–2007)
Donald Trump   CEO of The Trump Organization (1971–)
Scott Walker   Governor of Wisconsin (2011–)

Members of Hillaryland
(2016 unless otherwise stated)

Huma Abedin   Campaign Vice-Chairman
John Anzalone   Pollster
Charlie Baker III   Chief Administrative Officer
Joel Benenson   Chief Strategist and Pollster
Diane Blair   Hillary Clinton's best friend (d. 2002)
James Blair   Husband of Diane Blair
Neisha Blandin   Deputy Director of Grassroots Engagement
Andrew Bleeker   Digital Marketing Advisor
David Binder   Pollster
David Brock   Founder of American Bridge SuperPAC
Tony Carrk   Research Director
Guy Cecil   Political Director, Hillary for President
                            2008
Dennis Cheng   Finance Director
Brynne Craig   Deputy Political Director
Katie Dowd   Digital Director
Patti Solis Doyle   Campaign Manager, Hillary for
                            President 2008
Marc Elias   General Counsel
Brian Fallon   Lead National Press Secretary
Jesse Ferguson   Day-to-Day Press Secretary
Karen Finney   Strategic Communications Advisor/Senior
                            Spokeswoman
Ethan Gelber   Political and Research Consultant
Gary Gensler   Chief Financial Officer
Teddy Goff   Senior Advisor for Digital Strategy
Mandy Grunwald   Senior Advisor for Communications
Stephanie Hannon   Chief Technology Officer
Maya Harris   Senior Policy Advisor
Mike Henry   Deputy Campaign Manager, Hillary for
                            President 2008

Beth Jones	Chief Operating Officer
Don Jones	Pastor and mentor to Hillary Rodham
Elan Kriegel	Director of Analytics
Jesse Lehrich	Rapid Response
David Levine	Deputy Chief Operating Officer
Tracey Lewis	Primary States Director
Jenna Lowenstein	Deputy Digital Director
Jim Margolis	Media Advisor
Marlon Marshall	Director of State Campaigns and Political Engagement
Nick Merrill	Travelling Press Secretary
Jim Messina	Co-Director Priorities USA Super PAC
Cheryl Mills	Senior Advisor
Robby Mook	Campaign Manager
Ann O'Leary	Senior Policy Advisor
Jennifer Palmieri	Communications Director
Adam Parkhomenko	Director of Grassroots Engagement
Mark Penn	Chief Strategist, Hillary for President 2008
John Podesta	Campaign Chairman
Amanda Renteria	Political Director
Ian Sams	Rapid Response
Kristina Schake	Deputy to the Communications Director
Dan Schwerin	Speechwriter
Josh Schwerin	Rapid Response Spokesman
Jake Sullivan	Senior Policy Advisor
Neera Tanden	President of Center for American Progress
Buffy Wicks	Co-Director Priorities USA Super PAC
Maggie Williams	Campaign Manager, Hillary for President 2008
Howard Wolfson	Communications Director, Hillary for President 2008

Brits

Alastair Campbell	Downing Street Press Secretary (1997–2000) Downing Street Communications Director (2000–2003)

William Hague	UK Foreign Secretary (2010–14)
David Miliband	UK Foreign Secretary (2007–10)
Harold Macmillan	Prime Minister (1957–63)
Ed Miliband	Labour Party Leader (2010–15)
Jonathan Powell	Chief of Staff to Tony Blair (1997–2007)
Shaun Woodward	Secretary of State for Northern Ireland (2007–10)

Current US Office Holders

Samuel Alito	US Supreme Court Justice (2006–)
Jerry Brown	Governor of California (1975–83, 2011–)
Sam Brownback	Governor of Kansas (2011–) US Senator from Kansas (1996–2011)
Jim Cooper	Congressman from Tennessee (1983–95, 2003–)
Bill de Blasio	Mayor of New York City (2014–)
Ron Johnson	US Senator from Wisconsin (2011–)
Sheila Jackson Lee	Congresswoman from Texas (1995–)
John McCain	US Senator from Arizona (1987–) Republican Party candidate for President (2008)
Claire McCaskill	US Senator from Missouri (2007–)
Harry Reid	US Senator from Nevada (1987–) Senate Majority Leader (2007–15)
John Roberts	Chief Justice of the United States (2005–)
Charles Schumer	US Senator from New York (1999–)
Elizabeth Warren	US Senator from Massachusetts (2013–)

Past US Office Holders

Dean Acheson	US Secretary of State (1949–53)
James Baker	US Secretary of State (1989–92)
Edward Brooke	US Senator from Massachusetts (1967–79)
Zbigniew Brzezinski	National Security Advisor (1977–81)

Pat Buchanan	White House Communications Director (1985–87)
Dale Bumpers	US Senator from Arkansas (1975–99)
	Governor of Arkansas (1971–75)
Prescott Bush	US Senator from Connecticut (1952–63)
Howard Dean	Governor of Vermont (1991–2003)
Bob Dole	US Senator from Kansas (1969–96)
	Republican Party presidential candidate (1996)
Michael Dukakis	Governor of Massachusetts (1975–79, 1983–91)
	Democratic Party presidential candidate (1988)
John Edwards	US Senator from North Carolina (1999–2005)
	Democratic Party vice-presidential candidate (2004)
William Fulbright	US Senator from Arkansas (1945–74)
Rudy Giuliani	Major of New York City (1994–2001)
Barry Goldwater	US Senator from Arizona (1953–65, 1969–87)
	Republican Party presidential candidate (1964)
Edward Kennedy	US Senator from Massachusetts (1962–2009)
Joseph P. Kennedy, Sr	US Ambassador to UK (1938–40)
Robert F. Kennedy	US Senator from New York (1965–68)
	US Attorney General (1961–64)
Henry Kissinger	US Secretary of State (1973–77)
Melvin Laird	US Defense Secretary (1969–73)
Rick Lazio	Congressman from New York (1993–2001)
Joe Lieberman	US Senator from Connecticut (1989–2013)
	Democratic Party vice-presidential candidate (2000)
Eugene McCarthy	US Senator from Minnesota (1959–71)
Joe McCarthy	US Senator from Wisconsin (1947–57)

George McGovern	US Senator from South Dakota (1963–81)
	Democratic Party presidential candidate (1972)
Walter Mondale	US Vice-President (1977–81)
	US Senator from Minnesota (1964–76)
Daniel Patrick Moynihan	US Senator from New York (1977–2001)
Sandra Day O'Connor	Associate Justice, US Supreme Court (1981–2006)
Bob Packwood	US Senator from Oregon (1969–95)
Sarah Palin	Governor of Alaska (2006–09)
	Republican Party vice-presidential candidate (2008)
Rick Perry	Governor of Texas (2000–2015)
Nelson Rockefeller	Vice-President of the United States (1974–77)
	Governor of New York (1959–73)
Mitt Romney	Republican Party presidential candidate (2012)
	Governor of Massachusetts (2003–07)
Brent Scowcroft	US National Security Advisor (1975–77, 1989–93)
John Spencer	Major of Yonkers, New York (1996–2004)
Adlai E. Stevenson II	US Ambassador to the United Nations (1961–65)
Paul Tsongas	US Senator from Massachusetts (1979–85)

Other Significant Figures

Saul Alinsky	Community Organiser
	Author of *Rules for Radicals* (1971)
Bill Ayres	Co-founder of The Weather Underground
Marian Wright Edelman	President and Founder of the Children's Defense Fund
Hamid Karzai	President of Afghanistan (2004–14)
Sergey Lavrov	Foreign Minister of Russia (2004–)
Dmitry Medvedev	Prime Minister of Russia (2012–)
	President of Russia (2008–12)

Toni Morrison	US novelist and Professor Emeritus at Princeton University
Mohamed Morsi	President of Egypt (2012–13)
Hosni Mubarak	President of Egypt (1981–2011)
Ross Perot	Reform Party presidential candidate (1996)
	Independent presidential candidate (1992)
Anwar Sadat	President of Egypt (1970–81)
Alan Schechter	Professor Emeritus of Political Science, Wellesley College
Boris Yeltsin	President of Russia (1991–99)

Arkansas

John David Danner	Senior aide to Governor Bill Clinton (1978–80)
John Paul Hammerschmidt	Congressman from Arkansas (1967–93)
Rudy Moore	Senior aide to Governor Bill Clinton (1978–80)
David Pryor	US Senator from Arkansas (1979–97)
	Governor of Arkansas (1975–79)
	Congressman from Arkansas (1966–73)
Stephen A. Smith	Chief of Staff to Governor Bill Clinton (1978–80)
Frank White	Governor of Arkansas (1981–83)
Betsey Wright	Chief of Staff to Governor Bill Clinton (1982–89)

Members of Bill Clinton's Administration (1993–2001)

Madeleine Albright	US Ambassador to the United Nations (1993–97)
	US Secretary of State (1997–2001)
Sandy Berger	National Security Advisor (1997–2001)
Sidney Blumenthal	Assistant and Senior Advisor to President Clinton (1997–2001)

James Carville   Clinton '92 Campaign Director
Warren Christopher   US Secretary of State (1993–97)
Vincent Foster   White House Counsel (1993)
David Gergen   Counsellor to the President (1993–94)
Al Gore   Vice-President of the United States
                             (1993–2001)
                             Democratic Party presidential
                             candidate (2000)
Stan Greenberg   Pollster, Clinton for President (1992)
Morton Halperin   Director of Policy Planning, State
                             Department (1998–2001)
Webster Hubbell   Associate Attorney General (1993–94)
Harold Ickes   Assistant to the President & White
                             House Deputy Chief of Staff
                             (1993–97)
Anthony Lake   US National Security Advisor (1993–97)
Thomas 'Mack' McLarty   White House Chief of Staff (1993–94)
Ira Magaziner   Partner in Hillary Clinton's Task
                             Force to Reform Health Care
Dick Morris   Pollster, Clinton for President (1996)
Bernard Nussbaum   White House Counsel (1993–94)
Joseph Nye   Assistant Secretary of Defense for
                             International Security (1994–95)
Janet Reno   US Attorney General (1993–2001)
Nancy Soderberg   Deputy National Security Advisor
                             (1995–96)
                             Special Assistant for National Security
                             Affairs (1993–94)
George Stephanopoulos   Director of Communications/Senior
                             Advisor on Policy & Strategy (1993–96)

Members of George W. Bush's Administration (2001–09)

Condoleezza Rice   US Secretary of State (2005–09)
                             US National Security Advisor (2001–05)
Karl Rove   Special Advisor to the President (2001–07)
Donald Rumsfeld   US Secretary of Defense
                             (2001–06)

Members of Barack Obama's Administration (2009–)

David Axelrod	Senior Advisor to the President (2009–11)
Joe Biden	Vice-President of the United States (2009–)
Julián Castro	US Secretary of Housing and Urban Development (2014–) Mayor of San Antonio (2009–14)
Rahm Emanuel	Mayor of Chicago (2011–) White House Chief of Staff (2009–10)
Robert M. Gates	US Secretary of Defense (2006–11)
Gary Hart	US Special Envoy to Northern Ireland (2014–) US Senator from Colorado (1975–87)
Richard Holbrooke	US Special Envoy for Afghanistan and Pakistan (2009–10)
James 'Jim' L. Jones	US National Security Advisor (2009–10)
Caroline Kennedy	US Ambassador to Japan (2013–)
John Kerry	US Secretary of State (2013–) Democratic Party presidential candidate (2004)
Stanley McChrystal	US Army (ret.) Joint Special Operations Command Commander US and ISAF in Afghanistan (2009–10)
Michael McFaul	US Ambassador to Russia (2012–14)
Judith McHale	Under Secretary of State for Public Diplomacy & Public Affairs (2009–11)
George J. Mitchell, Jr	US Special Envoy for Middle East Peace (2009–11)
David Petraeus	Director of the CIA (2011–12) Commander of ISAF (2010–11) Commander of US Central Command (2008–10)
Samantha Power	US Ambassador to the UN (2013–)
Susan Rice	US National Security Advisor (2013–) US Ambassador to the UN (2009–13)

Philippe Reines	Deputy Assistant Secretary of State/Senior Advisor to Hillary Clinton (2009–13)
Alec J. Ross	Senior Advisor for Innovation, US State Department (2009–13)
Dennis Ross	Special Assistant to the President and Senior Director for the Central Region (2009–11)
	Special Advisor for the Persian Gulf and Southwest Asia (2009)
Anne-Marie Slaughter	Director of Policy Planning, State Department (2009–11)
Christopher Stevens	US Ambassador to Libya (2012)
Ann Stock	Assistant Secretary of State of Educational and Cultural Affairs (2010–13)

HILLARY RISING

By any measure, Hillary Diane Rodham Clinton has already lived an extraordinary life. She was the first student at Wellesley College to deliver a commencement speech, the first woman on the Walmart board of directors, the first First Lady with an office in the West Wing of the White House, the first First Lady to seek and win elected office, the first Secretary of State to visit more than 100 countries, and the first woman to seriously challenge for the presidency of the United States. In addition, she was the first First Lady to hold a postgraduate degree and the first First Lady to win a Grammy Award. She has also graced the cover of *Time* magazine more than any woman in history. Only because her skills are so formidable, her talent so obvious and her ambitions so clear, does this record of achievement not seem adequate. The one role that has eluded her to date is the American presidency. The presidential election of 2016 will reveal whether or not this is to be her destiny.

Having exploded onto the national and international stage in 1992, Hillary Clinton has served in one capacity or another in Washington, DC for twenty-four years: as First Lady, Senator and Secretary of State, as well as sitting on the board of directors at the Clinton Foundation. In these successive roles, Hillary has already held office in Washington, DC far longer than her husband, who was term-limited to his eight-year presidency. Now, with her second quest to claim the White House underway, she has positioned herself to eclipse her husband's achievements and emerge as a significant figure in her own right in US politics and history, both in terms of her electoral achievements and her potential to break the gender lock on the White House.

Hillary Rising explores the ascent to the pinnacle of American power by this remarkable woman. It reveals the key stages in her political career and the factors that have influenced her development from a child of conservative Republican parents to the Democratic Party's presumptive candidate for President of the United States. By tracing Hillary Clinton's path from a Republican adolescent and a student activist, through to her time as First Lady, Senator and Secretary of State, *Hillary Rising* addresses the policies she has endorsed, the personalities that have influenced her and the politics that have either helped or hindered her path to power. What emerges from this exploration of Hillary Clinton's past is the importance of a small number of core principles upon which her career and political ideology are based.

Hillary Rising does not claim to be a complete biography of Hillary Clinton's life and career. Instead, it addresses areas that have been overlooked in previous studies, which have fallen into three camps. The first is memoir-driven, written for posterity rather than the general population. They make important additions to libraries and for scholarly research, but are all too often impenetrable and seek to rewrite history from the vantage point of the author. Examples include Hillary Clinton's own memoirs, *Living History* (Simon & Schuster, 2003) and *Hard Choices* (Simon & Schuster, 2014). The second camp either demonises or lionises Hillary with regard to the polarising impact she has had in American politics. Such books include *The Seduction of Hillary Rodham* (The Free Press, 1996) by David Brock, *The First Partner* (William Morrow, 1999) by Joyce Milton and *Hillary's Choice* (Random House, 1999) by Gail Sheehy. The final camp focuses exclusively on one element of Hillary Clinton's career to the exclusion of all others, thereby presenting a narrow portrait of her impact on American political life. Examples include Kim Ghattas's *The Secretary* (Time Books, 2013), Jonathan Allen and Amie Parnes's *HRC* (Hutchinson, 2014) and Sally Bedell Smith's *For the Love of Politics: The Clintons in the White House* (Aurum Press, 2008).

Hillary Rising aims to distinguish itself from these accounts. It lays out the route that Hillary Clinton has taken from her childhood to the gates of the White House and offers readers an insight into what has driven her on her journey. It draws from a variety of sources including interviews, diaries and newly declassified materials that have only recently become available to trace the policies, personalities and politics that have defined Hillary's career and helped shape her character, with the aim of providing an insight into what can be expected if she becomes the first female President of the United States.

To understand Hillary Clinton's place in modern American politics, it is vital to appreciate the journey that she has taken, from her birth in Illinois through her formative years at college, her marriage to Bill Clinton and her time in the public arena as an advocate for the rights of women and children in particular. Accordingly, *Hillary Rising* considers the world into which Hillary Diane Rodham was born in 1947, explaining the conservative nature of the United States at that time, the impact that this had on her upbringing and the country, and how this prepared her for life at Wellesley College. It was here that Hillary Rodham first entered the public consciousness, becoming the first student to deliver the commencement address and subsequently appearing in the pages of *Life* magazine. Her time at university saw Hillary Rodham transition from a young Republican to the girlfriend of a future Democratic Governor and President, Bill Clinton, whom she met at Yale Law School in 1971.

After exploring Hillary's formative years, her time in Arkansas must be considered. Indeed, the rationale for her decision to move to one of the poorest states in the union at a time when she could have taken lucrative positions in Washington, DC or New York must be understood in an effort to dismiss oft-repeated allegations regarding the nature of her relationship with Bill Clinton. As a young, remarkably well-educated northerner, the transition to Arkansas was not easy, and it is important to consider the manner in which Hillary Clinton developed during the years she served as First Lady of Arkansas, the responsibilities she assumed and the success and failures she encountered during this time, as they provide a barometer for future events. Never was this more apparent than during the eight years that Hillary served as First Lady of the United States, a time that perfectly encapsulated the undulating relationship she had with her husband, as well as the one she had with the American public.

Hillary Clinton's initial time as First Lady of the United States was dominated by efforts to implement healthcare reform and the flaws in this effort reveal much about her and how she might function as President. The figure of Monica Lewinsky is unavoidable. However, she will not be addressed in the context of her affair with Bill Clinton, but instead by her impact on Hillary and her career after her husband's presidency. *Hillary Rising* takes the contentious position that the humiliation experienced by Hillary Clinton was essential for her to emerge as a candidate for the Senate in 2000, a move that established her own political power base for her future presidential bids. It is clear that Bill Clinton's affair with Monica Lewinsky had a direct impact on the Democratic Party's eligibility in 2000, aiding George W. Bush's election as President, and thereby contributing to the conditions that led to the Iraq War. If this is true, then by extension it must be acknowledged that the affair provided the public expressions of support for

Hillary Clinton that enabled her run for the Senate in 2000 and could, therefore, very well lead directly to the first female presidency in the history of the United States.

The many highs and all-too-public lows of Hillary's time in the White House provided the platform for her next endeavour, as a United States Senator from New York. Her years in the Senate risk being overlooked due to the roles that preceded and followed it, but they demonstrate her ability to work with others and achieve political results, both essential qualities in a President. It is important, therefore, to explore the years that Hillary spent representing the Empire State to understand what she did, how she did it and how she was perceived by those around her. From the moment she won election to the Senate, Hillary Clinton was expected to run for the White House, which she did in 2008. What no one expected, however, was that she would lose to a virtually unknown African-American Senator. To appreciate the campaign that Hillary will wage in her attempt to secure the presidency in 2016, it is vital to understand what occurred in her previous campaign: what went right and what went spectacularly wrong. If she is to persevere in 2016, personal, structural and political flaws from the 2008 campaign must be acknowledged and overcome.

Following the disappointment of her 2008 campaign, Hillary Clinton was appointed Secretary of State by President Obama. This four-year period saw her travel almost a million miles as she circumnavigated the globe advancing the cause of the United States in an effort to regain hearts and minds following the perceived failings of the George W. Bush years. This constituted a remarkable opportunity for Hillary to establish solid foreign-policy credentials with which to launch a second campaign for the presidency. Any consideration of her potential presidency must evaluate this time period with care and recognise the role that she has played as a global ambassador for the United States.

Having served four years as Secretary of State, Hillary Clinton stepped back from electoral politics and the role of Cabinet officer to recharge her batteries and consider the future. During this time she prepared her second memoir, *Hard Choices*, and joined the Clinton Foundation, a vehicle for global philanthropy established by Bill Clinton shortly after he left the White House. Doing so raised a series of questions, some old and some new, about the role of the foundation, its appropriateness and its relationship with foreign governments.

Irrespective of the outcome of the 2016 presidential election, the impact of the Clinton family on American political life since 1992 has given rise to speculation about the emergence of a new American political dynasty. Following in the footsteps of the Adamses, Kennedys, Rockefellers, Bushes and Roosevelts, the public fascination with powerful political families appears to be at odds with the founding principles of American political life, premised as the latter is on the concepts of equality and meritocracy. Indeed, the appropriateness of placing the Clinton family in this pantheon of American leadership is open to speculation. To date there has only been one generation of Clintons who has held office, albeit it at a senior level, but never at the same time; as Bill Clinton's elected career ended, Hillary Clinton's began.

Despite this, talk of a Clinton dynasty continues to thrive, with some even looking ahead to a political career for Chelsea Clinton, whose marriage and subsequent child have enabled Hillary to embrace a new role on the 2016 campaign trail that may prove decisive: grandmother.

If 'pragmatism' best described Bill Clinton, then perhaps 'endurance' best defines Hillary. Her career to date has been a seemingly endless journey of challenges, both personal and professional, and her tale is one of achievement, overcoming obstacles and heartbreak in the quest to push the boundaries of what is possible. She has seen her most precious ambitions rise and ebb, seen friends fall by the wayside and has become simultaneously the most vilified and admired woman on the planet. Married to the most powerful man in the world, she became the most publically wronged wife in the world, yet used this experience to forge her own unique role in American political life. By the dawn of the 2016 presidential electoral cycle, Hillary Clinton, remarkably enough, has become the grand dame of the Democratic Party; having arrived in Washington, DC in her mid-forties, she finds herself vying to become America's second-oldest President, bested only by Ronald Reagan.

The extent to which she can position herself within the Democratic Party, and within the nation, as a viable candidate for the presidency remains to be seen. Vilified by the right and never entirely trusted by the left, it was David Brock, whose initial writings caused so much damage to the Clinton presidency, who concluded in 1996: 'Hillary should be approached as neither an icon or a demon but as a real person who has had a remarkable life and, it could be argued, has been more important to America than her husband.'[1] Almost twenty years later, Hillary Clinton's achievements have become all the more pronounced. However, when she ran for the presidency in 2008 many Democrats feared a sense of inevitability about her approach to the candidacy. In 2015, little has changed, as some within the party still hanker after a competition, not a coronation, seemingly more determined to be idealistically pure than victorious in the general election. However, as Hillary Rodham noted in her 1969 Wellesley College commencement speech: 'We arrived at Wellesley and we found, as all of us have found, that there was a gap between expectations and realities. But it wasn't a discouraging gap … It just inspired us to do something about that gap.'[2] Almost fifty years, and countless personal and political reinventions later, Hillary Rodham Clinton finds herself facing, and once again needing to overcome, the gap between expectations and realities in her quest for the presidency of the United States.

CHAPTER 1

THE GOLDWATER GIRL

To truly appreciate Hillary Clinton's political and personal journey, it is vital to understand where she started. She was born into a Republican household in the heartland of the United States, and raised as a child during the golden years of Eisenhower's America. Far from being nurtured as the quintessential left-wing firebrand that Republican opponents and Tea Party activists portray her to be, Hillary Rodham was born to middle-class, hard-working parents and raised in a prosperous suburb of Chicago. Her transition to a more liberal persona began when she enrolled at Wellesley College in Massachusetts in 1965. It was at Yale Law School, however, where she eventually met the person who did the most to change the direction of her life: her future husband, Bill Clinton. Despite being labelled by opponents as radical members of the '60s generation, the quintessentially conservative nature of both Bill and Hillary Clinton ensured that neither of them was particularly rebellious as students or engaged in illegal activity at the height of the anti-Vietnam War movement. They certainly didn't 'turn on, tune in and drop out' as many of their generation did. Instead, they worked hard, studied hard, were embraced by the powers that be at the nation's top universities and sought to advance social change through peaceful participation in the electoral process. As she moved from her parents' home in Illinois to university in Massachusetts, to law school in Connecticut and to married life in Arkansas, family and faith remained at the centre of Hillary Rodham's life, as each move caused her to adjust to both her new role and to the differing expectations about the role of women in American public life.

THE STATE OF THE UNION: 1947

The United States into which Hillary Diane Rodham was born on 26 October 1947 appears on the surface to be a different country from the one she may well end up leading in January 2017. Often described as a golden age following the successful resolution of the Second World War and before the radical upheavals and assassinations of the 1960s, the era has been granted an almost mythical status. This was the height of America's post-war years, as the baby boomers came into the world, populating Norman Rockwell vistas of leafy suburbs where children could play safely, raised by stay-at-home wives whose husbands could earn a living wage and see the benefits of their hard work. Presided over by Harry Truman and Dwight D. Eisenhower, the late '40s and 1950s are portrayed as a time of plenty, seemingly free from the tumultuous global events that had dominated the 1930s and from the social tensions that erupted in the 1960s.

The United States during this time period was noted for its conservatism, its conformity and its consensus politics, presided over by the man who was, at the time, America's oldest President. Dwight D. Eisenhower had been Supreme Allied Commander in Europe and had overseen the D-Day landings in 1944. The success of this mission, and his media-friendly personality, propelled him to the status of a national hero, and finally to the presidency in 1953. As the first general to become President since Ulysses S. Grant in 1869, Eisenhower brought a conservative approach to the White House, becoming the first Republican President in twenty years.

President Eisenhower was a grandfatherly figure who appeared to transcend the political divide to such a degree that the harmony and bipartisanship of the era was dubbed 'The Age of Consensus'. Internationally, the late '40s and 1950s saw the implementation of the Marshall Plan to rebuild war-torn Europe and the establishment of NATO to defend Western Europe from the Soviet-backed Warsaw Pact alliance, while at home returning GIs set about rebuilding their lives and the nation in what became the Baby Boom era. In 1940, America's population had been 131 million. By the time of Hillary Rodham's birth in 1947 it had reached 144 million. By 1960, it had soared to 179 million, an increase of 48 million in just twenty years. This had been fuelled in part by a drop in average marriage ages. When Hillary was born, the United States celebrated marriage as 'the natural state for adults' and had an average marrying age of twenty-two for men and 20.3 for women, the lowest since records began in 1890.

With this population explosion came an increased demand for schools, transportation and services, which developed as the United States invested heavily in infrastructure and transportation systems. The Highways Act of 1956 set about connecting America's cities with gleaming new road systems to satisfy the nation's motorists, as well as to provide escape routes from urban areas in case of nuclear war with the Soviet Union. More roads were needed since car sales had risen dramatically with high employment rates. The US Bureau of Labor Statistics reported that the average national unemployment rate in the United States for 1947 was 3.9 per cent, well below what became the average unemployment rate of 5.83 per cent between 1948 and 2015, and that the average hourly wage in 1947 was $4.88. The United States during the 1940s and '50s, it appeared, was peaceful, prosperous and powerful.

At that time, Hillary Rodham's home state of Illinois was a microcosm of the nation, with a population of 8.3 million in 1947. Despite the large proportion of country-club Republicans, the dense Democratic population of Chicago saw to it that Democrats ran the state, ensuring a solid grip on power for successive generations of the Daley family. It also ensured that Democrats held the seat of power in the Governor's mansion, a position held in the late

1940s and early '50s by the esteemed liberal intellectual Adlai E. Stevenson. Stevenson was the grandson of a former Vice-President of the United States and was the unsuccessful Democratic Party candidate for President in 1952 and 1956, losing heavily to Eisenhower on both occasions. The political split between the decidedly Democratic Chicago and the more Republic rural element of Illinois reflected not only the divisions within the Rodham household, but also the political distinction of New York State, which Hillary Clinton represented in the Senate following the election of 2000.

Culturally, the United States in the 1950s was a time of hoop skirts, bubblegum and conformity, but it was also one of growing, simmering tension, political intimidation and effective apartheid for African-Americans, who were forced to live in segregated communities and barred from much of the new housing being constructed to accommodate the baby boomers that Hillary Clinton came to symbolise in later years. It was a time of great abundance in the United States, of seemingly untamed possibility for many, yet also one of great conservative conformity that appeared to dictate forms of political and social behaviour that constricted many and confused others. It was no time to question authority, although, as the decade wore on, such questioning came to be channelled through films such as *Rebel Without a Cause* and *The Wild One* and the 'beat generation' literature of Allen Ginsberg and Jack Kerouac.

The furies that exploded in the 1960s were fermenting throughout the era as the racial, social, gender and cultural tensions that defined the coming decades were beginning to rise. Even the overseas struggle in Vietnam that defined the 1960s had an earlier incarnation at this time in the Korean War, which divided opinion and resulted in an unsatisfactory stalemate. The political landscape was scarred by the charges of Senator McCarthy, ensuring that Eisenhower's consensus was driven, at least in part, by fear of deviation from the accepted mainstream. Conformity was in, consensus was mandated, and rebellion was quelled.

EDUCATING HILLARY

Hillary Rodham grew up in a house with strong transatlantic ties. Her father, Hugh, had English and Welsh heritage, while her mother Dorothy's family background could be traced to France, Scotland, Wales and England. Hugh Rodham, who had previously worked in a coal mine, owned a successful drapery and dominated the household with his strong anti-communist views and strict fiscal beliefs in thrift and probity, not uncommon for a generation that had experienced the Great Depression. His experience of the 1930s ensured that he routinely highlighted the plight of America's destitute underclass to his children to warn them against the folly of laziness and of the importance of hard work.

Hugh Rodham was averse to debt and credit and refused to use credit cards, even when his daughter was First Lady of the United States. Her father's strict belief in thrift ensured that Hillary Rodham grew up in a house in which the heating was switched off in the evening, which was far from ideal with winter night-time temperatures in Illinois averaging 18 degrees Fahrenheit. His thrifty reputation was matched by his gruff demeanour and seeming inability to lavish praise on anyone, even when his children exceeded at school or at sports. All accounts of Hillary's father portray a strict, reclusive, moody man with few kind words of support for anyone, about anything, irrespective of what may have been achieved. His children were denied a weekly allowance, even after completing chores, and straight-A report cards from school received sarcastic retorts regarding the apparent simplicity of the subjects. Hugh Rodham's bluntness and inability to conceal his inner feelings manifested themselves in his daughter, and, as subsequent chapters reveal, this came to cause problems for Hillary and those around her when she was required to interact with the world's media and her political opponents.

While Hugh Rodham ran the business, Dorothy remained at home, as was the expectation at the time, and raised three children, of whom Hillary was the eldest and the only daughter. Dorothy Rodham had great hopes for Hillary, who served as a vessel for her own stalled aspirations. As a child of the Great Depression, Dorothy had barely completed her school education and certainly had no initial career of her own due to family and societal pressures. As a mother, she was openly disappointed when Sandra Day O'Connor was appointed to the United States Supreme Court in 1981, meaning that her daughter could not be the first woman to serve on the highest court in the land. Her mother was determined Hillary must succeed in life based on merit and hard work, and not on superficial attributes such as clothes or make-up, all of which were frowned upon by Dorothy. The combination of her mother's puritanical approach to dress and her father's austere spending habits ensured that Hillary's senior prom dance was something of an underwhelming experience; a plain white dress was only provided on the understanding that her parents chaperoned her to the event. Unsurprisingly, her classmates at the time saw Hillary Rodham as rather unattractive and unfashionable. Even years later, as First Lady of Arkansas, Dorothy Rodham's influence was still apparent in her daughter's appearance, causing negative connotations for her husband and his election hopes.

Shortly after the birth of Hillary Rodham's older brother Hugh Jr, the family moved to the district of Park Ridge, a Republican stronghold in keeping with Hugh Rodham's conservative values and aspirations. Once there, however, the family tended to remain somewhat introverted. Dorothy Rodham was involved with her local church and taught Sunday school, but Hugh Rodham's reluctance to get involved appears to have been a more accurate reflection of their social involvement with the community. He was known to sit alone and aloof, even at local baseball games, tradition-ally known for their all-American social interaction and sense of community spirit.

In a house dominated by her father and with two younger broth-ers, Hillary Rodham grew up as something of a tomboy, playing softball and touch football, ice-skating and rooting for the Chicago Cubs baseball team. This was, in part, driven by her parents' encour-agement for her to participate with, and often beat, the local boys at their own games. It was while at school that Hillary Rodham developed her life-long love of swimming, which she continues to enjoy as a form of escape and relaxation to this day. Despite these outdoor pursuits, it was in the classroom that Hillary Rodham excelled, though this led to a reputation for being something of a teacher's pet at school. On one occasion she handed in a 75-page paper when no more than twenty had been expected from her. According to classmate Kenneth Reece, 'She was confident and had strong convictions and was able to follow through on them. She saw all sides of an issue, and she was able to integrate those and then make a judgement.'[3]

As a child, therefore, Hillary appeared eager to please her father, who had great difficulty expressing any form of positive emotion, and became the embodiment of her mother's stalled ambitions. Although never succeeding in her early desire to become an astronaut, she certainly succeeded in fulfilling her parent's ultimate aspiration that she be self-sufficient and successful in her chosen field.

KEEPING THE FAITH

In addition to imbuing her with these attributes, Hugh and Dorothy Rodham raised their only daughter in a religious household, which has had a profound and continuing impact on Hillary's life and career. Despite widespread international perceptions that the Republican Party has monopolised religion and has routinely portrayed Democrats as being godless and lacking in moral virtue, Hillary Clinton is a dedicated Methodist, a denomination that accounts for 6 per cent of the US adult population. Although she does not wear her faith on her sleeve, it is important to her, in a quiet, private way that has, on occasion, manifested itself in public. As she told the *New York Times*, her faith in salvation is 'there all the time. It's not something you have to think about, you believe it. You have a faith centre out of which the rest flows.'[4]

When David Margolick of *Vanity Fair* interviewed Tony Blair in 2003 about religion and its importance in his relationship with President George W. Bush, Downing Street Director of Communications Alastair Campbell interrupted the proceedings and insisted that, in the United Kingdom, 'We don't do God.'[5] Regardless of the political or religious merits of this statement, it is singularly not true for the United States. In 1966, John Lennon had remarked that the Beatles were 'more popular than Jesus now. I don't know which will go first, rock 'n' roll or Christianity. Jesus was all right but his disciples were thick and ordinary. It's them twisting it that ruins it for me.'[6] The backlash that greeted this remark when it was reported in the United States revealed the influence that those of a religious persuasion hold over both the cultural and the political spheres in the United States. To demean them or their beliefs is to risk incurring career-ending wrath.

The Constitution of the United States specifically prohibits the establishment of a national church and, therefore, the separation of church and state is absolute, designed to address what were seen as flaws in the UK system of government. Despite these clearly defined parameters, however, religion plays a vital role in American political life and in the life of its politicians. America has had Presidents of differing political backgrounds and traditions, as well as differing ethnicities. So far, however, it has not elected either a woman or an open agnostic. Indeed, the only non-Protestant President to date has been John F. Kennedy, who was forced to repeatedly declare that he would not place religion above the Constitution, and who was assassinated in his first term in office in a southern state, where he was loathed as a Catholic and a Communist sympathiser.

The United States has long been viewed as a melting pot of different races and religions, a place where many have travelled to become one people: Americans. Despite this apparent unity of purpose, however, religious divides continue to exist. As Dr Martin Luther King lamented in 1953, 'The most segregated hour of Christian America is 11 o'clock on Sunday morning.'[7] Thirty-seven per cent of Americans identify themselves as Protestant and 23 per cent as Catholic. Members of the Jewish and Mormon faiths account for 2 per cent each of the population, while less than 1 per cent of the population identifies as Muslim (0.9 per cent), Buddhist (0.7 per cent), Hindu (0.7 per cent) or Jehovah's Witnesses (0.8 per cent). With over 90 per cent of the population professing a personal belief in God, and 37 per cent regularly attending church on Sunday, religion and the views of the religious cannot be dismissed in the United States, and it is no place for a politician to keep their faith private. There is an expectation that politicians be open and faithful in their relationship with Christ, even if not in their personal relationships.

Hillary Rodham had been raised in the Methodist faith and was a regular attendee at the First Methodist Church and Bible class. In 1961, aged fourteen, she met the newly ordained Reverend Don Jones, appointed as Youth Minister at her church. He took a progressive approach in his attempt to reach the younger members of his congregation, drawing on folk music, poetry and movies to make religious studies as relevant as possible. Just as her father had previously driven her and her brothers to the slums of Chicago to see for themselves the dangers of sloth and laziness, Revd Jones arranged for Hillary and her church group to visit less affluent areas of the state to teach compassion and charity towards others. Such visits inspired Hillary's commitment to the needs of children and her belief in the importance of a strong family life.

Revd Jones took his students to hear guest lectures and sermons, including one by Saul Alinsky, the acknowledged father of modern community organising, who proved to be highly influential for Hillary.[8] In April 1962, Revd Jones arranged for the fifteen-year-old Hillary Rodham to join 1,000 other people in the Chicago Orchestra Hall to hear Dr Martin Luther King Jr deliver a sermon, 'Remaining Awake Through a Great Revolution'. She was personally introduced to Dr King and shook hands with him. Just as her future husband's meeting in the Rose Garden of the White House with President Kennedy in 1963 is attributed to having awakened his political ambition, Hillary Rodham noted that until meeting Dr King she had only been 'dimly aware of the social revolution' that was breaking out across America.[9] Dr King's warning of the dangers of ignoring those in need resonated deeply with her.

Revd Jones remained a mentor to Hillary long after she left for college and she wrote him letters detailing her progress and seeking guidance on issues of politics, philosophy and, eventually, social activism on campus. In later life, much has been made of

Hillary's determination to retain her maiden name as a symbol of her independence and steadfastness. Yet, this is also true in regard to her religious faith: raised in Illinois as a Methodist, she retained her commitment to the religion when she moved to Arkansas and married a man of the Southern Baptist tradition, surrendering neither her name nor her religion in the process.

UNIVERSITY LIFE

By the time Hillary Rodham came of age and started university, the great racial and social tensions that defined the 1960s in the United States were erupting. She attended the all-female Wellesley College in Massachusetts, arriving in the autumn of 1965. Despite the chaos that was breaking out across the nation as inner cities burned and anger mounted over the start of the land war in Vietnam, she remained removed from the radical nature of the times, hidden away on a college campus where the all-female student body was expected to dress for dinner, adhere to a strict honour code and obey a midnight curfew. It was a system that Hillary arrived embracing, but soon set about challenging with an increasing openness as her politics evolved and she left her father's strict conservatism behind once and for all.

Although seen by opponents as a radical, left-leaning ideologue, Hillary arrived at Wellesley carrying a copy of Barry Goldwater's *Conscience of a Conservative* and quickly became the president of the university's Young Republican Club. She identified with the moderate wing of the Republican Party, personified by New York

Governor Nelson Rockefeller. Throughout her first three years at
college, Hillary Rodham remained a Republican and interned on
Capitol Hill in the summer of 1968 for Wisconsin Congressman
Melvin Laird, who became President Nixon's Defense Secretary six
months later. She even attended the 1968 Republican Convention in
Miami that nominated Richard Nixon, a remarkable turn of events
considering the turmoil that the United States experienced that
year and an incredible one given her eventual role in the President's
impeachment process only a few years later.

It is clear that Hillary Rodham was experiencing a political transformation, for in the same year she also travelled to New Hampshire
to volunteer for the anti-war candidate Senator Eugene McCarthy,
whose success in securing 42 per cent of the vote in the Granite
State prompted Senator Robert F. Kennedy to enter the race and
contributed to President Johnson's decision not to seek re-election.
Intriguingly, one name that appears noticeably absent from any
consideration of Hillary's upbringing is Kennedy. Considering the
impact of her future husband's meeting with President Kennedy in
1963, his social, cultural and political impact on the nation, the significance of his murder and the subsequent career and assassination
of his brother, it is remarkable that neither his administration nor
his assassination appears to have made an impression on the future
First Lady. Instead, it was the sermons and assassination of Dr King
that appear to have galvanised a shift in Hillary's nascent political thinking, forcing her to challenge the mainstream Republican
attitudes of her upbringing and leading her towards the more progressive stance that emerged during her years at Wellesley College.

The political transformation that Hillary underwent at Wellesley was accompanied by a changing identity, commencing a pattern of personal and political reinvention that has continued throughout her life, depending on her role and location. Her self-awareness in this regard was remarkably pronounced, as she wrote to her pen pal, John Peavoy, explaining her evolving thinking on her own identity. Would she be an 'educational and social reformer, alienated academic, involved pseudo-hippie, a political leader, or a compassionate misanthrope?'[10] These were the options that Hillary Rodham saw for herself in her sophomore year at college during the spring of 1967.

Despite having arrived on the Wellesley campus as a conservative Republican, Hillary quickly set about challenging the campus regulations and honour code. The nation had begun tearing itself apart, as riots broke out that devastated large sections of America's cities, but at Wellesley the practical side to Hillary Rodham's nature demanded that she address those issues where she could make a difference. With only six African-American students in a year group of more than 400, Hillary Rodham petitioned for a greater representation of minority students. Yet she was also eager to retain the good grace of the university authorities and sought to work within the existing system, rather than to implement radical change. Having been elected student-body president, Hillary Rodham worked with the school administration to ensure that safe and organised protests against the Vietnam War took place on campus, without descending into the anarchy that had marked similar protests at other universities across the nation. This was a pattern of behaviour

that defined Hillary for her entire life, one that conservatives have
long ignored and liberals have long suspected.

In her senior year, guided by her tutor and second life mentor
Alan Schechter, Hillary Rodham wrote her senior thesis on Saul
Alinsky, author of the 1946 bestseller *Reveille for Radicals*, and his
efforts to address poverty in the United States, securing interviews
with her subject in the process. Alinsky became popular with the
New Left movement with the publication in 1971 of *Rules for Radicals*, which appealed to members of the generation born after the
publication of his previous work, who, like Hillary Rodham, were
now university activists. In 1968, she fitted the mould for those
attracted to Alinsky's philosophy of being opposed to the war in
Vietnam, in favour of civil rights and engaged in student government. Her thesis concluded that Alinsky, like Walt Whitman and
Martin Luther King, were feared 'because [he] embraced the most
radical of political faiths – democracy'.[11] Alinsky became another
older male mentor to Hillary Rodham, following in the footsteps
of her father, Revd Jones and Professor Schechter. Alinsky offered
her a job at his Industrial Areas Foundation Institute as a trainee
community organiser focusing on the middle class but, despite
being 'tempted', Hillary Rodham was already holding offers from
Harvard and Yale and declined his offer.

Having decided to accept an offer to attend Yale Law School,
Hillary's final months at Wellesley were punctured by national
tragedy. On 4 April 1968, news reached the campus of Dr King's
assassination in Memphis, Tennessee. Like her future husband,
Hillary experienced the euphoria of meeting a political giant only

to suffer the pain of his assassination, thereby establishing a personal connection with both the man and the murder.

Wellesley College was the making of Hillary Rodham and gave her a platform to thrive and develop her political and academic skills. As she later sought to do in the Senate, Hillary developed a reputation for consensus-building and hard work in her time at university, a reputation that ensured she became the first student to be asked to deliver the commencement address. The speech, however, was perhaps not what the authorities had expected when they selected her. She diverted from her prepared remarks to direct a rebuke to the other speaker that day, African-American Republican Senator Edward Brooke, whose remarks, Hillary believed, 'seemed out of touch with his audience: four hundred smart, aware, questioning young women. His words were aimed at a different Wellesley, one that predated the upheavals of the 1960s.'[12] The speech divided opinion, but she received a seven-minute standing ovation from the audience and it brought her to the attention of *Life* magazine. At twenty-one, Hillary Rodham found herself included in the publication as the personification of a new generation of future leaders, decked out in striped trousers and long hair, looking every inch the chic college student president she had long aspired to be.

YALE LAW SCHOOL AND BILL CLINTON

Having graduated from Wellesley College with a degree in political science and rejected an opportunity to become a community organiser, Hillary chose to pursue a career in law as a way to advance

social equality and justice. The first step on this route was the prestigious Yale Law School in New Haven, Connecticut, which she
joined in the autumn of 1969. Despite the conservative reputation
of Yale University, its law school had a more progressive reputation, with its Central Quad dominated by anti-war protests during
1969 and 1970. It was with such progressives that Hillary Rodham
spent much of her first year, as her journey from young Republican
to young liberal firebrand was accomplished. Rather than opting
to write for the university's renowned law review journal, she
chose instead to work for a publication dedicated to social action
and completed a series of internships, all dedicated to progressive
causes. She worked for the founder of the Washington Research
Project, Marian Wright Edelman, who became an early mentor
in Hillary's lifelong advocacy of the rights of women and children.
Hillary also worked on a Senate subcommittee chaired by future
Vice-President Walter Mondale that sought to aid migrant work-
ers. It was a long way politically and culturally from the work she
had done the previous summer for Melvin Laird, who was by now
running the Pentagon for President Nixon.

Irrespective of the classes she took and the causes she advocated,
the event that changed the course of Hillary Rodham's life came
in her second year at Yale, when she encountered a young, unruly
man sporting a bushy beard and bragging about Arkansas's prize-
winning watermelons. The meeting with Bill Clinton changed
Hillary Rodham's life in ways she could never have anticipated
and propelled both of them on a journey to the very apex of power
in the United States. At the time, however, it was Hillary who

was the more formidable student, working, as she always had, to impress her tutors and achieve all that was possible academically. Bill Clinton had a very different approach to studies, viewing Yale as an opportunity to engage in serious political networking as he ditched classes and worked on local political campaigns. With his lack of personal wealth or family pedigree, Yale Law School was a vital stage in Bill Clinton's political career, as he explained his intent to seek elected office: 'I'm goin' back to Arkansas, and I'm going to be Governor,' he told everyone, with absolute certainty.

Their journey together did not begin immediately after that first meeting. Hillary Rodham was dating someone else at the time and Bill Clinton didn't seem inclined to make the first move. Indeed, it wasn't until the spring of 1970 that they finally began spending time together, after an encounter in the law library when Hillary took the initiative and introduced herself to her future husband. He travelled with her when she spent that summer in Oakland, California, working for the law firm of Treuhaft, Walker and Burnstein, defending the working poor of Alameda County and members of the Black Panther movement. When she returned to Yale the following autumn, Hillary and Bill were an established, co-habiting power couple. Despite being a year ahead of Bill, Hillary delayed graduation and took various work placements, many of which centred on the role of child development.

The pair worked for George McGovern's presidential campaign in Texas over the summer of 1972; Hillary worked in San Antonio registering voters, while Bill worked for future presidential candidate Gary Hart at the McGovern office in Austin. Fate ensured that the lives and political careers of Gary Hart and Bill Clinton later became entwined, as they wrestled with the moral and personal dilemmas involved in seeking the presidency. It was at this time that they met Betsey Wright, who became an emphatic supporter of Hillary's and later joined Bill Clinton's team as his Chief of Staff in Arkansas.

The couple eventually graduated from Yale in the summer of 1973 and set off on a tour of England, where Bill Clinton had previously been a Rhodes Scholar at Oxford University. On the shore of Ennerdale Water in Cumbria, Bill proposed. Despite his renowned southern charm, however, Bill's proposal was rejected. Hillary knew that Bill Clinton was determined to pursue a political career in Arkansas, while she had secured a bright future for herself. She had the pick of any job in New York or Washington, DC and was not looking to hitch her wagon to anyone's star. Despite repeated attempts, she continued to rebuff Bill Clinton's proposals.

Returning to the United States, the couple initially went their separate ways. With President Nixon under investigation, Bill Clinton had been offered a job as a staff attorney in Washington, DC, but suggested his girlfriend for the role instead, as he was headed south to Arkansas to prepare for a first run at political office. As a staff attorney on the House of Representatives Judiciary Committee investigating the Nixon administration and its role at the Watergate break-in, Hillary Rodham worked diligently to investigate an impeachment case against the President, maintaining her relationship with Bill as he taught law in Fayetteville, Arkansas. She worked for Bernard Nussbaum, who later joined Bill Clinton's administration as Legal Counsel, analysing the secret recordings from the Nixon White House. In a move that returned to haunt her years later, she sought to apply as broad a rationale for impeachment as possible, including Nixon's actions in Cambodia.

In August 1974, President Nixon resigned, ending Hillary's responsibilities and opening up a world of possibility in Washington, DC and New York in the spheres of politics and law. Instead of pursuing a career of her own, however, she stunned friends and family alike by moving to Arkansas to be with the man she was already telling colleagues would one day become President of the United States. At the time, her peers were convinced that the move was a mistake that placed Hillary Rodham's bright future in jeopardy. Arkansas was a poor, uninviting state with little to offer a driven, politically engaged, career-minded young woman in her mid-twenties. She was going south to be the potential wife of a potential politician, when many of her friends and colleagues believed that she should be seeking political office herself. What they overlooked was that Hillary Rodham was not sacrificing her own political career, but was instead forming a formidable partnership with a man whose talents took them to the top of the American political system, but whose weaknesses almost cost them everything.

CONCLUSION

The extent to which Hillary could have risen as far and as fast as she did without Bill Clinton is impossible to address accurately, but certainly there was a world of options available to her in 1974, and her decision to move to Arkansas was one that took all by surprise. Bill Clinton became the latest, most important male figure in Hillary Rodham's life, following her father, Revd Jones, Alan Schechter and Saul Alinsky. Indeed, the only female mentor in Hillary's life, other than her mother, appears to have been Marian Wright Edelman. Unlike her insular and withdrawn father, Bill Clinton was warm, open, gregarious and fun. For Hillary to have followed him to Arkansas speaks to the mutual appeal and admiration between her and Bill Clinton. Each thought the other to be supremely capable of achieving elected office; both had been stars in their own right at Yale and both were supremely ambitious. A generation later it might have been Bill Clinton following Hillary Rodham to her home state of Illinois as she prepared to run for office, but this was 1974, and the southland beckoned.

CHAPTER 2

FIRST LADY OF ARKANSAS

Having graduated from Yale Law School, Hillary Rodham now began a new life for herself, not as a star in her own right in Washington, DC or New York as many predicted, but as the girlfriend and subsequent wife of a rising young star in Arkansas politics. The eighteen years that Hillary spent in Arkansas were marked by great highs and lows, as her husband became one of the youngest governors in the history of the country and then one of the nation's youngest ex-governors, all within a two-year period. During this time, she became a mother, established herself in the state's legal network and emerged as the main breadwinner in the Clinton household. However, the dividing line between Hillary's work in the worlds of politics, law and finance became blurred and proved to be a burden on Bill Clinton's presidency as well as on Hillary Clinton's own political career. Indeed,

Hillary's actions at this time and the lessons she learned from her experiences in Arkansas continue to haunt her as she seeks the presidency in 2016.

THE STATE OF THE UNION: 1978

When Hillary Rodham moved to Arkansas in 1974, the United States was in a very different political era from when she had been born in 1947. The intervening three decades had witnessed social, political and military upheavals that fundamentally impacted on the dynamic of the nation: assassinations, wars in Korea and Vietnam, civil unrest, rioting, the crimes associated with the Watergate break-in, and the perceived failures of the Johnson, Nixon and Ford presidencies contributed to a situation in which rising unemployment and inflation left the country in a far weakened position. Throughout Hillary's life, the United States had prospered and dominated the global economic markets. The 1970s, however, marked a change in the trajectory of the nation's finances. Unemployment rose, inflation soared and confidence collapsed, eroding faith in the federal government. No single incident caused this; instead, a steady stream of tragedies and calamitous events, as well as unexpected uprisings, diminished the United States to a point where even the observation of the nation's bicentennial in 1976 was a decidedly muted affair.

The economic record of the 1970s was dispiriting. Unlike the Great Depression of the 1930s and the Great Recession of the twenty-first century, there was no specific 'crash' to speak of, just a woeful record of underperformance and troubling economic results, with inflation exceeding 13 per cent in December 1979, having averaged 7.06 per cent throughout the decade. Interest rates reached 21.5 per cent in December 1980 and unemployment soared, a combination so unusual that a new name for it had to be created: stagflation. High inflation and unemployment in the United States ensured that the Misery Index reached 21.98 per cent by the end of the decade as the hope and optimism of the 1950s and early 1960s was replaced by a weary cynicism. The US domestic economic crises of the 1970s were compounded by the international situation; oil prices soared and supply declined, leading to queues at petrol stations as American motorists struggled to fuel their cars. Arkansas suffered more than most, ranking forty-ninth out of the fifty states in per-capita income in 1977, with a third of its citizens living in abject poverty.

Jimmy Carter was elected in 1976 as an apparent antidote to the excesses of what Arthur Schlesinger Jr had christened 'the Imperial Presidency', as well as the specific crimes associated with the Nixon administration. Unfortunately, Carter's single term in office proved to be a disappointment to those who believed that sweeping change would be easy to implement, as he proved ineffective and failed to establish a strong working relationship with Congress. Carter had previously served as Governor of Georgia, a largely rural southern state, and came to Washington, DC with his trusted aides, known as the Georgian Mafia, determined to do things in the nation's capital just as they had back home. Their inability to adjust to their new environment contributed to Jimmy

Carter's defeat in 1980 and provided a textbook example of how not to operate in Washington.

American ground forces had withdrawn from Vietnam long before Jimmy Carter arrived in office, but the conflict continued to cast a long shadow over his presidency as questions remained about what to do with those citizens who had avoided the draft. Carter continued the Nixon/Kissinger policy of *détente* towards the USSR right up until the Soviet invasion of Afghanistan in December 1979. He continued to support the Shah of Iran long after his overthrow, resulting in vehement anti-American sentiment and the 444-day hostage crisis that contributed to Carter's defeat to Governor Reagan in 1980. The sole success of the Carter administration was the Camp David accord between Israel and Egypt, although the subsequent assassination of Anwar Sadat demonstrated the fragility of any effort to secure peace in the Middle East.

The social, international and economic crises that first helped and then hindered Jimmy Carter had a profound impact on the life of Hillary Rodham. These forces contributed to Bill Clinton's election as Governor in 1978 and to his defeat two years later, as Democrats around the country were routed from office along with Jimmy Carter. The memory of the Carter presidency and the miserable economic record of that time ensured that when Bill Clinton ran for the governorship of Arkansas in 1982, and for the presidency ten years later, he deliberately positioned himself to the right of the Democratic Party, much to the chagrin of more progressive elements who have long remained suspicious of both Bill and Hillary's liberal credentials.

ARRIVAL IN ARKANSAS

Never at the centre of American political life, Arkansas was a backwater in the 1970s, routinely finding itself ranked among the poorest, least-educated states in the nation. This was not a place that anyone looking to make a name for themselves in national politics would choose to relocate. Neither was it a natural home for a well-educated northern woman who placed greater importance on intellect than appearance. When she moved to Arkansas, however, Hillary Rodham cannot have imagined that she would be there for long; Bill Clinton was running for Congress in 1974 and the Democrats were expected to sweep the board as President Nixon faced impeachment. What could possibly go wrong? Surely she would be back in Washington, DC as the wife of Congressman Clinton by 1975.

By the time Hillary arrived in Arkansas in the summer of 1974, Bill Clinton was deep into his first run for office. Aged twenty-seven and having only graduated from law school six months earlier, he had secured the Democratic Party's nomination for a seat in the House of Representatives and was running against the incumbent, Republican Congressman John Paul Hammerschmidt. The Clinton campaign worked to tie its opponent to the disgraced President and hoped that Richard Nixon remained in office throughout 1974 to further diminish Hammerschmidt's approval ratings. Nixon's resignation on 9 August 1974, however, enabled his successor, Gerald Ford, to begin resurrecting the Republican Party image, which benefited Bill Clinton's opponent and weakened the rationale for his removal from

office. Despite initial expectations of an easy re-election for Hammerschmidt, Bill Clinton's tireless campaigning, aided by Hillary's
work at his campaign headquarters, saw Clinton earn 48 per cent of
the ballot, losing by only 6,000 votes. A 2 per cent swing would have
been enough to secure victory, and at a time when ballot-rigging
was rife Hillary's steadfast refusal to engage in such chicanery may
have made a difference.[13] Her above-board approach of wanting
to win by merit, and to do so honestly, was admirable, but may be
seen to reveal a *naiveté* about the world of elected politics, in which
victory is rewarded and defeat is just a defeat.

As an entire new generation of Democrats arrived in Washington,
DC following the 1974 election, Bill Clinton was forced to reconsider
his options, languishing in Arkansas rather than taking office in the
nation's capital. Not for the last time, Hillary Rodham's decisive
impact at a key moment, along with Bill Clinton's acquiescence,
had a dramatic impact on both of their lives. With Arkansas's two
Senate seats being held by long-standing and popular Democrats,
David Pryor and Dale Bumpers, Bill Clinton's immediate route to
power in Washington, DC was stymied. The only remaining option
was the Arkansas state house, which was unavailable until 1978. The
result, however, ensured that rather than returning to Washington,
DC almost immediately as the wife of a US Congressman, Hillary
Rodham spent the next eighteen years in Arkansas as the wife of
the Governor of a deprived, rural state routinely identified as one
of the poorest in the nation. 'Thank God for Mississippi' was a
phrase routinely heard, signifying gratitude that at least there was
always one state faring worse than Arkansas.

Rather than returning to Washington, DC, Hillary Rodham began teaching at the University of Arkansas School of Law in Fayetteville, earning $18,000 per year, which helped fund her husband's political aspirations. It was during this time that she met Diane Blair, who quickly became her best friend. Blair had first met Bill Clinton in the summer of 1972, ahead of the Democratic National Convention which nominated George McGovern. As Clinton waxed lyrical about his girlfriend, she asked him

> why he didn't marry this wonderful woman and bring her back to Arkansas with him. He would love to, he said, but Hillary was so uncommonly gifted and had so many attractive options of her own that he felt selfish about bringing her to what would be his state and his political future.[14]

Three years later the two women became colleagues at the University of Arkansas. Neither had been raised in the south and sought solace in one another from the overt sexism that they encountered both in academia and in the law courts. As Diane Blair later recalled, 'It was not easy being a feminist in Arkansas in the 1970s, and Hillary and I were very glad to have each other for advice, comfort, and comic relief.'[15]

Despite her northern upbringing, Hillary Rodham quickly adapted to life in the south, but remained uncertain as to whether marriage to Bill Clinton was right for her. She was painfully aware that he was routinely engaging in relations with other women, including on the campaign trail, where his attempt to emulate JFK's nocturnal antics earned him a rebuke from his mentor, Senator Fulbright. Hugh Rodham and his younger son, Tony, had been dispatched to Arkansas during the 1974 campaign, ostensibly to assist in the election, but with the tacit understanding that they could keep an eye on the candidate and chase off unwelcome female attention. The recruitment of her father and brother as a chaperone for her future husband was hardly indicative of a regular relationship. Neither had Hillary Rodham been well received on her visits to Arkansas; campaign officials bristled when the candidate's girlfriend attempted to take charge of proceedings, she was subject to various rumours relating to her sexual orientation, and Bill Clinton's mother, Virginia, made little effort to hide her disdain. Considering her future, Hillary Rodham began exploring job opportunities in the north-east, far from Arkansas, and spent the summer of 1975 with friends in New York, Boston, Washington, DC and Chicago. As she noted in 1992,

> When we both graduated from Yale … he came right home to Arkansas to teach in a law school, and I was very unsure about where I wanted to be. I certainly was not ready to move completely to Arkansas yet, because I just didn't know whether that would be a decision that Bill could stick to. I really didn't know what to expect.[16]

Realising the implications of his girlfriend's summer sabbatical, Bill Clinton made a bold move by buying a house that Hillary had long admired and proposing, once again, upon her return in August. They were married with little fanfare in the house in a private ceremony on 11 October 1975, ahead of a honeymoon in the Mexican resort of Acapulco, where Hillary's parents and two brothers joined them. In keeping with feminist principles, but in defiance of southern tradition, Hillary elected to maintain her maiden name, a move that came to have serious, long-lasting implications for both her and her husband as Bill Clinton continued to seek elected office in Arkansas. On election day 1976, as Americans sent Jimmy Carter to the White House, Bill Clinton became Arkansas's attorney general, prompting a move from Fayetteville to the state capital, Little Rock. The move marked a career change for Hillary, prompting her to leave academia and secure a job practising law. She joined the prestigious Rose Law Firm, whose clients included local industry giants Walmart and Tyson Foods. She quickly established herself as the main income-earner in the family, benefiting from the political largesse of being the wife of the state attorney general when President Carter appointed her to the board of the Legal Service Corporation. It was at the Rose Law Firm that she became a colleague of Vincent Foster and Webster Hubbell, whose lives soon became consumed by the Clintons' political aspirations.

Hillary Rodham's drive and ambition, quite natural in her native Illinois or in Washington, DC and New York, were not universally acclaimed in Arkansas, where her views on feminism and fashion were in contrast to local trends. As a lawyer, she was a woman in a man's world and made little or no attempt to impress, except by means of her intelligence and intellect; her attire and appearance were not assets that she sought to exploit in any way. Hillary Clinton's appearance has undergone many changes throughout her career, but the polished, well-dressed woman of 2016 is in stark contrast to the young lawyer of the 1970s who wore thick reading glasses and no cosmetics and appeared to have little or no interest in hairstyles or fashion. Hillary Rodham, as she continued to be known following her marriage, was determined to succeed based on merit alone.

WHEELING AND DEALING

Despite Hillary's penchant for doing everything above board, rejecting shortcuts to power and winning by the rules, her positions as wife of a politician and as a local lawyer ensured that there arose, on occasion, the appearance of a conflict of interest. She took measures to avoid such situations and took time off to campaign for her husband, but then worked hard to make up for any salary shortfall. She took positions on the boards of companies including Walmart and engaged in a variety of business ventures and investments, often with friends, in an effort to secure her family's financial future. Such efforts, however, had long-term implications that persist unabated in 2016.

In 1978, Hillary Rodham traded in the commodities market for a short time, losing on some trades, gaining on others, but emerging with a profit of $100,000, three times what her husband eventually earned as Governor. The deals were done alongside James Blair, who was a counsel to Don Tyson, the poultry tycoon of Arkansas and husband of Hillary's best friend, Diane. Such financial gain from an initial investment of just $1,000 in a risky transaction in the commodities market, made with the guidance of a friend who worked for a major player in the poultry industry and who later became a donor to Clinton campaigns, roused considerable suspicion. The commodities investment paled in comparison, however, to the fiasco that centred on the Whitewater land deal and the Clintons' dealings with Jim and Susan McDougal. The land deal turned sour, resulting in the Clintons losing $46,000 and the McDougals losing $92,000. Because McDougal also owed Madison Guaranty Saving and Loan, which Hillary Rodham represented before Arkansas's Security Commissioner, serious questions were subsequently raised about conflicts of interest. Indeed, it was the initial concerns about this land deal that first prompted the appointment of a Special Prosecutor to investigate President Clinton in relation to his wife's steadfast refusal to turn over documents to the *Washington Post* in 1993. That investigation, which found no evidence of wrongdoing by the Clintons over Whitewater, led eventually to the move to impeach Bill Clinton over unrelated matters.

Interestingly, the drive to accumulate a financial safety net was driven by Hillary, not by Bill Clinton. Her upbringing in a household dominated by a strict father, who was controlling with money, make these deals appear all the more unusual. They seem to be at odds with her conservative nature and risk-free approach to all other aspects of her life and career. They also raise the uncomfortable and unanswerable question regarding the extent to which the deals were part of inside information made available by Bill Clinton's elected positions and her role at the Rose Law Firm, although no investigation has ever proved that this was the case.

Nevertheless, these trades and the failed Whitewater deal have haunted the Clintons for the remainder of their careers, as signs of greed, ineptitude, cronyism or simply criminal behaviour. Neither has ever been charged and insufficient evidence has been produced to substantiate the multitude of charges that have been levelled against them over the years. Such allegations were a high price to pay for a short-term financial gain on the commodities market and a land deal gone bad.

FIRST LADY OF ARKANSAS

Such scandals were in the future, however, as Bill and Hillary became the rising stars of Little Rock. He was attorney general and widely tipped to secure the governorship, while she was on track to becoming a partner in a leading law firm. By this time, Hillary had already worked on the presidential campaigns of George McGovern in 1972 and Jimmy Carter in 1976 and she now moved to help her husband as he sought the top job in Arkansas. Her role in the campaign continued to attract negative attention; even Bill Clinton's Democratic opponents sought to exploit the fact that the aspiring Governor's wife had failed to take his name. When asked, Hillary insisted it was merely her professional name.

As the campaign for the Governor's mansion progressed, Hillary Rodham became more involved and began making policy and personnel recommendations for her husband's potential team, just as she eventually did during the 1992 presidential election campaign. She also provided a contrast to her husband's optimism, which many read as political *naiveté*. Rudy Moore, Bill Clinton's campaign director at the time, noted,

> Bill sees the light and sunshine about people, and Hillary sees their darker side. She has much more ability than he does to see who's with you, who's against you, and to make sure they don't take advantage of you. He's not expecting to be jumped, but she always is. So she's on the defensive.[17]

It was a winning combination that saw the 31-year-old Hillary Rodham become First Lady of Arkansas following the 1978 election, as Bill Clinton became the youngest Governor in the United States since the 1930s, securing 63 per cent of the vote.

In many ways, Hillary's time as First Lady of Arkansas proved to be a precursor for her experience in the White House as First Lady of the United States. The allegations, jealousies and innuendos that were later levelled at her first came to light in Arkansas in the 1970s and 1980s in a recurring pattern of allegation, slander and lawsuits. The suspicion that surrounded them was understandable in Arkansas: Bill and Hillary were the vanguard of a generation that didn't want to play by the rules. They wore their hair long and dressed independently, she didn't take her husband's name and both had careers of their own. They were the ultimate power couple, with abilities and appetites on clear display. Hillary Rodham was a rising star in the law and a partner by 1979; Bill Clinton was now Governor; both were spoken of in the highest circles. And their worlds intersected in the byzantine corridors of Arkansas politics, where the personal was political and being the wife of the Governor granted Hillary access to the public policy decision-making process. As a couple, they have had a simple philosophy: 'It's better to get caught trying than to ask permission.' Just as Bill Clinton came to experience resentment due to his success, so too did Hillary Rodham, who had the added challenge of being a Yankee deep down in Dixie.

Not only did the Clintons not conform to expectations, but they also appeared to deliberately buck the system. In a rural, conservative state, Bill Clinton surrounded himself with a trio of bearded, liberal advisors: John David Danner, Rudy Moore Jr and Stephen A. Smith. The policies and appearance of the three did little to ingratiate the new Governor to his conservative constituents and, along with his wife, served to highlight Bill Clinton's distinctiveness from the mainstream Arkansas electorate. What was becoming commonplace in the north-east and in California was just not seen as acceptable in the Arkansas legislature, which took issue with the Governor, his wife and his staff, all of whom offended their conservative sensibilities.

Bill Clinton named his wife as head of his Health Care Advisory Board, a move that prompted accusations of nepotism and led to questions being asked about her influence and motivating factors. Not for the last time, Hillary was compared to Lady Macbeth, having arrived in Arkansas and taken up residence in the Governor's mansion.[18] The First Lady, however, was only one point of criticism for the new, young, incoming team of 'the Boy Governor', as Clinton was known locally. Rather than taking their time and seeking to placate special interests in the hope of instigating gradual change, Bill Clinton's first term in office was defined by his challenging of vested interests and his activist approach to government. Already unpopular in some circles, he infuriated the agricultural sector by levying an increase in car tax to pay for highway improvements. The disdain that this generated was compounded when Clinton acquiesced to a request from President Carter to house Cuban refugees in the state. Dick Morris, who later engineered Clinton's 1996 re-election campaign, started out working for him in Arkansas, noting, 'He was very idealistic, not pragmatic at all. There was no focus to his agenda. His first term resembled his first three months as President – a period of learning.'[19] That process involved making a lot of mistakes, which were compounded by concerns over the First Lady and his team of bearded advisors. Nonetheless, as his first term as Governor drew to an end, Bill Clinton decided to seek re-election in 1980.

With only an unpopular tax and more than a few new enemies to show for two years in office, Bill Clinton would have struggled for re-election at any time, but in 1980 he faced a national landslide for the Republican Party, re-galvanised by Ronald Reagan. Both nationally and locally, Democrats failed to appreciate the threat posed by the former California Governor until it was far too late. This was certainly the case in Arkansas, where the Clintons had a series of distractions that prevented adequate attention being paid to the 1980 campaign, as political issues compounded those of a more personal nature. Their family was completed with the birth of Chelsea Clinton in 1980, but almost ripped apart by

ongoing allegations regarding Bill Clinton's philandering. Not for
the first time, questions were asked regarding the state of the Clinton
marriage, but it was a union in which Hillary Rodham appeared
resolutely determined to remain. Her own private ruminations on
the matter have remained private and opportunities to lift the veil
on this aspect of her life have not been taken to date. It is clear,
however, that by Bill Clinton's own admission his actions at this
time caused great pain in his marriage and prompted a flurry of
speculation about what makes them work as a couple that shows no
sign of abating. With a baby daughter, a host of unpopular policies,
a disliked team of advisors and a wife who appeared to alienate
him from the Arkansas electorate, Bill Clinton suddenly found
himself out of a job as the voters rejected him after two years as
Governor. The Boy Governor was now the youngest ex-Governor
in the state's history.

FAITH

Bill Clinton's defeat in 1980 ensured that there was plenty of time
for soul-searching. Having retained her commitment to the Methodist faith after her move to Arkansas, Hillary Rodham developed
a greater sense of religious commitment in the 1980s following the
arrival of her daughter. Her church, the Little Rock First United
Methodist, was also home to the monthly meetings of the local
bar association, an indication of the large number of lawyers in
the congregation. As a mother, a lawyer and a Methodist, Hillary
Rodham regularly engaged in *pro bono* work for the church and

spoke regularly in support of central aspects of the church's teaching. Friends, including Diane Blair and Ellen Brantley, noted how religion appeared to become more important to Hillary during the 1980s as her public role increased and intrusions into her privacy became more prevalent. Writing in 2007, Carl Bernstein concluded that, 'along with her Methodism, Hillary's zealously guarded zone of privacy is essential to understanding her', a view echoed by her best friend, Diane Blair: 'No doubt about it. The fact that nobody has ever wanted their privacy more and had it more excruciatingly violated is still just staggering to me.'[20]

THE COMEBACK KIDS

Having made a concerted effort to present himself and his wife as a dynamic political team, Bill Clinton ensured that the election result of 1980 was as much a defeat for Hillary as it was for him. The policies that Bill Clinton introduced as Governor, as well as the national Republican sweep, contributed substantially to the 1980 result, but so too did the alienating figure of the First Lady of Arkansas. Her appearance, northern manners, assertiveness and use of her maiden name had all gone a long way towards distancing her from the Arkansas electorate. It was clear that fundamental change was required or the promising political career of Arkansas's golden couple would be over before it had really begun.

It was at this point that Hillary Rodham turned the focus of her energies toward ensuring her husband's political resurrection, for both of their sakes. While Bill Clinton wallowed in defeat and self-pity, she took charge of the situation, realising that, if she did not, their careers and perhaps even their lives together might never recover. Since they met at Yale Law School, their lives had become increasingly entwined; more than merely husband and wife, the Clintons were a power couple and at their best they were more than the sum of their parts. Like force multipliers, they drew the best from one another and galvanised themselves for the challenges that life threw at them. This process began in earnest after the 1980 defeat and contributed to Bill Clinton's successful campaign for re-election in 1982.

Changes were made across the board to ensure that the 1980 result was to be the final defeat in Bill Clinton's entire political career. Betsey Wright was recruited to help organise and manage Bill Clinton's return to power and although she did not go on to serve in the Clinton White House she was pivotal in working with Hillary to ensure that the 1982 re-election campaign was a success. Political consultant Dick Morris was brought in to offer guidance on what had gone wrong in Bill Clinton's first term and how to change public perceptions ahead of the 1982 election. Central to this effort was altering the public perception of the now former First Lady, who underwent a total makeover. Her appearance was radically altered; she began wearing contact lenses instead of her thick glasses, she recruited a consultant to help her with clothing and began wearing make-up and colouring her hair.

Not only did Hillary Rodham undergo a physical makeover, she also made the decision to adopt her husband's surname, despite having long been opposed to the idea. She now realised that the continued use of her maiden name was a political albatross that put everything she and her husband had been working for at risk. The issue had become increasingly problematic following Chelsea's birth and had been exploited by Bill Clinton's opponent in the 1980 campaign. Writing in her memoir *Living History*, she concluded, 'I decided it was more important for Bill to be Governor again than for me to keep my maiden name.'[21]

In public, the 'new' Hillary Clinton appeared more in keeping with the traditional role of political wives in the early 1980s: contrite, demure and silent. Behind the scenes, however, a very different Hillary Clinton was emerging as a dominant figure in her husband's political life. Furious rows ensued following the defeat as Bill Clinton spent the next six months trying to come to terms with his loss just as his wife's legal career was taking off and she was made partner at the Rose Law Firm. She maintained her ties with the legal establishment by continuing to work with the Children's Defense Fund, the American Bar Association and the Legal Services Corporation, and by networking extensively, long before it became common practice, gaining strong advocates in John Doar (Assistant Attorney General for Civil Rights), Burke Marshall (Assistant Attorney General) and Marian Wright Edelman (president and founder of the Children's Defense Fund).

With the help of Betsey Wright, Hillary worked to ensure that her husband's campaign team knew what was needed and that they produced as required. If prompting were needed, she delivered it, for while both she and her husband were known for their tempers, Bill Clinton was less inclined to wield the knife; Hillary had no such hesitation. In this way, Bill and Hillary Clinton developed a rapport akin to John and Robert Kennedy in the late 1950s and early '60s; JFK was the charming, outgoing public face who could do no wrong, while his brother worked the back rooms and made sure that the right people did their jobs as necessary or were removed. The parallel with the Kennedy brothers was to continue for much of the Clintons' political careers.

Vital to the campaign for re-election was a televised address by Bill Clinton in which he apologised for the mistakes he had made in his first term. Couched in southern colloquialisms, the address conveyed the former Governor's apparent sincerity and dismay at the hurt he had caused the people of Arkansas, and he asked for a second chance. In its own way, it was a modified version of the famous 'Chequers speech' that Richard Nixon gave on television at the height of the 1952 election when he had been accused of hiding a secret slush fund and appealed directly to voters to keep him on the Republican ticket, along with Dwight D. Eisenhower. It was not to be the last time that Bill Clinton would be required to make a televised apology to the American electorate, or that he would find his career eerily mirroring that of President Nixon, whom Hillary had worked so hard to drive from office.

The 1982 campaign, therefore, was a turning point for Hillary Clinton as well as for her husband. While the public focus was on her husband, she ensured that nothing was left to chance; defeat was not an option. Despite their previous importance to her husband, Hillary saw to it that the team of bearded advisors who had proved so toxic to Bill Clinton's first term was removed from the scene, as people, ideas and ideals were jettisoned in the pursuit of power, and new aides and consultants were recruited to ensure no further mistakes were made.

FIRST LADY ONCE MORE

On election night 1982, Bill Clinton became the first Arkansan Governor to be returned to office having previously lost the position, and no one was more pleased about it than the candidate's wife. Defeat was not a problem moving forward. For the next decade the Clintons dominated Arkansas, moving onward and upward, governing an essentially Republican state in a manner that soon became recognised the world over, adopting centrist policies and utilising adroit political footwork when necessary. A new team of older professionals better equipped to deal with the media, the electorate and the Arkansas legislature were recruited, and Hillary Clinton appeared poised and demure, in keeping with southern expectations.

The remainder of Bill Clinton's time as Governor of Arkansas proved to be a test-bed for ideas of government and an approach to leadership that was later adopted in the White House: the permanent campaign, in which there was no distinction between governing and campaigning. Instead, there was to be a concerted effort to ensure that policy implementation was accompanied by a public-relations exercise to guarantee that the electorate knew what was being done for them, and who they could reward with their vote. The press was by-passed via the use of direct mailing and advertising, while extensive polling was conducted to constantly test the public reaction to policies, ensuring that Bill Clinton never again got too far ahead of public opinion. The strategy was devised after Dick Morris was brought in to advise the new administration. His recommendation was that 'when you lead in an idealistic direction, the most important thing to do is to be highly pragmatic about it. And when necessity forces upon you a problem of great pragmatism, you need to use idealism to find your way out of the thicket.'[22]

The policy focus of Bill Clinton's time as Governor was education reform. Hillary Clinton was central to that effort, foreshadowing the role she later came to play in healthcare reform in the White House. The Arkansas Supreme Court ruled that the state's public education financing contravened the Constitution, as it was demonstrably inequitable. Poverty in Arkansas was hardly a new concept, but some teachers were receiving government-supplied food stamps and earning less than $10,000. In his first term, Governor Clinton appointed his wife chair of a committee examining health issues; now he named Hillary as chair of the Education Standards Committee. This, he stated, confirmed his own personal commitment to the issue; he couldn't chair the committee himself so he had appointed the person closest to him instead. As she later did at a national level for healthcare reform, Hillary barnstormed the state to engage policy-makers and voters. When she discovered that some teachers were teaching students about World War Eleven (due to their misunderstanding of the Roman numerals in 'World War II'), it was clear that a larger problem existed. She worked with Dick Morris and Frank White, whom her husband had recently defeated as Governor, to introduce competency-based testing for teachers and a 1 per cent rise in sales tax to pay for the necessary increases across all of Arkansas's school districts. Hillary Clinton's work and attention to detail won her plaudits from the public and lawmakers, with even opponents including State Representative Lloyd George noting, 'Gentlemen, we've elected the wrong Clinton!'

TO RUN, OR NOT TO RUN?

Having been successfully re-elected Governor in 1986, Bill Clinton seriously considered running for the presidency in the 1988 election. With Ronald Reagan constitutionally prohibited from seeking a third term, an opportunity existed to establish a new era in American politics. Vice-President George H. W. Bush was not particularly popular within his party and faced a serious challenge for the Republican nomination from Senator Bob Dole, no doubt encouraged by the fact that no sitting Vice-President had been elected to the presidency since Martin Van Buren in 1836. The Democratic Party nomination was also wide open, with no obvious front runner among a series of rather unimpressive, young and inexperienced candidates. A chance existed, therefore, for a dynamic and charismatic candidate to emerge as a symbol of generational change in the United States at the end of the 1980s. Could Bill Clinton, then aged just forty-two, be that candidate and become the youngest-ever President of the United States?[23]

Bill Clinton found his aspirations thwarted not by politics, but by his personal flaws. In 1987, Bill Clinton's former boss from the McGovern campaign, Gary Hart, had announced his intention to seek the presidency. Now a United States Senator from Colorado, Hart, like Clinton, did his best to exude a Kennedy-esque quality and was seen as a young, charismatic Democrat who could appeal to middle America in a post-Reagan era. Despite this, his candidacy evaporated almost overnight in a squall of accusations surrounding an alleged affair with a model named Donna Rice. Repeated denials became mute when photographs emerged of Miss Rice sitting on the Senator's knee, close to the moored yacht 'Monkey Business', which his campaign team had hired. As with Hart, rumours of infidelity had long surrounded Bill Clinton. In 1987, however, the allegations proved detrimental not only to his marriage, but also to Bill Clinton's career aspirations.

When Gary Hart was forced to quit the 1988 race, it became clear that whatever had transpired in Arkansas throughout the 1980s could not stay private in the heat of a presidential campaign. Despite this, Bill Clinton arranged a lavish press conference and gathered his friends and the media from around the world to the Excelsior Hotel in Little Rock in July 1987. On the day of the announcement, however, he stunned the gathered audience by announcing that instead of seeking the Democratic Party's nomination for the presidency he had chosen not to run. No one looked more crestfallen than Hillary Clinton, who wept openly, believing that this might be a great lost opportunity. The media focus on Gary Hart and questions about infidelity had convinced Bill Clinton that he and his marriage could not endure a similar firestorm in that year's campaign. For better or for worse, Bill Clinton passed on the opportunity, ensuring that Massachusetts's Governor Michael Dukakis secured the nomination and went on to eventual defeat by George H. W. Bush in the November election.

By deciding not to seek the presidency in the 1988 election, Bill Clinton suddenly called his entire future into question. What did it signify about his career that at the ideal political moment he could not seek the presidency due to his own personal shortcomings? If a bid could not be made for the presidency in 1988, with no incumbent and with such a weak Democratic field of candidates, was such a campaign ever going to be feasible? Bill Clinton had served as Governor of Arkansas dating back to 1978, with only the minor blip of the 1980 defeat behind him, but was this to be the extent of his achievements? Did he wish to go on serving as Governor indefinitely until an inevitable defeat left him with nowhere to go? Had the Boy Governor reached the end of his career? These questions had huge implications not only for Bill, but also for Hillary Clinton. Had she married him simply to become an Arkansas lawyer? Had she surrendered her own blossoming career to have her aspirations dashed by her husband's repeated infidelity?

Following the decision not to seek the presidency in 1988, suggestions began to emerge that Hillary Clinton should consider running for the governorship of Arkansas. Bill Clinton was clearly unsure about seeking another term as Governor and believed a presidential bid in 1992 was still a possibility. Hillary's past political performances had always been impressive and her directness and capacity to make decisions were matters of public record. The practicalities of a presidential campaign appeared, however, to be incompatible with a second gubernatorial challenge within the same marriage. Therefore, for the moment, Hillary Clinton's aspirations for elected office were put on hold; both she and her husband turned their thoughts north to Iowa and New Hampshire as campaign '92 beckoned.

CONCLUSION

When Hillary joined Bill Clinton in Arkansas in 1974, she could not have imagined that it would become her home for the next eighteen years. No doubt expecting her boyfriend to maximise the national tide of anti-Republican sentiment that existed due to the Watergate affair, she must have imagined that she would be back in Washington, DC by the spring of 1975. Indeed, many of Bill Clinton's campaign team had already begun house-hunting with similar expectations. When those dreams were dashed by a little under 6,000 votes, Hillary's entire future changed.

The eighteen years that she spent in Arkansas, between 1974 and 1992, brought great personal joy in her marriage to Bill Clinton and the birth of their daughter Chelsea. As a practising lawyer, she saw her career go from strength to strength as she was made a partner at the Rose Law Firm and established solid working relations with her colleagues, including Webster Hubble and Vince Foster. As the wife of the Governor, she was able to influence policy and gain the ear of powerful political figures, including President Carter.

She was a key informal member of her husband's inner circle. On the other hand, the years also brought great strain as Hillary was forced to accept her husband's infidelities, which became more than merely a private problem when they impacted on his ability to run for office, setting back their dreams and aspirations. Bill Clinton may have wanted to be a Kennedy-esque figure for the 1990s, but the private life that JFK led in the 1960s was not feasible for a poor boy from Arkansas in the 1980s. Hillary, therefore, repeatedly found her energies and skills being dedicated to propping up her husband in times of need, rather than being focused on a more positive agenda. A May 1992 memo noted, 'Hillary Clinton's problems are closely interrelated with Bill Clinton's problems … voters' perceptions of her are directly influenced by how voters see Bill Clinton. If voters did not see him as weak politically, they might view Hillary's strength in a more positive light and her role as less salient.'[24]

This see-saw effect of one being up and the other down, which was to later play out in Washington, DC, began in earnest in Arkansas long before it became a matter of national and international intrigue. The Arkansas years, therefore, provide a telling precedent for future behaviour, as Hillary Clinton and her husband sought to play politics by their own rules and survive politically in an increasingly conservative era.

— CHAPTER 3 —

FIRST LADY
OF THE
UNITED STATES

Hillary Clinton's time as First Lady of Arkansas proved to be a training ground for her next role as First Lady of the United States. There had been political power couples before, but, just as JFK and Jackie Kennedy had thirty years earlier, the Clintons personified a new generation. The baby boomers were taking control at a time of great upheaval and uncertainty in US and global politics. The significance of this generational shift cannot be underestimated. Indeed, it formed the basis for much of the ire that the First Couple faced during their eight years in power.

THE STATE OF THE UNION: 1992

In 1992, the United States was in an economic slump. Despite
having emerged 'victorious' from the Cold War, the United States
was masking serious economic challenges. The Soviet Union may
well have disintegrated due to the state of its economy, but the
United States was hardly in an ideal economic situation. The arms
race of the Cold War pushed both nations' economies to the brink,
preventing vital inward investment in US infrastructure. As Gary
Wills noted of Ronald Reagan, 'It is not given to many Presidents
to spend two world empires towards decline.'[25] The United States,
it appeared, had prevailed in the Cold War mainly because it had
better lines of credit than the Soviet Union.

The election of 1992 should have been the crowning moment
of George H. W. Bush's political career and seen him successfully
re-elected to a second term in the White House. During his time
in office, the Cold War had ended; US forces had toppled General
Noriega from power in Panama and prevailed in the 1991 Gulf
War. President Bush received sky-high approval ratings heading
into the election season and his campaign questioned the capability of his opponents to deal with potential international crises.[26]
His son, George W. Bush, joked with reporters, 'Do you think the
American people are going to turn to a Democrat now?'[27] Initially,
this appeared unlikely, and his father's polling figures discouraged
many leading Democrats from seeking the presidency that year,
believing Bush to be unbeatable.

Despite overseas successes and his reputation as a foreign-policy

President, however, George H. W. Bush and his administration failed to adequately provide a blueprint for the role of the United States on the world stage. The General Agreement on Trade and Tariff (GATT) talks and the North American Free Trade Agreement (NAFTA) negotiations had stalled; Europe was forming the European Union (EU), but found itself in a recession; China faced condemnation following the ending of pro-democracy protests in Tiananmen Square; Saddam Hussein remained in power in Iraq and had already begun to deliver vengeance on the Kurds and other opposition groups; a mass slaughter was occurring in the former Yugoslavia; starvation was rife in Somalia, and Haitians were fleeing their country and making their way to the United States on makeshift rafts following a coup. All of this appeared to receive scant attention at the White House, as the President's ill-defined New World Order failed to materialise. As Gavin Esler, the BBC's chief North America correspondent, noted, the United States 'had conquered the world and yet ... found little peace', as Americans were beset by political scandals and economic woes.[28]

This lack of vision was exacerbated by the downturn in the domestic economy that also went largely unaddressed by Bush and his team. Changes in geo-economics impacted on the United States as manufacturing jobs moved overseas and the nation struggled to find a role for itself in the immediate post-Cold War era. The United States was in a recession from July 1990 until March 1991 following eight years of solid economic results. On what became known as Black Monday, 19 October 1987, the stock market crashed, wiping over 20 per cent off the Dow Jones Industrial Average. This was exacerbated by the collapse of the Savings and Loan industry, the increase in interest rates and the rise in the cost of oil following the invasion of Kuwait. The US unemployment rate reached 8 per cent in June 1992, contributing to low consumer confidence and even lower confidence in the Bush administration. His inability to deliver what President Bush derisively called 'the vision thing' provided an ideal opportunity for his opponents to portray him as lacking in ideas or leadership. Domestic tensions were heightened by social unrest following the acquittal of Los Angeles police officers involved in the beating of Rodney King that resulted in fifty-three deaths and further exposed President Bush to claims of being out of touch.

It was this combination of foreign and domestic crises that convinced Bill Clinton to seek the presidency in 1992. A weak field of Democratic Party rivals ensured he was the front runner for the nomination from the moment he announced his candidacy in October 1991. His hopes were raised further by the bitter in-fighting among Republicans that ensured President Bush was forced to actively campaign for his own party's nomination, a process that had doomed recent incumbents to defeat. History revealed that incumbents who ran unopposed for their party's nomination won re-election, but that those who had to fight for their right to run again were defeated. In 1952, 1968, 1976, 1980 and 1992, incumbent Presidents faced internal challenges that forced them to actively campaign for their party's nomination and lost the presidency in the process: Harry Truman dropped out following poor polling in New

Hampshire, ensuring that most people forget he even considered running again;[29] Lyndon Johnson was undermined by the success of Eugene McCarthy in New Hampshire and the ensuing candidacy of Robert F. Kennedy and quit the race live on national television in March 1968; Gerald Ford fought off a bid by Ronald Reagan in 1976 but was weakened in the process, as was Jimmy Carter in 1980 when challenged by Ted Kennedy. Finally, Pat Buchanan dramatically undermined support for George H. W. Bush in 1992 by challenging him in the primaries.

Incumbents who avoided an internal party challenge during this time period (Dwight D. Eisenhower, Ronald Reagan, Bill Clinton, George W. Bush and Barack Obama) were re-elected. George H. W. Bush's political problems, therefore, became Bill Clinton's blessings, but also forced his campaign team to think the unthinkable: What if we win? Undeterred, Hillary Clinton immediately replied, 'Then we serve.'[30] It was a response that revealed much about the dominant force in the marital relationship and about the nature of the partnership that soon took power in the White House.

ELECTION '92

The 1992 election marked the Clintons' emergence onto the national political stage. It also became an election in which the two main party candidates were, to an extent, overshadowed by two other figures: Ross Perot and Hillary Clinton. Running as an independent candidate, Texan billionaire H. Ross Perot was

instrumental in capturing the national mood that had turned against
the Bush administration, but which had not fully embraced Bill
Clinton's candidacy. Using televised 'infomercials', Perot helped
soften George H. W. Bush for the Democrats to defeat in the
November 1992 election. To win the presidency, a candidate needs
270 Electoral College votes and, although Perot won no Electoral College votes, he won 18.9 per cent of the popular vote,
drawing heavily from Republican voters, ensuring that with just
37.5 per cent support, Bush received the lowest vote for an incumbent President since Herbert Hoover at the height of the Great
Depression in 1932. However, Perot's presence on the ballot that
year also meant that Bill Clinton was elected with just 43 per cent
of the national vote.

Ross Perot's presence guaranteed that the election focused on
the state of the economy, leading Clinton's campaign director James
Carville to remind his candidate that on every occasion possible
he should tell the voters, 'It's the economy, stupid.' However, it
was not only Perot who drew attention to financial issues. During the Democratic primaries, Bill Clinton's opponents sought
to highlight Hillary Clinton's role at the Rose Law Firm and her
husband's political activities as Governor of Arkansas to imply
a conflict of interest and of financial impropriety. Such suggestions became direct allegations of financial malpractice by former
California Governor Jerry Brown during the primary in Hillary's
home state of Illinois. Bill Clinton was forced to defend his wife
against false accusations made by Brown and the *Washington Post*
that he was 'funnelling money' to the Rose Law Firm as Governor

in an act of open 'corruption'. Clinton angrily attacked Brown in a live televised debate for besmirching Hillary's name: 'I don't care what you say about me, but you oughta be ashamed of yourself for jumping on my wife. You're not worth being on the same platform with my wife,' he insisted.[31] The incident was only one in a series in which Hillary Clinton threatened to overshadow her husband as he sought the Democratic Party's nomination.

Despite the airing of the allegation, the incident enabled Bill Clinton to demonstrate some righteous indignation and come to the vigorous defence of his wife. This was in stark contrast to the previous Democratic candidate, Michael Dukakis, who had given a soulless response four years earlier when asked about his view on the death penalty in the event of the theoretical rape of his wife. Unfortunately, however, speaking with reporters the following day, Hillary Clinton inadvertently compounded the issue by responding to a question regarding her career choice. Rather than deflecting the question, she sarcastically quipped that rather than pursuing a law career, 'I suppose I could have stayed home and baked cookies.' It was a response that resonated far beyond Sophie's Busy Bee Diner in Illinois and into political history as she spent the remainder of the campaign fighting the suggestion that her remark was an attack on stay-at-home mothers.

Hillary Clinton's caustic remark reminded many of her other verbal contribution to the campaign, which occurred at the height of its first major scandal. Appearing together on *60 Minutes* to refute allegations of a twelve-year affair between Bill Clinton and Gennifer Flowers, the Clintons spoke with Steve Kroft about their relationship and life together. Bill Clinton admitted to having caused 'pain in my marriage', but denied that he and his wife had arrived at an 'understanding', or an 'agreement' regarding their relationship. 'You're looking at two people who love each other,' he insisted. 'This is not an arrangement or an understanding. This is a marriage. That's a very different thing.' It was Hillary Clinton's response to this suggestion, however, that drew the most attention when she insisted,

> You know, I'm not sitting here – some little woman standing by my man like Tammy Wynette. I'm sitting here because I love him, and I respect him, and I honour what he's been through and what we've been through together. And you know, if that's not enough for people, then heck, don't vote for him.[32]

Her robust defence of her husband worked well in many quarters, but struck some as patronising and demeaning in its reference to little women who stood by their abusive husbands, as well as to an entire army of Tammy Wynette fans.

It was also the interview in which Hillary Clinton raised the concept of a 'zone of privacy', which later proved so toxic in her dealings with the media. Steve Kroft, who conducted the interview, later noted, 'She's got a ten-second delay … If something comes to her mind she doesn't think will play right, she cuts it off before anyone knows she's thinking it.'[33] Alas, this apparent built-in delay has not always been effective and has on occasion caused Hillary to reconsider statements that have appeared in retrospect to be 'inartful'.[34]

A further challenge that Hillary presented for her husband's campaign was the fact that voters reported that she reminded them of Nancy Reagan, whose influence over her husband had become the stuff of legend. A campaign memo drafted by the Clinton campaign's own pollsters in May 1992 revealed that Hillary Clinton's 'strong political and strategic role reminds voters very much of Nancy Reagan. They are sure, moreover, they don't want to have another Nancy Reagan in the White House.'[35] Not for the first time, Bill Clinton and his campaign team struggled to know quite how to position this most formidable of women in the eyes of American voters.

Bill Clinton had opted not to enter the presidential election in 1988 due to his concerns regarding the media and possible questions about marital infidelity. Now, four years later, he found himself facing tens of millions of Americans on a news programme broadcast directly after the 1992 Super Bowl, while Hillary single-handedly saved his candidacy and dismissed allegations regarding an affair with Gennifer Flowers. Her performance enabled her husband to move on to the New Hampshire Primary, where he came second, but, having been in free-fall, the result was seen as a remarkable comeback. The result was perfectly encapsulated by the candidate, who grabbed the headlines from the victor, Senator Paul Tsongas, by declaring himself to be the 'Comeback Kid'. After that, there was no looking back as the Clintons took the country by storm, secured the Democratic Party's nomination and defeated George H. W. Bush in November 1992. Americans had opted for Bill Clinton's offer of 'buy one, get one free'.[36] Now they were going to find out what that meant in practice.

CENTRE OF ATTENTION

Due to her contentious statements and high-profile role in the 1992
campaign, Hillary Clinton was a controversial character long before
she arrived in Washington, DC for her husband's inauguration in January 1993. This was only heightened when the First Lady announced
that she should be addressed as Hillary Rodham Clinton in a striking note of independence and assertiveness that was soon reflected
in her office allocation and role in the new administration. Indeed,
it was her independence and cool demeanour that helped fuel the
developing interest in her, but this also meant that she became the
focal point for intense political and media scrutiny as she moved to
establish herself as a new kind of First Lady for a new political era.
As the first First Lady of a new generation, she was a stark contrast
to Barbara Bush, who had positioned herself as America's favourite
grandmother and avoided the policy process altogether. The difference
between the incoming and outgoing First Ladies perfectly illustrated
the generational change that was coming to Washington, DC as Bill
Clinton's administration prepared to take charge.

Unsurprisingly, the media frenzy that accompanied the revelations surrounding Hillary Clinton's private life and finances on the
campaign trail did not disappear once the election was over and
continued unabated throughout the transition period. All too quickly,
Hillary came to the conclusion that: 'The press has big egos and
no brains.'[37] Despite the overwhelmingly positive press coverage
that the Clinton team received on the 1992 campaign, stories that
addressed the President's other women, the draft and financial affairs

did nothing to improve Hillary Clinton's view of the media. Indeed, her frustration with the press manifested itself as soon as she became First Lady. Where reporters had once been free to roam from their press area in the White House, the new First Lady insisted that a connecting doorway be closed, sealing journalists off from the various offices and work areas in the West Wing.

Unsurprisingly, the media were unimpressed and turned on Hillary with a vengeance. In hindsight, it should have been clear that, having established her role as Bill Clinton's wife/counsel/soulmate, Hillary was now ill-placed to attempt to establish a zone of privacy. To believe that such a concept was ever remotely feasible in the 1990s, with the emergence of 24-hour news channels and the eventual dominance of the internet, was unrealistic. While the zone of privacy that the First Lady had requested was extended to her daughter, Chelsea, government officials were not exempt from such treatment and the door was quickly reopened and a petty argument ended.

This, however, was not to be the end of Hillary Clinton's problematic relationship with the media. On the campaign trail, journalists had picked up on the Whitewater story and written a number of small reports about the incident. Now that her husband was President, interest in the story developed; more people in Arkansas recognised the potential to make money from the situation and the relatively inconsequential escapade developed a life of its own. Before the end of her first year in the White House, the *Washington Post* requested financial records from Hillary's past. The irony cannot have escaped the First Lady; as a young woman she had worked on the effort to impeach President Nixon. Now, as First Lady, the very newspaper that had begun the investigation into the Watergate break-in was asking for her private papers in an investigation that ultimately led to her husband's impeachment.

The request for data was debated at the highest levels of the White House and decided upon when the President was in Russia negotiating with Boris Yeltsin. Even though the President agreed with his aides that the documents should be released, Hillary Clinton refused to authorise it, ending the argument. It was a decision with unimaginable ramifications. Refusal to release the papers fuelled calls in the press and on Capitol Hill for a Special Prosecutor to investigate allegations of corruption in the failed land deal. Eager to move on with the legislative process and get the allegations behind him, President Clinton agreed to the appointment, which quickly turned into a roving searchlight for anything detrimental once it became clear that there was nothing of substance to the initial allegations.

The eight years that Hillary Clinton spent in the White House as First Lady were a seemingly endless round of skirmishes with the media, as political opponents, opportunists and a new breed of web-based writers took turns and sometimes worked in tandem to investigate, embarrass and humiliate the First Couple in a concerted attempt to derail their policy initiatives. Even when the Clinton White House was dramatised, Hillary appeared to be especially targeted: in *Primary Colors*, the fictionalised account of the 1992 campaign, her character has an affair with a character based on George Stephanopoulos. 'And so now,' said Hillary, 'they have [me] carrying on both with George and a lesbian vet.'[38] Later, in Aaron Sorkin's interpretation of the Clinton White House, *The American President*, the First Lady is killed off altogether.

The endless round of skirmishes and even the fictionalisations of Hillary had a profound impact on the White House, on the ability to enact policy initiatives and on the personal and economic lives of Bill and Hillary Clinton, as well as their staff. Legal bills mounted and the constant allegations did much to undermine faith in the administration and in the US system of government. Some issues erupted and then disappeared almost overnight, such as the First Lady's apparent involvement in the firing of seven long-standing members of the White House Travel Office in an effort to hire personal connections. Others, such as the suicide of her friend and former colleague, White House Counsel Vince Foster, lingered both personally and professionally. All, however, contributed to a sense of paralysis at the heart of government and contributed to the removal of trust in the administration.

Shortly after Hillary Clinton was born, 75 per cent of Americans said that they trusted the government to do the right thing; by the time she became First Lady, the same percentage stated that they did not.[39] Despite the repeated assertions of the President, it was not a figure that was set to improve during the 1990s. The Clinton administration's ability to utilise the media in this effort was stymied, in part, by the frosty relations with the First Lady, as the acrimony that began on the campaign and which was exacerbated by the doorway incident never really ended, ensuring that Hillary has spent the rest of her career in a testy relationship with the press.

THE CO-PRESIDENT?

In the United States, an eleven-week interregnum exists between election day in November and inauguration day in the following January. During this time, an incoming administration is required to assemble a team to govern the country for the next four years. Bill Clinton had promised a Cabinet that 'looked like America' and ensured that the First Lady was intimately involved in the selection process. The allocation of Cabinet-level appointments carried with it the opportunity to repay political debts from the campaign, to reward friends, punish enemies and to make statements of political intent. Part of the Clintons' selection process involved the use of an EGG test, determining the strength of candidates based on their ethnicity, gender and geography as the administration sought to build a team that reflected the United States of the 1990s, and not of the 1950s.

The incoming Clinton team made these decisions at the highest level, a process that continued once they had taken office, rather than entrusting them to the various heads of department, which delayed the process. Writing in the *Los Angeles Times*, Robert L. Jackson noted that 'Clinton and his wife, Hillary, are personally signing off on most choices – a factor that has caused added delay, especially in view of the President's propensity to take his time and to change his mind on such matters.'[40] While the quest for a diverse Cabinet resulted in a team where white males were in a minority, David Gergen observed that the 'obsessive demands for balance and the way [Clinton] agonised over choices prolonged the process so much that few other jobs were properly filled'.[41] During its first 100 days in office, however, the Clinton administration made 172 appointments, compared to 152 during the Reagan administration and ninety-six under George H. W. Bush. Over the years there had been a steady increase in the number of appointments to be made; when Kennedy was President he had 100 positions to fill, but by the time Clinton took office the number had reached 500.

There were also the character traits of the President and First Lady to consider, for there was, according to Joe Klein, 'always the sense that Bill and Hillary thought they could do it all themselves'.[42] Both were used to being the centre of attention in Arkansas, something they were determined to continue at the White House, ensuring that Hillary was given the specific remit of identifying the first woman to be US Attorney General. However, this initiative led to a series of problems for the administration that rocked its first weeks in power, as Zoe Baird became a by-word for failures in the vetting system. Identified as the ideal candidate, Baird was forced to withdraw her name from consideration following congressional hearings that dwelt on her use of an illegal alien as a live-in domestic servant. The second choice, Judge Kimba Wood, was announced to the press and then withdrawn once it emerged that she had also hired an illegal nanny and had also trained to be a Playboy bunny, a far-from-appropriate training ground for the head of the United States' Justice Department.[43] At the third attempt, Janet Reno was nominated and confirmed to serve as the first female US Attorney General, remaining in the position throughout the eight years of the Clinton administration. Despite the eventual success in nominating Janet Reno, the backlash against Baird and Wood was a tremendous distraction for the first Democrat administration in twelve years and drew attention away from early legislative successes. To nominate candidates with such obvious flaws showed poor political judgement and presented the administration's allies in Congress with no option but to signal their discomfort with the new President and his team.

Beyond her extensive involvement in selecting members of the Cabinet, the most tangible example of Hillary Clinton's immediate influence in Washington, DC came with her office allocation at the White House. Since 1961, First Ladies had worked out of an office in the East Wing. Hillary, however, was designated an office in the West Wing complex and a suite of offices in the East Wing, as well as in the Executive Office Building next door to the White House that became known as Hillaryland. On the basis that proximity to power equates to actual power, the West Wing of the White House is the most valuable office space in the world. It is also in extremely short supply, with too few offices designed to accommodate too many officials, all of whom would rather work in a broom-cupboard-size office in the West Wing than in a much larger office elsewhere in the White House complex. The physical space in the West Wing is so limited that even the Vice-President did not have an office there until President Carter made room for Walter Mondale in 1977. Hillary's office on the second floor of the West Wing, up a flight of stairs from the President's Oval Office, placed her in immediate proximity to the Vice-President, the Chief of Staff and the National Security Advisor. The allocation of office space confirmed Hillary Clinton's influence on a broad range of policy issues as she quickly emerged as the most influential First Lady in US history. It was a position that was at odds with public sentiment, however. Clinton's campaign pollster, Stan Greenberg, warned the campaign in May 1992, 'Voters are particularly wary of the concept of having a co-President ... They don't want any suggestion that someone who has not been elected will exercise presidential authority.'[44]

When President Kennedy was asked who he wanted by his side when he made decisions, the answer was his brother, Robert Kennedy, whom he appointed Attorney General. When Bill Clinton was asked the same question, he instinctively replied, 'Hillary', but a 1967 change in the law prevented Hillary Clinton from serving in her husband's administration in an official capacity. Title 5, §3110 of the United States Code states: 'A public official may not appoint, employ, promote, advance, or advocate for appointment, employment, promotion, or advancement, in or to a civilian position in the agency in which he is serving or over which he exercises jurisdiction or control any individual who is a relative of the public official.' Therefore, a role needed to be found for Hillary that enabled her to advise the President without being a government employee.

HEALTHCARE

In the early 1990s, there was common consensus, particularly among Democrats, that the US healthcare system needed to be addressed as a matter of urgency. When Bill Clinton became President, he came to Washington, DC with a Congress and a Senate both controlled by the Democratic Party, and with Republicans effectively locked out of any governing role. To many, this presented a rare opportunity to push through legislation that may otherwise have struggled to overcome partisan opposition. Having campaigned on the issue, and with apparent party support, healthcare reform became a domestic policy priority for the new Clinton administration. Indeed, the White House focus on the issue was such that even foreign policy initiatives were considered in light of any detrimental impact that they may have on the passage of the healthcare proposals.

To signal the administration's commitment to the proposals, President Clinton appointed the First Lady to head up the task force drawing up the necessary legislation for congressional approval. It was a move that reflected the President's admiration for his wife's abilities in a clear continuation of her previous role in Arkansas. If the proposals succeeded, they would constitute the most significant contribution to the American welfare state since the New Deal policies of the 1930s and a completion of the Great Society programmes of the 1960s. However, the manner in which the effort was implemented demonstrated an ignorance of the polarisation of politics in the 1990s, as the administration initially promised to present legislation during its first 100 days in office. By placing so much political and personal capital into the policy, opponents only needed to target the healthcare initiative to potentially derail the entire Clinton presidency. It was a precarious situation that Hillary appeared to regret almost immediately, confiding in her best friend Diane Blair as early as 1 February 1993 that she regretted taking the position.[45]

Despite initial concerns, Hillary adopted a similar approach to the one she had previously taken in Arkansas, actively engaging with the general public in a series of meetings designed to convey both her personal commitment and a sense of urgency. The First Lady listened intently to personal tales of woe from members of the 10 per cent of Americans who were uninsured. With the vast majority of Americans already having some degree of healthcare, the Clinton administration recognised that their proposed policy required a human face. Her plan was to ensure that even Americans who were already covered recognised the potential risks that came from being registered as uninsurable in the future, or from unemployment and the eventual loss of medical benefits. As she said many times in many places throughout 1993 and into 1994, 'Until all people are secure, no one is.'[46] Unfortunately, Hillary Clinton's attempts to meet and engage with America's uninsured were all too often met with organised protests and the vehement opposition of vested interests. Her opponents suggested that her efforts amounted to socialised medicine and the level of personal animosity the proposals aroused ensured that she acquiesced to a Secret Service request to wear a bulletproof vest when she visited Seattle to promote the policy.

Despite such organised opposition, the exercise was a remarkable opportunity for Hillary Clinton to engage with the American public in a way that no First Lady had done before. The initiative perfectly encapsulated Bill Clinton's notion of 'buy one, get one free', as Hillary initially earned high praise for her efforts, both from the general public and lawmakers; she gave speeches without notes, met powerbrokers and the uninsured in both back rooms and town halls. There was, essentially, nothing new or revolutionary in the healthcare proposals that her task force devised. They were, instead, an amalgamation of various reform proposals that had been discussed for many years. They aimed to provide universal healthcare to all US citizens, in part by incorporating the existing Medicaid system, while also overhauling and improving the US Medicare system. The plan called for this to be paid for, in large part, by employers and overseen by regional Alliances. Eighty per cent of an individual's premium was to be paid for by a business with more than seventy-five employees. Those not covered directly by their employers would deal with the local Alliances, which were designed to offer a range of coverage dependent on the individual's requirements. These efforts, however, ultimately failed to result in the passage of legislation, as the Clinton administration's healthcare reforms collapsed before ever being voted on in Congress. As the head of these efforts, it is important to appreciate the role that Hillary Clinton played in the plan's ultimate failure as an indicator of her approach to policy negotiations.

Despite her efforts to engage with the American people and their lawmakers on Capitol Hill, the process by which Hillary and her healthcare task force went about devising the plan, the scale of the 1,364-page Bill and the reaction to alternative solutions all helped doom the initiative. Hillary worked with Ira Magaziner to lead a task force made up of six members of Bill Clinton's Cabinet and many top White House advisors. In addition, over 500 people, pulled together from various government agencies and congressional offices, as well as healthcare experts, contributed to the process in a vast undertaking that was likened to the invasion of Normandy in terms of its unprecedented scope. Despite the wide range of input, four factors that Hillary insisted upon helped cripple the process. Firstly, the American Medical Association and other groups who were opposed to the plans were excluded from the process. This ensured that those who were believed to have a vested interest had no way to impact on the process without going public, which they did by organising a highly successful advertising campaign lambasting the size, scope and cost of the proposals.

The second mistake involved the secrecy that surrounded the process. Having excluded those believed to be opposed to the plan, the task force conducted hearings in private with the administration, refusing to identify who was working on the plan or what was being discussed. The excessive secrecy, bordering on paranoia, appears to have originated from Hillary Clinton personally, since Ira Magaziner denied responsibility for it and subsequently identified it as a major mistake. Omitting relevant members of the administration *and* Congress ensured that both the executive and legislative elements in Washington, DC felt excluded and increasingly hostile towards the process, despite early support and, in many cases, sympathy with the need for healthcare reform.

Hillary also insisted that only a final bill be submitted to Congress, rather than liaising on a draft proposal. This meant that Congress believed it was being presented with a *fait accompli*, which offended their sensibilities and practices. This decision, which deliberately sought to avoid the traditional congressional practice of adding amendments and attachments to legislation, was also designed to prevent outside interference from the healthcare industry and insurance companies. It was another example of the control that Hillary Clinton sought to maintain over the process and a continuation of practices that had worked in Arkansas, but ultimately failed to impress in Washington, DC.

Finally, efforts to provide universal healthcare coverage also failed due to an inability to recognise viable alternatives, such as one proposed by Democratic Congressman Jim Cooper of Tennessee. The Congressional Budget Office concluded that this proposal ensured that 91 per cent of all Americans would have healthcare, up from a figure of 85 per cent, by adding an extra 15 million uninsured citizens. The Cooper plan was incremental and had the backing of powerful figures in Congress, including Senator Daniel Patrick Moynihan, chairman of the Finance Committee, whom Hillary eventually succeeded when he retired. He observed, 'With this fairly minimal bill, 90-plus per cent of the population would be insured within eighteen months. That's pretty impressive.'[47] It was also a compromise between maintaining the status quo and the more radical changes called for by Hillary Clinton's task force, and, therefore, occupied the all-important middle ground in American politics.

However, it was *not* the plan that Hillary Clinton had advocated and was, therefore, seen as being in direct competition with the White House. The goal should have been to find a solution that extended healthcare coverage to as many as possible as quickly as possible. However, the issues had become personalised and politicised within the White House due to the involvement of the First Lady. Bill Clinton's entire *modus operandi* as a politician and as President had been to seek compromise and achieve what was achievable. However, Hillary insisted on an all-or-nothing approach and prevented the President from compromising on the healthcare initiative. Senator Bob Packwood, the ranking minority member of the Senate Finance Committee, mused, 'If you can get what we pretty much all agree is universal coverage – none of us think we are going to get a *hundred* per cent ... why have the compulsion?'[48] Hillary was seen smiling as President Clinton promised to veto any legislation that failed to offer universal healthcare coverage, but issuing such a red line proved self-defeating and ultimately yielded nothing, as healthcare reform became impossible for another twenty years.

Failing to compromise with a fellow Democrat on the issue helped doom the White House healthcare initiative and set up the disastrous mid-term elections of 1994. Instead of heading into those elections with broad support for a Bill that would have dramatically increased coverage, with a view to steadily increasing membership once it was established, the White House had nothing to show for its efforts except an embarrassing failure. The 1994 mid-term elections saw huge Democrat losses as the Republicans took control of both Houses of Congress for the first time in forty years, ensuring that Bill and Hillary Clinton's political opponents now controlled the levers of power on Capitol Hill, including the capacity to hold hearings, investigate and eventually impeach the President.

Hillary Clinton observed in her 2003 memoir that the 'most critical mistake was trying to do too much, too fast' and that is partly true.[49] In reality, however, a range of challenges prevented the passage of healthcare reform in 1994. These included the opposition of the insurance companies and other vested interests, but Hillary's personal role was also central to the reason for its collapse. President Clinton chose her because he felt she was the most competent person possible to lead the operation, but doing so made her a lightning rod for all of his enemies and a target for Republicans eager to reclaim the White House in 1996. This decision, along with Hillary's unwillingness to accept anything but full implementation of her plan revealed the couple's *naiveté* about how Washington, DC worked, treating the nation's capital as an extension of Little Rock. Alas, what worked in Arkansas failed to cut it in Washington, DC, as the Clintons learned a series of painful lessons about the use of power, and the chance for healthcare reform was lost for a political generation.

FIRST STEPS OVERSEAS

Hillary Clinton's initial foray into domestic affairs and the debacle over healthcare did not end her involvement in policy guidance during the Clinton administration. It was initially announced that she was to contribute on domestic affairs and healthcare, but as time went on her role expanded to a point where she provided input on foreign policy, despite a total lack of experience in this area. A key ally in the Clinton White House was Madeleine Albright, who served as UN Ambassador in the first term. Outspoken and engaging, Albright formed a close working relationship with the

First Lady that worked to their mutual advantage, providing Hillary with a grounding in foreign policy that later proved helpful when she became Secretary of State and granting Albright a powerful ally in the administration. Albright conceded that her relationship with the First Lady 'was a departure from tradition', and that she was 'once asked whether it was appropriate for the two of us to work together so closely' as she and Hillary Clinton commenced an 'unprecedented partnership' that coincided with a more hawkish approach to foreign policy by the administration.[50]

The relationship proved especially beneficial for Madeleine Albright as she received Hillary Clinton's vital support to be nominated as Secretary of State in Bill Clinton's second term, becoming the first woman to serve in the post that Hillary herself filled eight years later. In her memoir *Living History*, Hillary addressed the need to intervene in the former Yugoslavia in 1993, although US military action was not forthcoming until 1995. Like Madeleine Albright, Hillary Clinton was adamant that US foreign policy had to be backed by force and dedicated to the defence of the innocent. Her faith and commitment to Methodist principles, along with her belief in an American mission, combined to ensure support for the promotion of democracy, which formed a central tenet of her husband's grand strategy.[51]

THE WRONGED FIRST LADY

Perhaps the most monumental turning point in Hillary Clinton's time as First Lady came in January 1998 when it was revealed that her husband had engaged in a relationship with an intern. This was not the first time that allegations had been made about Bill Clinton's private life, but it was clear from the beginning that the situation regarding Monica Lewinsky was different from previous rumours. Firstly, the relationship with the woman Hillary privately referred to as a 'narcissistic loony toon' had been conducted while he was President and appeared to involve an attempt to encourage perjury by potential witnesses.[52] The President vigorously denied the allegations as he wagged his finger at the American public and issued the most remembered quote of his entire presidency: 'I did not have sexual relations with that woman.' Having been secluded with lawyers for several days prior to this statement, there was a sense that perhaps the President was indeed being set up. This was certainly the approach that Hillary Clinton took in her first interview after the story broke, in which she told Matt Lauer of NBC's *Today Show*, 'The great story here for anyone willing to find it and write about it and explain it, is this vast right-wing conspiracy that has been conspiring against my husband since the day he announced for President.'[53]

The 'vast right-wing conspiracy' was eventually found and written about by Joe Conason and Gene Lyons in their book *The Hunting of the President*, which detailed the workings of the Arkansas Project, designed to undermine and destroy Bill Clinton's credibility and electability. Their work was reinforced by the subsequent revelations of former Clinton critic David Brock in his book *Blinded by the Right*, which detailed the conservative efforts to thwart the Clinton presidency. However, the President had indeed been involved in what he later admitted was 'an inappropriate relationship', which rather overshadowed the revelations of the concerted effort to undermine his administration. Even after the President had confessed his guilt, Hillary Clinton was determined to find a way to forgive him, noting the tragedies he had faced since taking office, including the death of his mother, his father-in-law and Vince Foster. Diane Blair noted that

> Ever since he took office they've been going thru [sic] personal tragedy [Vince, her dad, his mom] and immediately all the ugly forces started making up hateful things about them, pounding on them. They adopted strategy, public strategy, of acting as tho [sic] it didn't bother them; had to. [Hillary] didn't realize the toll it was taking on him.[54]

Ultimately, Hillary questioned her own responsibility for the situation, as Blair noted: 'She thinks she was not smart enough, not sensitive enough, not free enough of her own concerns and struggle to realise the price he was paying.'[55]

What was clear, however, was that the legal effort to undermine and disrupt the Clinton White House took a toll on personnel and policies. White House aides left the administration owing thousands of dollars in legal fees due to politically motivated depositions. Meetings with the President were interrupted by lawyers forced to address personal law suits brought against Bill Clinton for events alleged to have transpired prior to his time in office and, for the first time in US history, both the President and the First Lady were compelled to appear before a grand jury investigation.

The spectre of suspicion never strayed far from the First Couple despite repeatedly being cleared of any wrongdoing by a succession of juries, judges and investigative panels.

ASSET OR LIABILITY?

A popular joke from 1992 depicts Hillary Clinton flirting with a petrol station attendant while her husband waits patiently in the car. She later reveals that she once dated the attendant, prompting Bill Clinton to retort that she could now be the First Lady of a petrol station if history had taken a different turn. No, Hillary insists, the petrol station attendant would now be President of the United States. The joke, which has lost its lustre from repeated retelling, was both amusing and telling, as it was widely believed that Hillary Clinton was the driving force in the relationship, that it was she who actively encouraged her husband to achieve all that was possible and that without her he would have remained another charming, roguish politician from a dirt-poor Southern state that no one outside Arkansas had ever heard of. Even once elected, White House aides recognised the perception problem extended far beyond humour; it was suggested that that the President and First Lady should never appear together on live television because Hillary 'makes him look soft & weak – her like his mother. She strongly enhances him; not sure what he does for her.'[56]

If the joke has a resonance in reality then it naturally raises the question to what extent Hillary Clinton was an asset or a liability for her husband. Was she responsible for his rise to the Oval Office, or for his near-calamitous removal from the presidency? Despite the obvious personal failings of the President that did so much to jeopardise his administration, many of the scandals originated with the First Lady, not with the President: her suggestion that she could have stayed at home and baked cookies, which did much to undermine the campaign with female voters, came in response to a question about her financial affairs; it had been her determination to make quick money that resulted in the scandals over Whitewater and her commodities investments; it had been her feud with the media that fuelled journalists' refusal to take the White House at face value and continue to dig for dirt; it was her refusal to turn over documents to the *Washington Post* that led to the appointment of a Special Prosecutor; it had been her decision to fire the White House travel service; it was Hillary who moved to seal Vince Foster's office after his suicide. Finally, it was Hillary who led the healthcare reform effort that crashed so memorably, due in no small part to her approach. And it was this that led directly to the 1994 mid-term election catastrophe resulting in a return to Republican control of Congress that did so much to undermine the Clinton agenda in the 1990s.

It must be recognised, though, that Hillary Clinton had been instrumental in getting Bill Clinton to the White House in the first place. She remained loyal through all of the scandals in Arkansas and through the Gennifer Flowers revelations, sat with him through the humiliating *60 Minutes* interview, stayed with him as Arkansas State Troopers revealed they had procured women for the Governor and when it was revealed that he had indeed been in a relationship with Lewinsky. At any one of these points her departure would have signalled the end of Bill Clinton and his political career.

Despite being husband and wife, and President and First Lady, there was a constant tension during the White House years between their apparently competing agendas. The Clinton presidency, for all of its aspirations and progressive instincts, resembled a see-saw on the Potomac, with either the President or First Lady riding high and the other sinking in popularity. This lack of equilibrium in the White House in the 1990s had significant implications for what was achieved over the eight years of the administration. There was always too much going on and too little focus on getting one thing done at a time, which is how governments tend to work best. The ability to address any single issue was routinely compromised by the competing power bases in the West Wing of the White House. An early example was the decision to press ahead with both healthcare reform and passage of the North American Free Trade Agreement (NAFTA) in the autumn of 1993. Hillary was adamant that all attention should focus on healthcare, but the White House prioritised the NAFTA agreement, much to the First Lady's chagrin.

The Clintons exercised extraordinary power as President and First Lady during the 1990s, continuing at a national level many of the same policies and approaches to power they had initiated previously in Arkansas. Alas, they often received a similar reaction, as Hillary Clinton adopted a forthright role in her husband's administration and became an easy target for his political opponents, who routinely asked who had voted for her to take on such an enhanced position.

For eight years she maintained an effective veto on policy to an unprecedented degree for an American First Lady as her husband continuously kowtowed to her policy aspirations and directives. This led to a confused chain of command in which Cabinet secretaries and White House staff were left unsure who was responsible for the final approval of policy.

There can be no doubt that on many occasions Hillary Rodham Clinton was a remarkable asset for her husband and his administration. As the most educated First Lady in US history, she made a perfect contrast with her husband, offsetting his southern, laid-back approach with a brisk and assertive northern manner that ensured much-debated ideas were actually implemented and not merely discussed. She was also remarkably adroit at presenting policy in committee hearings, demonstrating a solid grasp of the issues and the politics involved. Despite the eventual demise of her healthcare reform initiatives, congressmen on both sides of the political aisle remarked on her polished performance before their hearings. However, her triumphant appearance before congressional committee was tempered by her subsequent grilling by a grand jury, another less welcome 'first' for Hillary Clinton as First Lady. This unrelenting pattern of positive and negative, driven partly by rampant political opportunism among Clinton's opponents, meant that the American people were rarely presented with a consistent view of their First Lady.

As the decade progressed and the popularity of the internet grew, Hillary was increasingly vilified by the right and defended, if not ever quite adored, by the left. Her role in the Clinton administration arguably never developed as she had hoped. Denied an official role in government by regulations preventing the appointment of relations, her lack of official stature was frustrating for her and those around her as she sought to influence and direct policy in a bureaucratic bubble. She was neither a government employee, political appointment, nor merely First Lady, but a unique combination of all three, ensuring that her contribution to the Clinton White House remained nebulous and contentious.

CONCLUSION

Hillary Rodham Clinton's time as First Lady was a rollercoaster ride of great highs and historic lows, as her husband became the first Democrat to be elected to two full terms since Franklin Roosevelt, but also only the second President to be impeached in US history. The impeachment scandal, caused at least in part by the President's relationship with Monica Lewinsky, brought obvious embarrassment and discomfort to his wife as she weighed both her political and marital future. Often forgotten, however, is Hillary Clinton's role in the incidents that led to the President's impeachment, a process that could have potentially been prevented had records relating to Whitewater been released to the *Washington Post* in 1993. Attempting to hide the losses from a land deal and financial gains made from commodities trading in Arkansas in the 1980s led to the appointment of a Special Prosecutor determined to uncover wrongdoing of any kind and exploit it for political ends.

With her husband's second term decimated by the impeachment process, the opportunity for Hillary to maximise the role of First

Lady was diminished, and all energies were turned to political survival rather than the implementation of the progressive policies that she would have liked to advocate. When it mattered most, however, Hillary Clinton's popularity figures were at their peak and it was at that point that she struck out on her own to run for the Senate and for a place in history on her own terms.

CHAPTER 4

THE JUNIOR MEMBER FROM THE GREAT STATE OF NEW YORK

As her husband's career as an elected politician drew to a close, Hillary Clinton moved to claim her own place at the seat of American power. Having loyally assisted her husband's political career for thirty years, Hillary moved to ensure that, whatever else happened after she left the White House in January 2001, she would not be moving back to Arkansas. Instead, she struck out on her own for the very first time and became the first First Lady to seek elected office. The risks were huge; a defeat would surely mark the end to any potential role as an elected official and even victory did not guarantee acceptance among Washington, DC's power brokers. However, public sympathy and a vast supply of campaign resources

ensured that her first foray into elected politics was a resounding
success, as she secured a place in the United States Senate and
in the history books.

THE STATE OF THE UNION: 2001

The United States that Hillary Clinton faced as she entered the
Senate in 2001 was to change drastically during her time in office.
As she took the oath, the country was at peace, was prosperous
and appeared set for several years of continued growth. Under her
husband's leadership, the nation had emerged from a recession and
enjoyed the longest era of growth in its history. Unemployment and
inflation were down, wages were up and the mood was buoyant and
optimistic. As the twenty-first century began, talk of a Second
American Century was in the air.

This all changed just eight months later, as Hillary Clinton's
own constituents came under attack high above the streets of
Manhattan. The sunny optimism and laid-back detachment
of the 1990s suddenly appeared lackadaisical and irresponsible
as the United States declared an unconditional War on Terror.
The US Bureau of Labor reported that the national unemployment rate in the United States was 4.2 per cent in January 2001,
a figure that leapt to 5.7 per cent less than a year later and which
reached 7.8 per cent by the time Hillary left the Senate in January
2009. The budget surplus of $280 billion that President Clinton
bequeathed to his Republican successor was quickly erased and
replaced with a deficit of $6 trillion by 2011; eight years' worth

of work by the Clinton administration to erase America's debt and return the nation to a solid economic footing was wiped out by the Bush administration's tax cuts and the cost of fighting in Iraq and Afghanistan.

The new administration brought back many old faces to Washington, DC, as those who had been exiled by the Clintons were recalled and decisions agreed during that eight-year period were reversed. The new Republican administration walked away from international treaties designed to address global warming (Kyoto) and dismissed a long-standing agreement with Russia, partly on the precept that the Anti-Ballistic Missile Treaty had been signed with the USSR, which technically no longer existed.

International terrorism, which the Clinton administration had dealt with as criminal activity, was now designated as warranting a military response, which prompted land wars in Afghanistan and Iraq. A Saudi financier and his group of radical Islamists replaced the leaders of the now defunct Soviet Union as Public Enemy Number One and a global manhunt was launched for Osama bin Laden and his associates. Suddenly, the era through which Hillary Clinton had served as First Lady felt like a distant memory, and its relevance was open to speculation as George W. Bush's administration placed the nation on a permanent war footing, at odds with anything Americans had experienced under Bill Clinton. From her office on Capitol Hill, Hillary looked out over Washington, DC and saw a changed America, one to which she would again be required to adapt in order to remain relevant.

RUNNING FOR THE SENATE AND RUNNING FOR HISTORY

The very possibility of Hillary Clinton running for the Senate sprang from the public humiliation brought on by her husband's publicised affair with 'that woman', Monica Lewinsky. As Bill Clinton's impeachment process dragged on and the inevitable end to his presidency (either enforced or as constitutionally scheduled) loomed large, Hillary began to consider her future. Indeed, it was on the very day that the Senate voted on articles of impeachment against Bill Clinton that she met to devise a strategy for elected office. The concept of Hillary seeking elected office had been considered previously. When her husband seriously considered not running for re-election as Governor of Arkansas in 1990, key backers in the state briefly, but seriously, considered Hillary Clinton as a potential successor. The implications and logistics involved convinced all concerned that it was not a viable option, however, and her role as the steadfast First Lady of Arkansas continued unabated.

By the end of her husband's time in the White House, Hillary Clinton was in a very different situation. The see-saw on the Potomac that continued throughout the 1990s had placed her in a powerful position: her commitment to Bill Clinton had been vital during the impeachment process, she was riding high in the polls and the President was beholden to her as never before. As Republican Senators voted to impeach one member of the Clinton family, the other was making plans to join their distinguished ranks on Capitol Hill. Speculation was rife that Hillary planned to divorce her husband once they left the White House, but as Hillary met with key advisors, including Harold Ickes, to plan her path to independence and power, she made the decision to continue in her marriage. Simultaneously juggling her personal and political future was no easy task and it involved much soul-searching. In her memoir *Living History*, she later revealed, 'The most difficult decisions I have made in my life were to stay married to Bill and to run for the Senate from New York.'[57] The scandal surrounding the impeachment was a very public humiliation for Hillary, but she was determined to survive and maximise the opportunity that arose from the resulting public support.

Hillary Clinton's historic announcement that she had decided to compete for a seat in the Senate ended years of speculation as to what she might do at the end of her husband's administration, but raised both questions and eyebrows as she sought to position herself as a New Yorker. When long-term Democratic Senator Daniel Patrick Moynihan announced his intention to retire, a series of potential successors received consideration, including both John Kennedy Jr and his cousin Robert Kennedy Jr, whose father had held the seat forty-five years earlier. These considerations were silenced once it emerged that Hillary Clinton intended to seek the nomination. This was not going to be an easy election, however, as her campaign raised obvious challenges of nepotism, not to mention naked opportunism. Like Robert F. Kennedy before her, Hillary faced allegations of carpetbagging that were hard, if not outright impossible, to deny. Born in Illinois, educated in Massachusetts, resident of Arkansas and Washington, DC, Hillary

Clinton had no natural affinity for or claims to a relationship with the Empire State.

To succeed, Hillary was required to do what she had done throughout her life and career: reinvent herself for a new constituency. In the past she had morphed from a young Republican to an advocate of progressive Democratic principles at Wellesley; from a feminist determined to retain her maiden name to a doting political wife in Arkansas; from a co-President to a more traditional First Lady. At every step of her career, Hillary Clinton adopted a position and was then forced to address its merits in the face of public scepticism. In this case, however, her enthusiasm backfired. She was a well-known, lifetime fan of the Chicago Cubs baseball team, yet sought to ingratiate herself with potential constituents by wearing a New York Yankees cap. Despite this early misstep, she drew on a long-standing team of political consultants that had coalesced around her husband in his 1992 and 1996 campaigns to devise an electoral strategy designed to combat the carpetbagger label and re-humanise her from her elevated stature as First Lady. Working with Harold Ickes, Mandy Grunwald, Mark Penn and the future Mayor of New York Bill de Blasio, Hillary Clinton's team devised a state-wide strategy designed to out-campaign and out-charm her opponents.

The campaign received an early and unexpected stroke of good fortune when the anticipated opponent, outgoing New York Mayor Rudy Giuliani, dropped out of the race long before he could turn his sights on Hillary. Often forgotten in the aftermath of 9/11 is the extent to which, by 2000, Giuliani had become the forgotten man of New York politics due to his high-profile affairs, political losses and ill-health. Indeed, it was the latter, a diagnosis of prostate cancer, that was premised as the rationale for Giuliani's withdrawal from the race, a decision that ultimately proved to be the end of his political aspirations. In his place, the Republican Party nominated a little-known congressman from Long Island, Rick Lazio, whose key electoral advantage was believed to be his affinity to the local community and lack of star power. His strategy was to use both assets in stark contrast to the outsider superstar candidate from Illinois, Arkansas and Washington, DC. However, it was a strategy that singularly failed to ignite, for while Lazio appeared content to remain in the vicinity of New York City (a Democratic Party stronghold), Hillary Clinton routinely travelled north into the Republican stronghold of upstate New York, far from the urban centre of Manhattan. In a move that she eventually replicated at the start of her 2016 campaign for the presidency, Hillary hit the road in a van and visited all of New York's sixty-two counties in an effort to overcome perceptions of her as a superstar candidate, happy to be parachuted into high office.

Hillary's Senate campaign embraced a deliberately low-key approach designed to challenge convention and expectations. She did not need to introduce herself to the electorate; she already had near-universal name recognition. In the aftermath of the Lewinsky scandal and after eight years of her husband's presidency, however, this did not necessarily equate to universal adulation, and her opponent dwelt on the scandals of the 1990s. It proved to be a flawed approach, however, which enabled Hillary's campaign to portray Lazio as looking backward rather than forward. Lazio's campaign was further damaged when the congressman appeared to physically challenge his opponent during a live televised debate, in a stunt that dramatically backfired and generated sympathy for the First Lady. Ultimately, her tenacity, determination to engage and refusal to give in gained her the begrudging respect of New Yorkers and helped secure her victory on election night 2000. It was a rare moment of joy for the Democrats on a night that saw Bill Clinton's Vice-President, Al Gore, lose his bid for the presidency despite receiving half a million more votes than George W. Bush.

WORKING HARD, MAKING FRIENDS IN THE SENATE

It was, therefore, with all too obviously forced smiles all around that outgoing Vice-President Al Gore, serving in his capacity as President of the Senate, posed for photographs as he re-enacted Hillary Clinton's oath of office. Despite the perception of Hillary as having been a virtual co-President for eight years, her campaign made it abundantly clear that neither the voters nor her colleagues in the Senate would forgive her for grandstanding in her new office. She had been granted an opportunity to serve the people of New York and it was that concept of service that she needed to demonstrate most during her time as Senator. Thankfully, the need to ingratiate herself with the voters and the Senate leadership appeared to come naturally to Hillary as she worked to gain their trust and support. At school she had gained a reputation as a teacher's pet, and she adopted a similar approach to life in the Senate, arriving early to meetings and committee hearings despite not being required to. She prioritised floor votes at the expense of meetings and external events, ensuring that during her first two years in office Hillary only missed five roll calls. Despite making a deliberate effort not to act like a celebrity in the Senate, her status ensured that she was sought out by colleagues, eager to get attention for their own legislative efforts. As a result, while Hillary Clinton sponsored 711 of her own Bills during her time in the Senate, she co-sponsored more than 2,500 pieces of legislation brought to her by colleagues who recognised her unique ability to draw attention to even the dullest regulations due to the continuing press interest in her and her aspirations.

When the Clintons arrived in Washington, DC, they were courted by party elders such as Pamela Harriman at her Georgetown residence. A decade later, the Clintons were the hosts, as their Washington residence became a hub for politicians and strategists. This was part of a strategy designed to ensure that Hillary Clinton remained central to political life in the United States. Indeed, one of the challenges that Hillary faced in 2001 was entering the very legislative body that only two years previously had considered articles of impeachment against her husband and which was still dominated by many of the same Republicans who had vehemently opposed President Clinton and vilified Hillary as First Lady. These former opponents were now colleagues with whom she needed to develop working, if not necessarily cordial, relations in order to be seen to be doing her part to get along in a particularly exclusive club.

As one of only 100 Senators drawn from across the United States, there was nowhere for Hillary Clinton to hide.

The American system of government was deliberately designed to frustrate rather than facilitate the passage of legislation, as Hillary Clinton's own Senate record demonstrates. Between 2001 and 2009, she sponsored 711 Bills, yet only four of these were approved by both the Senate and the House of Representatives and only three became law. Moreover, these three laws are unlikely to ever be studied by legal experts for their influence on the American legal or political system. One renamed a stretch of road in New York State after the TV presenter Tim Russert, another renamed a New York post office building and the final Bill established the New York home of nineteenth-century union activist Kate Mullany as a national historical site. In addition, of Hillary's 2,676 pieces of co-sponsored legislation, only seventy-four eventually became law.[58] This is not an indictment of Hillary's legislative capabilities, or necessarily of the American legislative system, but it is a reflection of the difficulty in passing legislation and of implementing political change in the United States.

Hillary Clinton worked hard to overcome personal perceptions and to reach across party lines. This charm offensive was designed to demonstrate her ability to gain a bipartisan approach to politics with a view to an eventual run for the presidency. There was, however, a downside to this cross-party effort: many of her fellow Democrats were already suspicious of her liberal, progressive credentials and her efforts to engage with what were viewed as hard-line conservatives merely fuelled such concerns. This was exacerbated by Hillary

Clinton's efforts to introduce the Flag Protection Act of 2005 to ban flag burning and her legislative efforts to restrict sales of violent video games. Yet her efforts were recognised by the least likely of colleagues, including those who had worked tirelessly to bring down the Clinton presidency. She formed a friendship with Republican Senators Sam Brownback from Kansas and John McCain (R) from Arizona, against whom Hillary anticipated running in 2008, and won effusive praise from Republican Senator Lindsey Graham, who noted in his profile for *Time*'s 100 most influential people of 2006 that in the Senate her 'high-profile status, combined with a reputation as a smart, prepared, serious Senator, creates real influence'. He concluded, 'Those who underestimate Hillary Clinton do so at their own peril.'[59]

FIRST TERM

Hillary made domestic politics her priority upon entering the Senate, specifically requesting assignments to committees that enabled her to act in the best interests of her constituents in New York and allowed her to continue her lifelong work in the defence of women and children. In that role she opposed the Bush administration's efforts to reduce taxes in 2001 and 2003, arguing that such efforts undermined the achievements of her husband's administration and would bring about the return of a growing budget deficit. She also voted against two separate efforts to change the American Constitution which sought to define marriage as being between a man and a woman and followed the Democratic Party line by refusing to endorse the nomination of Samuel Alito to the Supreme Court or of John Roberts to serve as Chief Justice of the United States. She also attempted to initiate hearings into the handling of Hurricane Katrina, which devastated the Louisiana coastline in August 2005, causing damage in excess of $108 billion, but her efforts ultimately proved fruitless.

Hillary also worked outside the Senate in helping to establish a liberal network to counteract what she had previously referred to as the 'vast right-wing conspiracy'. One of the most prominent people with whom she worked was David Brock, whose 1993 article 'His Cheatin' Heart' in the *American Spectator* revealed claims by Arkansas State Troopers that they had procured women for Bill Clinton during his time as Governor. Brock, however, had a change of heart and wrote of his transformation in *Blinded by the Right*. Seeking to rectify his past endeavours, he sought out and gained Hillary Clinton's assistance in establishing Media Matters for America, an organisation dedicated to monitoring and correcting conservative news outlets in the United States. In 2003, Hillary assisted in the start-up of Citizens for Responsibility and Ethics in Washington, DC, designed to address unethical political behaviour. Perhaps most important, however, was her work with her husband's former Chief of Staff, John Podesta, to establish the Center for American Progress (CAP), a progressive think tank which came to serve as a hub for once (and potentially future) Clinton administration employees and to do for Hillary what the Progressive Policy Institute had done for her husband in the 1990s: provide ideas, support and support staff for the development of her policies, both in the Senate and with a view to her future career in Washington, DC.

As a first-term Senator representing New York State, however, Hillary Clinton had to be mindful of the specific requirements of her constituents and not get too carried away thinking about future jobs in other white buildings at the other end of Pennsylvania Avenue. To this end she worked with Republican Senator Lindsey Graham, who had managed her husband's impeachment trial, to pass the American Manufacturing Trade Action Coalition, designed to aid the nation's manufacturing base. She also demonstrated her willingness to disagree with policies that her husband's administration had endorsed by refusing to support ratification of the Central America Free Trade Agreement (although this was subsequently agreed upon despite Hillary's opposition).

INTO THE CRUCIBLE: 9/11

Trade talks and manufacturing issues, however, suddenly became of secondary importance, both to the United States and to Hillary Clinton in particular as a Senator representing the state and city of New York, when the Twin Towers of the World Trade Center were suddenly torn from the iconic skyline. Hillary's status as former First Lady and United States Senator ensured that she was afforded unprecedented protection in the wake of the attack; heading to work on Capitol Hill she was taken to a secure location and separated from the world until the immediate danger had passed. As a mother, she was also separated from her daughter, Chelsea, who was in Manhattan at the time and could not be reached, in part because so much of the city's communications equipment had been perched atop Tower One at the World Trade Center. As a wife, she was also separated from her husband, who was in Australia on a speaking tour.

It was into a changed world that Hillary Clinton eventually emerged, and one in which her relevance was suddenly in doubt. In the wake of the tragedy, the nation and the world sought guidance and leadership, neither of which was immediately forthcoming. She may have been a high-profile member of the Senate, but Hillary was not the senior member from New York and was outranked by her colleague Charles Schumer. The President of the United States was flown from one secret secure location to another and so her former political adversary, Rudy Giuliani, suddenly emerged as the nation's *de facto* political leader on the debris-strewn streets of Manhattan. Only when George W. Bush made his way to Ground Zero several days later did the political impetus return to the White House as the President found and asserted his authority.

The robust military response that the White House initiated through its War on Terror totally altered the political landscape of the United States. The 1990s and the touchy-feely approach to politics personified by President Clinton suddenly belonged to another era, which posed a dilemma for Hillary Clinton. As a former First Lady, she was intimately associated with that era and could no more divorce herself from it than she could from her husband, something that few now spoke of as a possibility. Instead, Hillary did what she had done on previous occasions when faced with an existential crisis: she reinvented herself. The caring, nurturing former First Lady who had written books about White House entertaining and of the importance of strong communities to raise children, set about metamorphosing into a strong, robust and determined warrior figure, determined to appear as resilient as any of her male colleagues.

The Senate committee assignments that Hillary Clinton had been granted only months beforehand were now shockingly irrelevant in the new, deadly era that called for a focus on national security, not education or budgetary issues. The Senate leadership, however, was not about to simply hand Hillary a prize assignment to the Foreign Relations or Intelligence Committees. Instead, she secured a seat on the Senate Armed Service Committee, which served her purposes. It enabled her to visit military bases, work alongside top generals and develop a rapport with the Pentagon that had always eluded her husband, who had been viewed with suspicion due to his efforts to avoid the draft in Vietnam.

In the immediate post-9/11 era, it was not politically viable to be viewed as anything other than pro-military and virtually impossible to be too much in favour of armed intervention in retaliation for the attacks. Despite the eventual withdrawal from this muscular approach, it was a mood that the nation and its citizens and politicians wholeheartedly embraced in the immediate aftermath of the attacks. Hillary Clinton was no exception as she moved to both anticipate and reflect the mood of the electorate. Speaking on the floor of the Senate, she made remarks that were indistinguishable from those of George W. Bush, insisting that she planned to

> stand united behind our President as he and his advisors plan
> the necessary actions to demonstrate America's resolve and com-
> mitment ... Not only to seek out and exact punishment on the
> perpetrators, but also to make very clear that not only those who
> harbour terrorists, but those who in any way aid or comfort them
> whosesoever, will now face the wrath of our country.[60]

As a representative of New York, Hillary Clinton was perfectly placed to assist in the planning of the rescue effort in Manhattan. Her constituents had been victims, family members, police officers, fire fighters, first responders and regular citizens either caught up directly or impacted in one of a thousand ways by the calamity that had devastated the city. With her fellow Senator from New York Charles Schumer, Hillary obtained $21.4 billion to help rebuild the devastated area where the World Trade Center once stood. She also took an early lead in investigating health conditions at Ground Zero and the potential implications for first responders, earning the respect and electoral support of the Uniformed Firefighters Association and New York City's Uniformed Fire Officers Association.

As a Senator, however, Hillary Clinton was also called upon to vote on a series of contentious bills in the wake of 9/11. At the time it appeared impossible to be too gung-ho in the defence of the nation or in the persecution of its enemies, as public sentiment verged on vengeance in the face of the destruction visited upon the United States. As a result, Hillary and many of her colleagues in the Democratic Party supported US military action in Afghanistan in direct response to the terrorist attacks and voted for the USA Patriot Act, despite concerns over the Bill's implications for civil liberties. These votes were entirely in keeping with the mood of the nation in the aftermath of 9/11, as Hillary sought to position herself as a strong, defence-minded Democrat who could work with the Pentagon and the White House in a bipartisan fashion to ensure America's future security needs were met. Hillary neither led the charge for extra vigilance, nor sought to block moves by the administration in this area, but was in the mainstream of political thinking. Only several years later, when the political climate cooled, did Hillary's voting record come to have negative implications for her career aspirations.

IRAQ

In the interregnum between his election in November 1992 and his inauguration in January 1993, Bill Clinton implied that Saddam Hussein could be welcomed back into the family of nations if he changed his ways. 'I'm a Baptist,' he said. 'I believe in deathbed conversions.'[61] The backlash that this suggestion received from members of Congress and the outgoing Bush administration forced the President-Elect to retract the statement almost immediately, and ensured his new team continued the no-fly zone and sanction policies put in place by George H. W. Bush. Bill Clinton, however, had no intention of continuing the clash of wills that existed previously and did what he could to diminish the Iraqi leader's military capabilities without engaging him directly or unnecessarily raising tensions. Throughout the 1990s, Saddam was viewed as an irritant, but nothing more, by the Clinton administration. The Iraqi leader was 'kept in his box', apparently out of harm's way, but otherwise ignored.

On the afternoon of September 11th, as the Pentagon burned and the World Trade Center collapsed, Bush administration officials sought to discern if the attacks, mounted by fifteen men from Saudi Arabia, two from the UAE, one from Egypt and one from Lebanon, financed by a renegade Saudi based out of camps in Afghanistan, could be tied to Saddam Hussein's regime in Iraq. This reflected concerns among many in the new Bush administration that Saddam should have been dealt with in the early 1990s and that George H. W. Bush had erred by not finishing the job.

In the eighteen months following the attacks of 9/11, the White House steadily ratcheted up the pressure on Saddam to comply with existing United Nations resolutions governing weapons inspections. Ahead of an impending vote on the authorisation of force, the White House provided Senators with a National Intelligence Estimate, detailing what the Bush administration believed to be Iraq's failure to comply with UN resolutions and its justification for a military response. Hillary Clinton was briefed on its contents but did not read it and instead repeated claims by the White House that Saddam had aided bin Laden's terrorist activities. When the Iraq War Resolution came to be voted on, Hillary refused to support an amendment put forward by fellow Democrat Carl Levin that called for the White House to assemble an international coalition or to subsequently seek congressional support for any unilateral operations. She insisted that her decision was 'influenced by my eight years of experience on the other end of Pennsylvania Avenue, in the White House, watching my husband deal with serious challenges to our nation', as she voted to grant President Bush the authorisation to use force in Iraq. At the time, the vote was entirely in keeping with her foreign policy stance, wherein she sought to position herself as a tough, determined defender of US national security. She had no way of knowing that the vote would prove to be a decisive factor in denying her the White House in 2008.

The deployment of US forces to Iraq and Afghanistan demonstrated the overlap between foreign and domestic policy as troops usually stationed in New York State, including the 10th Mountain Division, were sent into battle. As a result, Hillary Clinton's domestic commitment to her constituents was combined with her responsibilities on the Armed Services Committee. While never apologising for her vote, she broke with the administration once it became clear that the rationale for war was flawed. However, by not apologising for her vote, Hillary managed to alienate members of her own party and voters on the left. Yet, by also criticising the administration's execution of the war plan, she alienated voters on the right and distanced herself from any successes that occurred. As a result, Hillary placed herself in a politically uncomfortable position of having voted for an unpopular war without really supporting it, and then having sought to distance herself from it without making a clean break. As she wrote in 2005, 'I take responsibility for my vote, and I, along with the majority of Americans, expect the President and his administration to take responsibility for the false assurances, faulty evidence and mismanagement of the war.'[62] Ultimately, however, few politicians ended up paying as high a price for their vote to authorise the war in Iraq as Hillary Clinton.

SITTING OUT 2004

The attacks of 9/11 altered millions of lives around the world, including Hillary Clinton's, as her political aspirations suddenly required revaluation. With George W. Bush's uncertain victory in the 2000 election, his re-election in 2004 was by no means guaranteed. As a leading member of the Democratic Party, Hillary was a viable contender, despite only having been in the Senate a matter of months. Her name recognition and personal network ensured that she had to be considered a front runner for her party's nomination. As the President's approval ratings spiked to record levels after the attacks, however, the political landscape suddenly looked less inviting. Just as his father's ratings after the Gulf War persuaded senior Democrats not to seek the presidency in 1992, so now George W. Bush's standing caused his opponents to reconsider their options.

Instead of Hillary Clinton, John Kerry emerged as the Democratic Party's candidate in 2004, determined to exploit his war record in Vietnam to demonstrate his capacity to serve as Commander-in-Chief in a time of conflict and highlight George W. Bush's dubious service record in the Texas Air National Guard during the 1960s. However, as George W. Bush's strategist Karl Rove predicted, by the time the Republicans finished manipulating Kerry's service record it was difficult to discern the accuracy of his heroism. The most egregious incident occurred with the publication of a forged photograph that depicted Kerry with Jane Fonda, known for her outspoken criticism of the war. Although Kerry ultimately lost the 2004 election, George W. Bush won by the smallest margin of votes of any sitting President since Harry Truman in 1948.

The highlight of the Kerry campaign, however, came on 27 July at the Democratic National Convention in Boston as the keynote speech was delivered by a young candidate for an Illinois Senate seat: Barack Hussein Obama. Hillary Clinton was in the audience as Obama made his debut on the national stage and electrified the hall in Boston. Unlike many, however, Obama was no stranger to Hillary, who had campaigned for him in Illinois and was delighted with his speech and the reaction it received. She could have had no idea that she was witnessing the emergence of her own political nemesis, who would arrange her defeat just four years later.

SECOND TERM

With the 2004 election out of the way, Hillary Clinton could finally begin considering her run for the presidency in 2008. To do so, she needed to secure a convincing re-election as Senator for New York and use this as a springboard towards the party nomination. A strong showing in the November 2006 election would enable Hillary to present herself as a strong, unity candidate capable of drawing cross-party support to lead the United States in the aftermath of the George W. Bush era. She secured 83 per cent of her party's support in the primary and her strength in the state ensured that she faced no serious opposition from her Republican opponent in the November general election. The former Mayor of Yonkers John Spencer secured just 31 per cent of the vote to Hillary Clinton's 67 per cent in an electoral landslide that made headlines but came at a high price. To ensure victory, Hillary Clinton's campaign spent $36 million dollars compared to her opponent's budget of just $5 million. With Hillary safely re-elected, her campaign quietly transferred $10 million that had been unspent into a new account dedicated to her 2008 presidential aspirations.

The remainder of Hillary Clinton's second term in office consisted of preparing a presidential campaign, dealing with the Iraq War and the actual run for the presidency. Returning to the Senate after her 2006 campaign, Hillary was faced with the deteriorating situation in Iraq and the continued political fallout of the conflict. Bombarded with mounting calls to withdraw US ground forces, President George W. Bush did the exact opposite and initiated a surge in an attempt to quell the insurgency and provide an environment within which Iraq could begin to govern itself. This was initiated under a new Defense Secretary when Donald Rumsfeld was removed and replaced with Robert Gates, with whom Hillary eventually developed a close working partnership. As a candidate for the presidency, however, Hillary was in no place to support the Bush administration's initiatives in Iraq. Her vote to authorise military action was contentious enough and she was not prepared to compound this by continuing to support the White House efforts.

This ensured that she adopted a hard-line approach against the conflict, against the surge and in favour of a troop withdrawal.

The need to legislate during an ongoing campaign ensured that the war became increasingly politicised as politicians from both main parties manoeuvred to position themselves into the best light possible. Facing the unexpected challenge from Senator Obama, Hillary Clinton was forced to walk a very thin line in regard to Iraq, having voted in favour of the authorisation for war, but being unwilling to concede that this was a mistake or to apologise for her vote out of fear that it might appear irresolute. Having suggested that General Petraeus's report to Congress on the Situation in Iraq 'require[d] a willing suspension of disbelief', Hillary subsequently used his appearance before the Senate Armed Service Committee in April 2008 to call for an orderly withdrawal of US ground forces. Unsurprisingly perhaps, Hillary later admitted that her stance on the Iraq War during this time was driven more by her presidential ambition than by any national security considerations.[63] Having no sooner been re-elected to the Senate, Hillary Clinton announced her intention to seek the presidency on 20 January 2007, ensuring everything that occurred during her second term in the Senate was viewed through the prism of its impact on her candidacy for the White House.

CONCLUSION

Hillary Clinton's most significant contribution to American political life as a United States Senator was largely symbolic, as she became the first First Lady to seek and gain elected office. Her tenure in office produced no direct legislative results of note, but her continued presence in Washington, DC provided a much-needed voice for women's issues and a positive role model. It also provided her with a credible platform from which to seek the presidency of the United States. Her time in office, however, was marred by national tragedy and personal disappointment. The events of 9/11 ensured that Hillary Clinton's expectations changed dramatically as she was required to reposition herself as a robust defender of the national interest rather than as a smart and dedicated defender of the weak and the under-represented members of American society.

Mindful of the need not to arrive on Capitol Hill and flaunt her superstar status, Hillary worked diligently to ensure that she was able to develop cross-party working relations, even with Republicans who had been openly critical of her and had sought to remove her husband from the presidency. Doing so was all part of the big-picture project of seeking the presidency and being able to present herself as a candidate capable of putting past differences behind her to work with her opponents and get things done in the name of the national interest. This was Hillary Clinton's pitch as she launched her historic campaign for the presidency in January 2007, a bid that resulted in her leaving the Senate behind her and returning to the executive branch of government, though not in the capacity for which she had hoped.

CHAPTER 5

THE CANDIDATE IN 2008

On 20 January 2007, Hillary Clinton made the announcement that many had anticipated ever since she arrived in the Senate: she would challenge for the presidency of the United States. She chose to do so at a time of financial and military turmoil for the country. Offering an approach that appeared robust and which drew on her years of experience in Washington, DC, Hillary seemed to be the right person, at the right time, in the right place to make history and restore a sense of normality to the United States. She became the first former First Lady to run for the presidency and the first woman to have a serious chance of being elected, entering the race as the clear front runner.

However, while her campaign should have been an epoch-defining moment, Hillary Clinton found herself outmanoeuvred by Senator Barack Obama, who successfully framed the election as an opportunity to break the Colour Bar, not the gendered Glass Ceiling. As a result the 2008 presidential election proved to be deeply disappointing for Hillary and her supporters. The nomination had been hers to lose, and lose it she did. How did this happen? Hillary Clinton entered the 2008 campaign with every imaginable advantage: exceptional financial backing, universal name recognition, apparent party support and plenty of political IOUs to cash in. She entered as the presumptive nominee for the Democratic Party and amassed a huge war chest that she expected to be able to spend on defeating her Republican rival in the general election. Yet all of these advantages came to nothing. The cash dried up, her status was turned into a negative, the party leadership turned on her and political debts were forgotten. Her 2008 campaign was a classic example of what a vicious, mean and utterly cutthroat business politics really is. Poor campaign management, flawed electoral tactics and a sense of hubris contributed to her failure to secure the Democratic Party's nomination and the demise of her presidential aspirations in 2008.

If Hillary Clinton is to be elected President of the United States in 2016, it is vital that her campaign learn from the mistakes that were made in 2008 and not merely attempt to win using the same flawed tactics. With no obvious Obama-like challenger within the Democratic Party, her chances appear improved, but the United States of America is in a very different position from 2008 and

Hillary's campaign will need to adequately reflect these changes if she is to be victorious this time around.

THE STATE OF THE UNION: 2008

The United States that Hillary Clinton sought to lead in 2008 was a country that appeared to be on the brink of calamity, if not total collapse. Much had changed in the eight years since Hillary had left the White House as First Lady and taken her seat in the Senate. A national surplus had become a national debt of staggering proportions, swelling to $9,986 billion by the end of the financial year in 2008. The most serious economic downturn in almost a century was destroying jobs and threatening the principles inherent in the American Dream; the US military was bogged down in Iraq and Afghanistan; Osama bin Laden continued to elude capture; and the Bush administration appeared to thrive on universal unpopularity. The growing sense of national pessimism was reflected in the economic figures released by the US Bureau of Labor. The national unemployment rate in the United States was 5.5 per cent but spiked to 9.3 per cent the following year as average wages in the country hit a record low of $9.88 an hour in July 2008. With wages down, confidence was depleted; the national birth rate fell; and the Dow Jones Industrial Average plummeted to 8,776.39, losing almost 34 per cent over the course of the year. Faith in the government to rectify the situation was at an all-time low. The Dow finally hit bottom on 5 March 2009, at 6,594.44, down from a high of 14,164.43 on 9 October 2007, a loss of 50 per cent. The Wall Street Crash of 1929 had seen a more calamitous impact on the stock market as 90 per cent of its value had been lost over three years, but the crash of 2008 was more constricted. Occurring in just eighteen months, 240,000 jobs were lost in October alone. In the space of a little more than two weeks, the Dow experienced its two worst trading-day losses, losing 777.68 points on 29 September and 733.08 points on 15 October. The stock market, which had been the engine of US economic success in the 1990s, was in meltdown.

To become President in 2008, Hillary Clinton needed to win two election battles: the first was for the right to be the Democratic Party's nominee for the presidency, the second would be in a general election against the Republican candidate to determine who occupied the White House for the next four years. The initial assumption heading into the election season was that whoever secured the Democratic Party's nomination was virtually assured of winning the presidency, since the Republican brand was considered toxic following eight years of the George W. Bush administration. The race to secure the Democratic Party's nomination took place in state-by-state elections starting with the Iowa caucuses on 3 January 2008 and ending with the primary elections in Montana and South Dakota on 3 June. To win the nomination, Hillary needed to secure 2,117 of the 4,233 delegates at stake ahead of the nominating convention in August 2008. Assuming she was successful, she would then name a vice-presidential running mate and campaign across the country against her Republican opponent ahead of the general election to be held on 4 November 2008.

GREAT EXPECTATIONS

With George W. Bush at the end of his two terms in office and Dick Cheney choosing not to run for the presidency, 2008 marked the first time in decades that neither the sitting President nor the Vice-President was running for election. After a gruelling contest, the Republican Party nominated Arizonan Senator John McCain as their candidate to succeed George W. Bush. Both men had sought their party's nomination in 2000 but the methods that Bush had used to secure victory, particularly in the crucial South Carolina Primary, caused great bitterness in the McCain camp that still lingered eight years later. To have any hope of winning the presidency, however, Senator McCain needed President Bush's support. In the name of political expediency, McCain was required to offer his support for the war in Iraq that he had long felt to have been poorly executed. He was further handicapped by his difficult relationship with the Republican Party leadership, which had never taken kindly to the candidate's self-proclaimed role as a 'maverick' and his tendency to make up his own rules as he went along.

This was perfectly encapsulated by McCain's selection of Alaskan Governor Sarah Palin as his vice-presidential candidate. McCain had wanted to name Senator Joe Lieberman as his running mate, however, the Republican Party steadfastly refused to place Al Gore's partner from the 2000 election, now an Independent member of the Senate, a heartbeat away from the presidency, especially considering McCain's age. Therefore, at the very last minute, McCain was forced to make a snap decision, which he and his party hoped would change their electoral fortunes. With McCain fighting alongside the feisty Governor of Alaska, the Republican Party believed they might have a formidable team that could hold on to the White House despite the economic downturn and the challenges faced in Iraq and Afghanistan. This was not the widespread opinion in the country, however, which appeared weary following eight years of the George W. Bush administration. Contentious from the start with its failure to win the popular vote, the administration had made few efforts to gain a governing consensus and had acted as though it had secured a sweeping mandate for reform in the 2000 election.

In Hillary Clinton, the Democratic Party believed that they had an ideal front runner to become a historic candidate for reform and for a place in the history books as the first female President of the United States. As the campaign season prepared to get underway, few doubted the apparent inevitability of such an assumption. Hillary was well prepared, well financed, well briefed and well placed, neither too far to the left of the Democratic Party to alienate independent voters nor too far to the right to frustrate more traditional liberals. The level of disdain for the direction of the country heading into the election of 2008 was such that it was assumed that whoever secured the Democratic Party's nomination would go on to be elected President. This was certainly the case within Hillary's campaign, which expected the primary season to be effectively over by February 2008. A coronation, rather than a competition, appeared to be on the cards for the junior Senator from New York ahead of an easy victory against the irascible Senator from Arizona in the general election. That was the idea. The reality, however, proved all too different for Hillary, whose 2008 presidential campaign was flawed from the start.

THE UPSTART

Although Hillary Clinton was the clear favourite heading into 2008, there was a cloud on the horizon which steadily grew to rain on her parade: the precocious, media-friendly, first-term Senator from Illinois, Barack Hussein Obama. In a twist of fate that was as remarkable as any Greek tragedy, the man who defeated her in 2008 owed much of his political start to Hillary Clinton. Obama had burst onto the national political stage with a speech nominating John Kerry for the Democratic Party's nomination in 2004. In that single speech, Obama became a star. As Hillary noted later, 'I thought that was one of the most electrifying moments that I can remember at any Convention. I have campaigned and have done fundraising for him.'[64]

The Clinton campaign had expected the fight for the nomination to come from John Edwards, the former Senator from North Carolina who had sprung to national prominence in the 2004 campaign and had been selected as John Kerry's running mate that year. Young, wealthy, with an apparently happy marriage and solid political pedigree, Edwards was seen as a natural front runner and a formidable opponent for Hillary to overcome. He had been viewed as a Robert F. Kennedy-style politician who could unite the party and the country, but this assessment appeared to be based more on his boyish haircut than on any particular legislative or political achievements to date. As it was, it was another young, dashing candidate with his own apparent Kennedy-esque qualities who took the nomination and broke Hillary Clinton's political heart that year.

Before Hillary began to haemorrhage votes to Barack Obama, however, she was losing the fundraising war. Hillary Clinton entered 2007 with $10 million in the bank left over from her Senate re-election campaign. However, her advisors worried that this was not enough and that far too much had been spent on the re-election campaign. To ensure a landslide, Hillary needed to spend over $35 million, but this necessitated a huge drive to enable her campaign to remain solvent. The push was effective and her presidential campaign raised $20 million in the first quarter of 2007, a remarkable figure by any estimates. But in the same quarter the Obama team revealed figures of $23.5 million. Over the course of the year, the two candidates desperately sought to raise the funds necessary to finance their presidential aspirations going into the election year of 2008. Despite her best efforts, Obama outpaced Hillary's campaign by over $5 million over the course of 2007, as his team raised $98.5 million to her $93 million.

Hillary faced opposition not only from declared candidates, but also from the Democratic Party leaders whose trust and commitment she had attempted to win during her time in the Senate. Party elders such as Senator Harry Reid of Nevada and her fellow New York Senator Chuck Schumer believed that she brought far too much personal and political baggage to the campaign and that her presence would inevitably raise the issue of her time in the White House and the accompanying scandals. With only 41 per cent of Democrats apparently committed to supporting Hillary, they believed an alternative was required. It was they who approached Barack Obama and convinced him to run in 2008 against his former champion, Hillary Clinton. The party hierarchy that Hillary had courted during her eight years in the Senate ensured that her presidential moment was delayed for at least a further eight years.

THE SOPRANOS AND CLINTON FAMILY VALUES

Unlike her husband, one of Hillary Clinton's greatest challenges has been projecting a sense of accessibility and charm. Those who know her and have worked with her attest to her personal warmth. However, much like Al Gore or Richard Nixon before her, Hillary has an unfortunate tendency of alienating an audience by attempting to try too hard to be liked and to appear at ease with popular-culture references. A prime example emerged in 2007 as her team unveiled the final choice of a campaign song to accompany the candidate and her rallies in the months to come. Rather than selecting an apt song from her youth, as her husband had done with Fleetwood Mac's 'Don't Stop', Hillary Clinton canvassed opinion on her website. Despite the effort to utilise the internet to generate interest and direct engagement, the initiative instead further enhanced a growing reputation for a lack of decisiveness by the Clinton campaign.

The song selected was an eminently forgettable track by Celine Dion, entitled 'You and I', designed to convey a sense of solidarity between the candidate and the electorate. The song's selection was totally overwhelmed by the production that was put into unveiling it. To premiere the selection, the campaign released a video on 20 June 2007 starring both Hillary Clinton and her husband in a parody of the series finale of *The Sopranos*, which had recently ended its run on HBO. This was a bizarre decision for many reasons. Firstly, the video effectively cast Bill and Hillary in the roles of Tony Soprano, the head of a leading New Jersey crime family, and his wife Carmela, whose marriage was riddled with distrust, adultery and unhappiness. Furthermore, Hillary was a Senator from New York, yet chose to parody a show based across the Hudson River in New Jersey, which was odd considering the great rivalries that exist between the two states. The scene being parodied from *The Sopranos* ends ambiguously, but with the distinct implication that Tony and Carmela, as well as their children, are about to be murdered. In an effort to engage with a social and cultural phenomenon, the campaign had produced a video that raised a whole host of uncomfortable parallels with a show whose protagonists were about as far as they could possibly be from presidential role models.

Sopranos family values were patently not what the Clinton campaign wanted to advocate, yet the video made such comparisons inescapable. It spoke to having been assembled by a team of insiders who had tied their careers to Hillary Clinton but could not quite fathom how to make her accessible to the public. The video's producer, Mandy Grunwald, had worked on Bill Clinton's

1992 campaign and it was part of a concerted effort to show that Hillary didn't take herself quite as seriously as many people believed. It followed the launch of the YouTube initiative to find a campaign song in which Hillary Clinton announced that, whatever the result, she would not sing it, having famously been caught singing the national anthem off key. The campaign also released an online video featuring feedback received on the initiative that was far from positive. The entire process appeared to be a classic example of a joke that was funny to campaign staff but which should, perhaps, never have been released to the public. However, the competitiveness between members of Hillary's campaign team, with each determined to call the shots, had a detrimental impact on the campaign far beyond the relatively minor infractions of the election's soundtrack.

BEHIND FROM THE START

The Sopranos video not only raised questions as to the judgement of the campaign, but also directly referenced the fact that the campaign was struggling over six months before the first votes were to be cast. 'How's the campaign going?' Bill Clinton asks. 'Well, like you always say, focus on the good times,' Hillary replies, using dialogue from the TV show but also revealing the fact that all was not well in the face of unexpected opposition from Barack Obama.

Hillary Clinton's hopes for 2008 were impacted on by decisions made during her 2006 re-election campaign for the Senate. She had run for her first six-year term in 2000 pledging to serve a full term and not seek the presidency in 2004. No one had any such illusions about her presidential ambitions for 2008, two years into a second term in the Senate. However, Hillary had to be careful not to telegraph her ambitions too early, as this could have weakened her support in New York and led to a diminished re-election result that would have raised doubts about her viability in 2008. On the calendar, two years existed between Hillary Clinton's Senate re-election campaign and the next presidential election. However, she could not simply arrive in the snows of Iowa and New Hampshire in January 2008 and expect to win. Both states relied heavily on 'retail politics' and the electorate was used to being courted for their vote. Hillary, therefore, faced a dilemma: courting voters in Iowa risked alienating her constituents in New York, whose support she needed to be re-elected to the Senate, but avoiding Iowa risked alienating voters whose support she needed to secure the Democratic Party's nomination for the presidency in 2008. Deciding that re-election was vital to any subsequent campaign for the presidency, Hillary decided against making early and conspicuous visits to Iowa and New Hampshire. Although this decision was seen as vital for her Senate re-election hopes, it meant that both Barack Obama and John Edwards could invest time, money and effort in Iowa, leaving Hillary Clinton to play catch-up months later.

Not surprisingly, perhaps, when Hillary's team eventually began canvassing opinion in Iowa they discovered that she was polling third behind Obama and Edwards, primarily on the basis that voters claimed not to like her. Her competence and ability were not issues, but in Iowa, where voters are inundated with presidential candidates and often meet them three times before deciding to vote for them, Hillary Clinton's absence created a void that her opponents filled, as well as giving the impression that she was removed from the process. If Hillary inadvertently made Iowans believe that she didn't need them, they were more than prepared to make it clear that they did not need her.

At the last minute, Hillary's campaign flooded Iowa in a desperate attempt to convince voters that she was not taking their vote for granted. Hillary, Bill, Chelsea and even Dorothy Rodham ended 2007 pounding the snow-swept streets of Iowa, shaking hands, meeting and greeting in a rear-guard action designed to prevent an embarrassing start to what had been viewed as a virtual coronation only weeks before. However, the injection of over 300 volunteers, the entire Clinton family and various dignitaries could not compensate for the fact that with only weeks to go before voting, Barack Obama had visited sixty-eight of Iowa's ninety-nine counties, compared to Hillary Clinton's mere thirty-eight.

Early Iowa polling presented Hillary with an age-old dilemma that spoke directly to lingering issues about her character and personality. Her intelligence and abilities were not in dispute, but, in an age in which voters openly admitted to voting for a candidate that they would rather have a beer with, Hillary Clinton's likeability was a vital factor to consider. This had been a challenge during her time as First Lady of Arkansas, during her husband's presidency, on her 2000 campaign for the Senate and now, as she sought the highest office in the land, doubts about her personality threatened to undermine her undisputed intellectual abilities.

The feedback from Iowa also addressed Hillary's gender and related issues of toughness and aggression. Hillary Clinton's gender could not be ignored, but the candidate refused to embrace it or the historic nature of her candidacy. Indeed, if anything, Hillary appeared determined to run a gender-neutral campaign. Like John F. Kennedy in 1960, she refused to campaign as a minority, merely as a candidate who happened to be a minority. Had this been any other campaign season, Hillary Clinton's decision may not have become an impediment. Unlike her opponent, whose supporters were more than prepared to champion his cause on the basis of overcoming historic prejudice, Hillary's refusal to stress her gender proved self-defeating.

Hillary Clinton's 2008 campaign strategy was premised on the belief that rather than appealing to the 50.8 per cent of the population who were female, she must instead appear as tough and decisive as any male candidate. Emotion, femininity and histrionics were barred from her campaign, replaced with stoicism, gender neutrality and steadfastness. This presented one final political debate that dated back to the time of the Medici: should Hillary seek to be liked or feared? Should she run a positive campaign, advocating her experience and attempt to introduce a warmer personality to her message, or alternatively run a negative campaign, hammering both John Edwards and Barack Obama for their near-total lack of experience and stressing their own character flaws? Ultimately, her campaign never adequately settled on a single strategy and her message and her approach to her opponents fluctuated widely.

CAMPAIGNING

Hillary Clinton's entire gambit in 2008 was based around a simple concept: 'Ready to Lead on Day One'. However, given the sudden threat posed by Barack Obama's grassroots candidacy, her campaign needed to swiftly incorporate a more progressive component than had originally been intended. Hillary's advocacy of essential continuity would not suffice in the face of a candidate promoting 'Change We Can Believe In'. To that end, her campaign attempted to stress her ability to achieve results as opposed to merely deliver speeches calling for change and to promote her political journey from Illinois to Wellesley to Arkansas to Washington, DC and to New York. Hillary Clinton's communications director, Howard Wolfson, noted, 'We think voters are asking, at a time when every candidate is talking about change, who actually has a record of accomplishing it their entire adult life.'[65]

However, when the results were announced in Iowa, Hillary Clinton's numbers had barely moved and, as predicted, she came in third with 29.5 per cent of the vote, narrowly behind John Edwards on 29.8 per cent, but considerably behind Barack Obama's winning number of 38 per cent. The campaign tried to present it as an anomaly, insisting that Hillary was in for the long haul; this was a marathon, not a sprint. However, the result shattered the illusion of Hillary Clinton's invincibility. Her campaign team appeared uncertain as to what to do next or as to what had gone wrong, as revealed by a conference call the next morning that Hillary ended tersely, noting, 'This has been a very instructive call, talking to myself.' In hindsight, campaigning in Iowa may have been the greatest single mistake of the campaign.

Following the result, Hillary Clinton's supporters flooded into New Hampshire in a do-or-die operation, as Barack Obama's support rocketed by 10 per cent, demonstrating the momentum that comes from success in Iowa. Remembering that her husband's presidential ambitions had risen, phoenix-like, in New Hampshire in 1992, Hillary desperately needed to become 'the comeback kid' in her own right if she were to have any hope of continuing her campaign. Surprisingly, two incidents which played upon her gender helped swing the vote Hillary Clinton's way and provided her with a vital victory to breathe hope back into her faltering campaign. The first incident occurred at a debate at St Anselm College in Manchester, New Hampshire, when Hillary Clinton's personality was openly addressed. The same issue that had been raised in the early polls in Iowa was being repeated in New Hampshire: Hillary's competence was beyond doubt; what gave voters cause for concern was her cool, detached personality and perceived lack of a likeability factor. What would she tell voters who professed to prefer Barack Obama on a personal basis and were inclined to vote accordingly? 'Well, that hurts my feelings,' Hillary conceded, smiling bravely, but clearly wounded at the suggestion. She noted that Senator Obama was 'very likeable' and observed, 'I don't think I'm that bad.' Her grace and generosity, however, were met with a withering put-down from Obama, who remarked quietly, 'You're likeable enough, Hillary.'

Hillary's femininity and grace may never have been better demonstrated as she quietly replied that she appreciated Obama's compliment, meant, or otherwise. What became clear immediately, however, was that voters did not appreciate his remark, as his support dropped sharply, especially with female voters, who interpreted the retort as being condescending and cutting. Suddenly the state was back in play as the women of New Hampshire threw their support behind Hillary Clinton, who choked back tears in response to the situation, telling customers in a small coffee house in Portsmouth, New Hampshire, 'I couldn't do it if I didn't just passionately believe it was the right thing to do. I have so many opportunities from this country, and I just don't want to see us fall backwards as a nation. This is very personal for me.'[66] Having refused to exploit her gender for political gain, voters in New Hampshire suddenly responded to Obama's sexist remark and her human frailty, ensuring that Hillary emerged the surprise victor.

However, the rear-guard action in Iowa had crippled the campaign's finances and, in an election season that was gearing up to be the most expensive in history, Hillary Clinton could not win if she were outspent by her opponent. Her campaign had already parted with $100 million, but had insufficient funds to mount an adequate ground game in many of the forthcoming states where victory was needed. The momentum that Hillary hoped to develop following New Hampshire failed to materialise. Obama won state after state, shoring up supporters, delegates and vital financial donations to be used in subsequent battleground states. The differences in the campaigns became all too apparent at this point. Obama's team announced it had raised $32 million in January alone, while Hillary was forced to lend the campaign $5 million of her own money simply to limp on into the primaries to be held on 5 February.

Each state carried a varying number of delegates to the Democratic National Convention, with highly populated states such as California and New York providing 370 and 232 delegates respectively and sparsely occupied states such as Delaware and North Dakota yielding only fifteen and thirteen delegates each. Certain states were, therefore, more important than others and received a disproportionate amount of attention from the candidates. Barack Obama devised a winning strategy, whereby he sought to keep the pressure on in the largest states where Hillary should be ahead, while also concentrating on much smaller states that carried a disproportionate number of delegates. No single day was as important as Super Tuesday, when twenty-three states and territories voted, with 1,681 delegates up for grabs. It proved to be a devastating day for Hillary Clinton's campaign due to the manner in which delegates were awarded. Despite her winning 50.2 per cent of all votes cast, Barack Obama won thirteen of the twenty-three states and 847 delegates, ensuring the momentum was at his back.

At this point, the lack of loyalty in politics became apparent. Long-time Clinton supporters, including Missourian Senator Claire McCaskill and Massachusetts's Senator John Kerry, endorsed Barack Obama. The cruellest defection, however, came with the loss of the Kennedys. During Bill Clinton's presidency, the Clintons had courted the former First Family and helped rehabilitate the career of Ted Kennedy following the 1991 rape trial of William Kennedy Smith in Florida. President Clinton had presided over

Jackie Kennedy's funeral in 1994 after Hillary Clinton had previously sought her advice on raising Chelsea in the White House. When John F. Kennedy Jr's plane was lost off the Atlantic coast, President Clinton committed far more resources than expected in a vain hope to save the lost son of Camelot. Despite these efforts, Senator Edward Kennedy led his family to back Senator Obama, primarily on the basis of his ethnicity and for the historic significance that his potential presidency would have for the country and as an apparent culmination of policies that both John F. Kennedy and Robert F. Kennedy had campaigned for in the 1960s. When President Kennedy's daughter and sole surviving child, Caroline, released a video talking about how Barack Obama made her think of her late father, the die was cast.

Despite the obvious flaws in her campaign strategy and her assembled team, Hillary sought to stay as loyal as possible for as long as possible. She resisted calls for sweeping change after the Iowa result, and victory in the New Hampshire vote had briefly caused a sense of optimism. However, by 10 February 2008, change became inevitable as Hillary Clinton replaced her campaign manager with her former White House Chief of Staff as First Lady, Maggie Williams, but refused to fire pollster Mark Penn. With money running out and with a markedly reduced series of options available to win the nomination, Hillary gambled on a string of victories on Super Tuesday II (4 March 2008), when four states, including Texas and Ohio, voted. It was also at this point that her campaign launched the most contentious advert of the year, directly questioning Barack Obama's preparedness to lead the nation in a time of crisis.

HITTING OBAMA HARD, BUT NOT
HARD ENOUGH

Political advertising can take a variety of approaches, fluctuating between positive campaigns that stress a candidate's credentials and negative approaches that attack an opponent's perceived weakness. In 1984, President Reagan famously ran an advert heralding the return of 'Morning in America' in which the land was bathed in golden sunlight, the flag was flying high and Middle America was booming. Yet his campaign for re-election also ran an advert depicting a bear loose in the woods as a metaphor for the Soviet Union, stressing the need to stand up to aggression. In 2008, Hillary Clinton's campaign was torn between which approach to take with regard to Barack Obama. For months they had played it safe and played nice. In March 2008, however, the gloves came off. John Edwards had dropped out of the race earlier in the year, and Mark Penn believed that Hillary had to appeal to Edwards's former supporters who might be disinclined to vote for Barack Obama. These were mainly white men, who might be wooed on the grounds of defence and national security issues, areas in which Hillary had a natural advantage. He produced an advert which featured a phone ringing in the middle of the night. 'It's 3 a.m., and your children are asleep,' the voiceover announces, 'but in a dangerous world, who do you want answering the phone?' The message was clear: only Hillary Clinton had the experience and the intelligence to address the challenges the United States faced in 2008.

This approach depicted Hillary Clinton as strong, resilient and as capable of acting as Commander-in-Chief as any of her male challengers, but it carried risks. She was already recording high 'unfavourable' scores within the Democratic Party and this scorched-earth approach only exacerbated this. It also had the potential to damage Barack Obama in the general election should he prevail in the primaries, thereby handing the Republican Party a new line of attack. However, despite such reservations, the advert ran and caused a sensational response, both positive and negative. The most important, short-term impact was to help Hillary win the primaries in Texas and Ohio, but the message failed to gain traction moving forward as the campaign continued to vacillate between portraying 'good' Hillary and 'tough' Hillary. She prevailed in Pennsylvania but failed to win in North Carolina. Even victories were tainted due to the introduction of proportional representation, ensuring that even as she won in states such as Indiana, she only won a little over half of the delegates on offer; even in defeat, therefore, Barack Obama continued to maintain his lead.

The sole remaining path to the nomination was in the form of the 800 superdelegates, who constituted almost 20 per cent of all the delegates that would ultimately decide who received the nomination. Such support from the superdelegates would have eclipsed Obama's lead of 150 delegates heading into the convention. However, for the second time in the primary season, Hillary found herself abandoned by the party elders she had courted during her time on Capitol Hill. The leadership made it clear that the superdelegates should not overturn the results of the primaries. Hillary Clinton's fate was effectively sealed by a further bureaucratic setback as the

Democratic National Committee ruled against her petition to be awarded the delegates from Michigan and Florida, which had been denied due to the unauthorised decision by these states to move their primary dates in order to be more relevant in the process. This decision ensured that Barack Obama had secured the necessary number of delegates by the beginning of June, despite Hillary Clinton's success in the Puerto Rico and South Dakota primaries.

Over the course of the primary season, Hillary Clinton received more votes than any woman had ever won in any election ever held in the United States. As she conceded defeat and endorsed Barack Obama at the National Building Museum in Washington, DC, she noted,

> Although we weren't able to shatter the highest, hardest glass ceiling this time, thanks to you, it's got about 18 million cracks in it, and the light is shining through like never before, filling us all with the hope and the sure knowledge that the path will be a little easier next time.

As she stepped from the stage, few doubted that she planned to mount another campaign for the presidency. It was just a matter of when.

WHERE DID IT GO WRONG?

Hillary Clinton's front-runner status and her campaign's air of invincibility also rendered it bloated, inefficient and slow to react. The dinosaur analogy is not altogether inappropriate, as it was outwitted, outpaced and outsmarted by the nimble, sleek and altogether more up-to-date strategy enacted by Barack Obama's campaign. Hillary's campaign made a series of mistakes that proved fatal to her presidential aspirations in 2008. The extent to which these wounds were self-inflicted merely accentuates the fact that she received more votes in the 2008 primary season than any previous winning candidate, yet still failed to gain the Democratic Party's nomination. Ultimately, five flaws served to undermine her 2008 campaign and ensured that, once again, Hillary was forced to take a detour on her path to power.

1. A Reactive Campaign

As the front runner, Hillary should have been setting the pace, calling the shots and ensuring that nothing was left to chance. She should have been the first to announce, the first to raise the necessary funds and the candidate everyone was watching. Instead, the Clinton campaign, from the start, became reactive to the tone, strategy and timings of the Obama campaign. Hillary wanted to wait until late spring 2007 to announce her candidacy, but was bounced into doing so on 20 January by Obama's announcement four days earlier. Her launch was a success but its timing and use of an online announcement was entirely reactive and immediately conceded the momentum of the campaign season to Barack Obama.

The Obama campaign not only had the steal on Clinton in terms of timing and its use of social media, but also in terms of fundraising and online material. The Clintons, so often at the vanguard of modern campaigning in recent years, suddenly looked very analogue in a new digital age. Between January and April 2007, the Obama campaign spent $6.8 million on web advertising, compared to the Clinton team, which spent just $350,000. This enabled Obama to build a reputation and a presence that proved insurmountable. Hillary's approach was to draw upon a long-standing network of established donors who had contributed to her previous campaigns for the Senate, as well as to her husband's presidential bids. Barack Obama's tactic of drawing on small contributions from a groundswell of supporters numbering in the millions was based on Howard Dean's approach from 2004. When Hillary resolved to seek online contributions and actively encouraged such donations in February 2008, her campaign witnessed a huge surge in funding, predominantly in small donations of under $200. By that point, however, the Obama campaign had already been doing this for a year. Hillary's new funding source amounted to 50 per cent of her income, up from 20 per cent previously. Unfortunately, it was a classic example of too little, too late and provided further evidence of the campaign's lethargic, reactive nature.

2. The Role of Gender

The 2008 campaign for the presidency always promised to produce a historic outcome. The United States would either elect its oldest President (McCain), its first female President (Clinton) or its first African-American President (Obama). All three candidates, however, appeared unsure as to how best to address their relative status. McCain refused to commit to only serving one term on the grounds of his age, Hillary vacillated on how to address gender and

Obama fluctuated on his stance on the extent to which race would play any part in his campaign. None of them wanted to be seen as 'the old candidate', 'the female candidate' or 'the black candidate', yet all three were happy to draw support from seniors, women and the African-American community respectively when it suited.

Hillary Clinton's stance on her position as a gender role model was clearly conflicted. She was advised by Texas Congressman Sheila Jackson Lee to deliver a keynote address on gender, partly in response to a speech Obama had given in March 2008 on race in America. Such a move again played into a perception that the Clinton campaign was reacting to terms that were being dictated by the Obama camp. Despite Hillary's apparent inclination to deliver such a speech, members of her team thought it could backfire and persuaded her not to. A central argument was that Hillary would be accused of equating racism with sexism – not a debate that was sought by the campaign. However, the decision not to address gender and the apparent unease of doing so for fear of offending spoke to a lack of intent in the campaign. Hillary could no more escape her gender and the potential history-making nature of her candidacy than Barack Obama could deny his ethnicity and equally historic potential. But, whereas the Obama campaign made great inroads with the African-American community, Hillary Clinton's team never quite made the same effort or achieved anything like the same success with American women. When the breakdown of the United States is considered, the flaw in this plan becomes apparent: African-Americans constitute less than 13 per cent of the American population, whereas women account for almost 51 per cent of all US citizens. A gender-based appeal to American women in 2008 would have had a vastly larger constituency to draw upon and would have been far more geographically dispersed.

3. The Strategists

The team that Hillary assembled constituted a third flaw in her campaign, as demonstrated by the indecision and internal conflict over the viability of a gender-based approach. Her advisors were drawn from former members of her husband's administration and members of Hillary's inner circle (Hillaryland), as well as from the upper echelons of the Democratic Party. Most, if not all, had a long history of working with the Clintons, with some having been involved since 1991. This did not mean, however, that they all agreed on everything, or in some cases anything. Internal division proved decisive in derailing Hillary Clinton's 2008 campaign as advisors openly fought over policy, strategy and message. Issues of style and substance were fought over and debated, revealing fundamental differences of opinion as to how Hillary should campaign, what policies should be advocated and what message she should convey to American voters on any specific occasion.

The team was openly divided, with Bill Clinton and Mark Penn advocating an aggressive approach, to take the fight to Barack Obama and challenge his lack of experience. They also wanted to question his ties to less-reputable members of American society, such as former member of the anarchist movement 'The Weather Underground' Bill Ayres. Others, however, such as Howard Wolfson, Harold Ickes, Mandy Grunwald and Patti Solis Doyle, advocated a far more positive campaign that was less aggressive in tone and that sought to focus on Hillary's achievements and strength of character. Those seeking a positive approach prevailed for much of the primary season, while the more aggressive technique tended to emerge in times of crisis, leading to accusations of panic in the campaign. Had one approach prevailed, or had an intelligent combination of the two approaches been adopted for different stages of the campaign or for differing demographics, then the ensuing chaos could have been avoided. However, the inability to adequately shape a message doomed Hillary Clinton's campaign in 2008. The fundamental dilemma was whether to portray Hillary as an agent of change or a symbol of essential continuity and experience. It was a question that was never fully resolved and resulted in wild undulations on the campaign, as Hillary appeared with her daughter, Chelsea, in university settings as she sought to stress her progressive policies to young voters and then in more formal settings with her husband and members of his entourage in an appeal to more conservative elements.

The central figure in Hillary's 2008 campaign was Mark Penn, who started working for Bill Clinton in the 1996 re-election campaign and became instrumental in his second term, offering polling-based advice on a variety of issues, including how best to deal with the impeachment crisis. However, his personality and demeanour went a long way to undermining his own ironclad faith in his numbers-based approach to politics. Having helped steer Bill Clinton to re-election in 1996 and Hillary to a Senate seat in 2000, Penn sought to dominate the campaign, designating himself as Chief Strategist and earning the disdain of his colleagues in the process. His apparent infallibility, even in the aftermath of defeat, only served to heighten internal tensions as others around him were jettisoned from the campaign staff.

Whatever personal shortcomings Penn may have exhibited, however, he devised a strategy for victory that appeared logical and was designed to address a variety of elements. He urged a campaign that demolished the myth of Barack Obama as the new JFK and, in an unmistakable echo of Richard Nixon's 'Silent Majority' strategy, called for Hillary to appeal to 'Invisible Americans'. Penn had no interest in positioning Hillary Clinton as anything other than a strong, resilient leader, whose capabilities were beyond question. He advocated an electoral strategy that began with an appeal to women, made a positive pitch to middle-class and poor Americans and defended her past actions to men and wealthy Americans by stressing her years of experience. Furthermore, he was unconcerned about addressing issues of Barack Obama's heritage, suggesting that Hillary wrap herself in the flag and stress her Midwestern roots, her years of service to the country and her all-American heritage, in stark contrast to Obama's diverse upbringing and heritage. Penn's approach had much to recommend it, but many elements were rejected as the campaign chose to play nice instead of playing to win. Hillary's strategists would have done well to remember that, in a presidential election, there are no prizes for the *nicest* candidate.

4. The Strategy

The primary season in the United States requires a strategy to secure victory. It is not simply a case of entering every race and hoping for the best. Some campaigns will forego elections in certain states, while others will make a targeted focus on certain geographical regions. To be truly competitive, however, requires a national focus and the ability to develop momentum. With momentum comes support, donations and a winning aura of invincibility: nothing succeeds like success. It became apparent very quickly that Hillary's campaign team did not have an adequate ground game to compete with the structure that Obama had put in place, a remarkable conclusion considering the assets at her disposal and the network of support that she had assembled over several decades.

Hillary Clinton's campaign strategy problems were driven in large part by an apparent inability to recognise that the 'winner-takes-all' approach to delegates that had prevailed previously was no longer in effect. This meant that winning a primary in a narrow result (51 per cent/49 per cent) produced great headlines but was an effective tie in terms of delegate allocation. Not all were blind to the problem. Harold Ickes made several attempts to highlight the potential flaw in the campaign strategy that went ignored for far too long.

Also key to winning is knowing where to fight. Hillary failed to invest time and resources in Iowa, at least in part due to her Senate re-election campaign in 2006. This ensured that her two rivals could secure local support while she was still courting voters in New York. As early as May 2007, her campaign was advised to avoid the Iowa caucuses altogether on the basis that she could not win and could only embarrass herself. She was advised that the effort would drain much-needed financial resources and that she might unintentionally aid her opponents by taking part. However, this advice from Mike Henry, the deputy campaign manager, was not heeded and was instead leaked to the *New York Times* – an indication of the internal divisions that were ripping the campaign apart.

Hillary Clinton committed to campaigning in Iowa, despite the fact that her husband had secured the presidency without campaigning there in 1992. Unfortunately, she committed to the state with only a matter of weeks to go. By that point, John Edwards and Barack Obama had become virtual residents in the state and had secured all the necessary endorsements and support. As a result, Hillary invested over $20 million to finish third in the race, a result that would have ended most campaigns and which undermined any remaining sense of inevitability. She would have been far better off to have avoided this race altogether. Instead, her decision to campaign in Iowa actually aided Barack Obama by dividing his opposition and ensuring that he left Iowa as a surprise victor. Had Hillary avoided the state, John Edwards would almost certainly have won the vote, undermining Obama's candidacy, perhaps fatally. Had this occurred, John Edwards would have been a candidate that Hillary Clinton's team could have been far better placed to defeat in the ensuing primaries and may well have resulted in Barack Obama being named as her vice-presidential candidate in the November election.

Neither was there any coherent plan in place following the Iowa result. Hillary Clinton's initial campaign manager, Patti Solis Doyle, rejected a series of plans that had been devised by campaign field director Guy Cecil, yet failed to implement an alternative strategy.

The folly of this approach, or rather the lack thereof, became all too apparent when Hillary failed to campaign in a series of vital state caucuses. Once again, the campaign had been alerted to the challenges that such an approach presented by its senior consultant, Harold Ickes, who was again ignored. By failing to compete in smaller state caucuses, where results tend to require a grassroots operation, Hillary ceded vital delegates, as well as a reform mantra, to Barack Obama. Her decision to focus on large state primaries also proved to be financially and politically costly. Hillary Clinton's campaign's strategy unravelled at this point, as Barack Obama's victories in small state caucuses more than offset her headline-grabbing victories in larger state primaries. The lack of a credible campaign strategy undermined Hillary's claim to be organised and ready for power, cost her valuable delegates, misallocated increasingly rare funds and stripped her of a winning aura, yielding all such credentials to her opponent. With a series of small state victories, Barack Obama was able to redefine his position, gain vital momentum and maintain a steady flow of donations that propelled him to further success. For a campaign that was built on its apparent inevitability, to miscalculate so poorly proved to be catastrophic and exacerbated a sense of hubris among the senior advisors and potentially in the candidate herself.

5. Iraq

Long before the dark clouds of recession rolled in, the expectation was that the 2008 presidential election would focus on US foreign policy and the war in Iraq. The conflict had become increasingly unpopular and was viewed as a mistake executed by a President who was not on the ballot in 2008. Therefore, attention turned to who had or who had not supported it. In this regard, Barack Obama was in a fortunate position: he had not been in the Senate when the vote to authorise action in Iraq was debated. Hillary Clinton and John Edwards had both approved the action, in line with the prevailing national sentiment in 2002. Much had changed in the intervening years, however, including the justifications for war and the inability to locate the weapons of mass destruction that the Bush White House had insisted were the precursors for the invasion. As a Democrat, a woman and a candidate for the presidency, Hillary was in an unenviable position. If she recanted her vote, she would be portrayed as irresolute, with the potential to be portrayed as a 'flip-flopper', as John Kerry had been branded four years previously to devastating effect. If, however, she chose to stand by her vote, she risked yielding the reformist platform to Barack Obama, who could claim not to be tainted by the decision.

Barack Obama's constant use of the Iraq vote to distinguish himself from Hillary caused a furious reaction from Bill Clinton that threatened to dominate the debate. Noting the similarity of Obama's Senate voting record to Hillary's, Bill Clinton referred to Obama's opposition to the Iraq War as a 'fairy tale', ensuring that the former President became a talking point, rather than Obama's specific policies. In an effort to address her predicament, Hillary visited Pakistan, Iraq, Kuwait and Afghanistan in January 2007, days prior to announcing her candidacy, in an attempt to project her capacity to lead and reform US foreign policy. As she explained in her announcement address on 20 January 2007, 'The President's team is pursuing a failed strategy in Iraq as it edges closer to collapse, and Afghanistan needs more of our concerted effort and attention.' She then promised to 'bring the right end' to the war in Iraq.

Whereas John Edwards tried to explain and retract his vote to authorise military action, Hillary repeatedly refused to do so, believing that this appeared feckless and could undermine her credibility as a potential Commander-in-Chief. However, before the American electorate could consider her for this role, Hillary Clinton had to win her party's nomination. Her ability to do so, however, was severely undermined by her vote in 2002 and her continued refusal to distance herself from it, an approach that reinforced the perception of Hillary as an agent of the status quo and cemented Barack Obama's position as the candidate of change.

CONCLUSION

History was made in the 2008 presidential campaign, but not the history that Hillary Clinton had hoped for. Instead of electing its first female President, the United States elected another man, the country's first African-American President. The roles of race and gender were clearly exhibited in the presidential campaign of 2008, though neither Obama nor Hillary chose to run as a minority candidate. Despite these choices, issues of race and gender refused to disappear, and in this regard Hillary Clinton's decision to appear as tough as her male challenger in an effort to pass the commander-in-chief test appears to have been a mistake. Changes had also been introduced to the US electoral system, which Senator Obama was able to exploit and which Hillary Clinton's team failed to take sufficient notice of, to her detriment.

The 2008 campaign that was designed to propel Hillary Clinton to the presidency served instead to highlight a series of challenges that she needed to overcome to be a serious contender in the future. Many of the flaws were a result of a top-heavy campaign team, overloaded with consultants, all eager for jobs in a future administration, too certain of their methods, too confident in their candidate's inevitable nomination and too reactive to events when they should have been the ones in the driving seat. Yet the candidate cannot escape ultimate responsibility for what occurs on their campaign. It is they who signs off on all major decisions, in whose name the campaign is waged and who must fall or succeed with its merits.

Mark Penn attempted to position Hillary Clinton as a 'responsible progressive', further alienating her from the liberal wing of the Democratic Party to whom she first needed to appeal in order to win the nomination. It is clear, in retrospect, that Hillary's campaign team appeared to take the Democratic Party's nomination process for granted, assuming they were assured of victory. The campaign was looking ahead to the November general election against the Republicans when it should have been focusing on how to secure the nomination of the party. What it failed to recognise was that Hillary was being outmanoeuvred by a candidate of equally historic importance and who was being openly encouraged and courted to run by the very party elders on whom she had counted for support.

However, technical issues, campaign strategies and in-fighting were compounded by a fundamental question surrounding what was believed to be Hillary Clinton's greatest potential flaw: her own electability. Unlike her husband, famed for his charm and soft skills, Hillary was portrayed in a similar light to Al Gore: a potentially capable and effective President who lacked the necessary people skills to secure the office in a general election in which personal likeability was a crucial factor. Hillary's demeanour was framed all the more clearly by her husband's presence on the campaign. Bill Clinton's southern style threw into stark relief his wife's northern manners and suggested once again that he remains Hillary's greatest liability as well as her greatest asset.

Presidential campaigns are a training ground for power, during which, ideally, the successful candidate accrues the knowledge and experience to take office and govern effectively. All too often it appeared that Hillary Clinton's 2008 campaign was prepared to believe its own slogan: 'Ready to Lead On Day One'. This approach, coupled with the assumption that the nomination was a foregone conclusion, undermined the sense of the campaign as an opportunity for Hillary to develop and evolve. Rather, throughout the campaign, her fundamental instincts and character remained unchanged. It was in the months ahead that Hillary Clinton did begin to evolve – not as a candidate for the presidency, but as a member of Barack Obama's Cabinet, a position that neither she nor anyone else could have forecast when her presidential odyssey began.

— CHAPTER 6 —

SECRETARY OF STATE

When her 2008 presidential ambitions were quashed, many speculated as to what the future held for Hillary Clinton. With a young and popular Democrat in the White House, her career path appeared to be stalled for at least the next eight years. Few expected President Obama to draw upon Hillary Clinton's unique stature and nominate her as Secretary of State for his first term in office. As America's chief diplomat, the role offered Hillary a remarkable opportunity to gain invaluable international experience as well as to serve her country at the highest Cabinet level, placing herself within the presidential line of succession.

After eight years in the Senate, Hillary had achieved much but had fallen short of her ultimate ambition, the presidency of the

United States. Having been offered the consolation prize of Secretary of State, she realised it was an opportunity to add greatly to her résumé. The alternative was to remain in the Senate for at least eight more years as a new generation of politicians was elected around her, creating an aura of stagnation to her career. The longer she remained in the Senate, the less likely it was that she would ever become President. Since John F. Kennedy in 1960, only Barack Obama had won the presidency while running as a sitting member of the chamber, as Americans repeatedly elected former state governors to the White House. John Kerry discovered in 2004 that a long Senate career produces a list of votes on a vast range of subjects that can easily be manipulated and distorted by opponents and Hillary Clinton's time in the Senate had already contributed to her failure to secure the presidency in 2008 due to her floor vote on Iraq.

With her global brand and international celebrity status, Hillary was a fascinating choice to serve as Obama's globetrotting emissary. Following in the footsteps of Henry Kissinger and James Baker, Hillary Clinton had an opportunity to be the second most visible member of the Obama administration and to gain a reputation as a team player at the same time. During the election, debate had centred on whether America would have a black President or a female President. Now, two former rivals were working together to present a refreshed image of the United States to the world as the Obama administration sought to reset a series of relationships that had been tarnished throughout the previous eight years under George W. Bush.

As First Lady, Hillary had sought to bring a new approach to the White House, an ambition she maintained as Senator for New York. Now, as Secretary of State, she attempted to bring this approach to the world stage. She may not have been the President, but she was the next best thing: the face of America to the world at large, able to promote those policies that had been dear to her throughout her career and in a manner that was in keeping with her philosophical approach to power and policy. Under the direct supervision of Secretary of State Clinton, a new era of American Smart Power was about to begin. To her would go the spoils if it succeeded and the blame if it failed.

THE STATE OF THE WORLD: 2009

The world that Hillary Clinton faced as Secretary of State in 2009 appeared to be one of total pandemonium, not least due to the perceived position of the United States on the global stage. For the eight years following the tragedy of September 11th, the United States had adopted an aggressive approach to international affairs. The events of 9/11 influenced the direction and tone of US foreign policy for the remainder of George W. Bush's time in office as the nation adopted the President's perceived 'swagger' on the world stage. Changing this perspective of the United States was a priority of the new administration, but was something that could not be achieved immediately. Despite years of warfare, American troops were still actively engaged in Afghanistan, hunting in vain for America's nemesis, Osama bin Laden. Furthermore, Iran was allegedly

developing a nuclear weapons capability, relations with Pakistan
were deteriorating, Benazir Bhutto had been assassinated, US forces
in Iraq were engaged in a surge in a desperate attempt to stabilise
the country, and tensions were mounting on the Korean peninsula.

During his campaign, Barack Obama insisted that the world
would look differently at the United States if he were elected President; the practical job of ensuring this happened, however, fell in
large part to Hillary Clinton. The worldview of the United States
was not encouraging as she took office. The Pew Research Center
revealed that majorities in nineteen of twenty-four surveyed countries 'had little or no confidence' in outgoing President George W.
Bush, including Britain, Spain, Turkey and Jordan, where opposition
ran as high as 89 per cent. This contributed to fears of a spread of
American cultural influence, with only six of forty-six surveyed
nations believing that increased US cultural presence was a benefit. This level of international resentment proved to be a major
challenge for the Obama administration as it sought to rebuild
the image of the United States overseas. Nominating Hillary was
a key element in this process. The White House strove to present
an image of domestic harmony and unity between former political
opponents and to utilise Hillary's global standing to advance the
causes of the United States around the world.

A SECOND LIFE

The invitation to serve as Secretary of State was a mixed blessing for Hillary and she knew it. The job had once served as a

springboard for the presidency, in much the same way that British politicians often head government departments before becoming Prime Minister. Between 1801 and 1841, all but one President had previously served as Secretary of State, but not since before the US Civil War had America's former top diplomat gone on to secure the presidency. Hillary realised that the position would either be a springboard to a second run at the White House in 2016 or it would be the final posting in her political career. A seat on the Supreme Court had appeared a more likely reward for her support in the final stage of the 2008 campaign, and one that would have reflected Hillary Clinton's legal expertise. However, that would also have ended any future political aspirations that she might have had. Her new role as Secretary of State presented challenges that could draw upon Hillary's unique place in American life, allow her to audition for the presidency during Obama's first term and openly run for office during his second term. It was a second chance at greatness and a second life in the public sphere.

Much like her husband, however, Hillary Clinton had a wary relationship with foreign policy. In 1992, Bill Clinton ran on a domestic agenda against George H. W. Bush, who was identified as being the 'foreign-policy President'. Once in office, his advisors were divided over the task of espousing a doctrine with which to address the post-Cold War world. His first Secretary of State, Warren Christopher, had told the Senate that he had no interest in placing 'the foreign policy of the United States into a straitjacket'.[67] Hillary had watched her husband make mistakes and achieve successes in international affairs as President, and her experience convinced her of the need to be tough on national security issues, placing her on the hawkish side of the Democratic Party. This stance served her well in the initial stage of the War on Terror, but returned to haunt her during the 2008 campaign due to her vote in favour of the Iraq War. She was now in the unusual position of being a hawkish Secretary of State serving a President who was perhaps less inclined to intervene militarily, and working alongside Secretary of Defense Robert Gates, who had been appointed by George W. Bush, the man who started the wars Obama had been elected to end. It was, in many ways, a strange and complicated relationship from the start. Scheduling errors that resulted in Hillary turning up for non-existent meetings at the White House fuelled initial insecurities and led to terse email exchanges: 'I arrived for the 10:15 mtg and was told there was no mtg. Matt said they had "released" the time. This is the second time this has happened. What's up???'[68]

The role of Secretary of State fluctuates from administration to administration and its impact depends on global events and the remit that the specific President wishes to bestow on it. Some Presidents wish to serve as their own *de facto* Secretary of State and immerse themselves in global challenges, whereas others have been more domestically focused and content to grant their emissary a wide remit. As Hillary Clinton began her new role, it was not clear which approach President Obama planned to take, considering the myriad challenges he faced upon taking office in January 2009. What was clear was that Hillary was going to be very busy as she became America's face in the world, shuttling between trouble spots in the Middle East, Asia, Europe and South America.

Her time in office coincided with upheavals in the Arab world, with-drawals from Iraq and Afghanistan, the return to power in Russia of Vladimir Putin and continuing challenges in the Middle East. What was required was a new strategy to deal with the new world she was encountering.

A SMART APPROACH

Hillary Clinton became Secretary of State with a unique background and a similarly unique set of skills. Her previous experience ensured that she arrived at the State Department headquarters in the Foggy Bottom district of Washington, DC with some strong ideas about the future direction of US foreign policy and about how America should position itself on the world stage at the start of Obama's presidency. A key influence in the formulation of her thinking was the Harvard scholar Joseph Nye. Nye had been Assistant Secretary of Defense for International Security Affairs under Bill Clinton, and had been touted as a potential National Security Advisor had John Kerry become President in 2004. Nye's influence on the Clintons came, in part, from his work on the concept of 'soft power', which stressed the importance of presenting an attractive model for other nations to emulate. In terms of policies, culture and values, soft power stood in stark contrast to aggressive, 'hard-power' concepts of coercion, which often involved the use of force.

As President, Bill Clinton embraced Nye's soft-power approach to policy and attempted to implement the concept as a component of his grand strategy initiatives. Hillary had drawn on the 'soft-power' concept as First Lady as part of an overall strategy designed to make the United States a beacon for human rights and democracy. Speaking in Beijing in 1995, Hillary Clinton touted the US record on such issues and insisted that: 'Human rights are women's rights and women's rights are human rights – one and for all.' Fourteen years later, as Secretary of State, she was able to take this approach to the next level by incorporating Nye's latest concept: 'smart power'. Building on his previous concept, Nye defined smart power as the combination of both hard and soft power according to the specific requirements of a situation. He did so, in part, 'to counter the misperception that soft power alone can produce effective foreign policy'.[69] Hillary Clinton was an early advocate of smart power, which came to be defined as a rebuke to the preponderance of hard-power policies implemented by the George W. Bush administration, and referenced it in her confirmation hearings before the Senate.

The smart-power approach that Hillary Clinton sought to instil in her State Department was evident in the travel plans of Under Secretary of State for Public Diplomacy and Public Affairs Judith McHale. In April 2010, she travelled to Doha to meet with the heads of the Aljazeera network and Prime Minister Hamad bin Jassim bin Jaber al-Thani, as well as with CENTCOM staff at the Al Udeid Air Base. 'Travel well,' Hillary wrote, 'I'll look forward to hearing your report.'[70] What McHale reported back, however, is unknown, as the nature of her briefing at Al Udeid remains redacted from the emails that have been released.

As Secretary of State, Hillary Clinton combined Nye's smart-power concept with what she termed 'convening power' in an attempt to draw together outside agencies and organisations for the advancement of common interests. Her efforts reflected many of the attempts made by her husband's administration in the 1990s to move beyond a preponderance of power and advance a cultural and social approach to foreign policy, presenting the United States as a model to emulate. This included a commitment to the use of public diplomacy and development in the furtherance of national security, spending $8 billion on global health issues in 2010 alone. She made a conscious decision to break from practices enacted by the Bush administration and sought new organisations with which to partner in a concerted effort to expand the reach and impact of the State Department, without inflating its budget. This approach reflected the desire of the Obama administration to reduce the focus on hard-power options as it moved to disengage from Afghanistan and Iraq without undermining the United States's role on the world stage. As such, the Obama–Clinton effort can be compared to the Nixon–Kissinger initiative to withdraw from Vietnam forty years previously.[71] The extent to which either has proved successful in the long term is open to speculation and interpretation.

The State Department's use of soft power was evident when Assistant Secretary of State for Educational and Cultural Affairs Ann Stock engaged with America's pre-eminent cellist:

> I saw Yo-Yo Ma this week and we spoke about his Silk Road Project.
> Three members of his company are Iranian and he is very interested
> in touring in and furthering cultural engagement with Iran once
> the country opens up. He asked that I pass on this message to the

Secretary, explaining that if and when this kind of engagement becomes possible, he and the Silk Road Project are ready to embrace the opportunity.[72]

Such opportunities for cultural and diplomatic interaction were at the heart of Nye's smart-power concept and continued to play an important, if intangible role in US foreign policy under Hillary Clinton.

Hillary thus embraced an approach to diplomacy in stark contrast to Henry Kissinger's Metternich-inspired embrace of a rather more Machiavellian philosophy in which power and national interest were paramount. Her effort to implement a human-to-human approach to diplomacy was one that Kissinger had repeatedly rejected, but in a new era of instant communications it was one that appeared, initially, to produce results. Hillary encouraged positive engagement with activist groups through the use of the internet and social media, becoming personally committed to the use of Facebook and Twitter as a means of communication with the disenfranchised and the disillusioned. Needless to say, the extent to which US grand strategy or the intricacies of international relations could be communicated in 140 characters was doubtful. It was also clear that Hillary Clinton's efforts to engage in social media came up against her own personal lack of technical know-how. Emailing her senior advisor Philippe Reines in July 2010, she was forced to confess, 'I don't know if I have Wi-Fi. How do I find out?'[73] Even older technology appears to have been problematic, as Hillary was forced to ask her aide Huma Abedin about a fax machine: 'HRC:

I thought it was supposed to be off hook to work? HA: Yes but hang up one more time. So they can re-establish the line.'[74]

Hillary Clinton's efforts were seen as a concerted attempt to re-engage with the world in a manner totally at odds with the efforts of the previous George W. Bush administration. This went far beyond her personal work and became ingrained in the entire State Department for the duration of her time in office, as career service diplomats were tasked with using social networking and provided with courses in how best to use popular platforms such as Facebook and Twitter. The use of smart power as an expression of US foreign policy was revealed in an email to Cheryl Mills from Alec J. Ross, Senior Advisor for Innovation at the State Department. Reporting on the use of social media in Syria, in September 2010 Ross noted:

> This past week a campaign went viral on Facebook in Syria (even though Facebook is outlawed in Syria it is widely accessed through proxies) showing teachers in Syria abusing their pupils. Thousands of Syrians made public their support on Facebook (the fact that people made their identities known is notable) for the campaign to remove these teachers, and the Ministry of Education intervened and fired the teachers.[75]

Such initiatives were later encouraged in Egypt, Libya and Tunisia with varying degrees of success.

Hillary made efforts to hold American-style town hall meetings when she went abroad and to engage with regular citizens in the countries she visited, not just with leaders and the press. Director of the Policy Planning Staff Anne-Marie Slaughter insisted, 'She's the one who kept saying, "You've got to have government-to-government, government-to-people, and people-to-people contacts." She's been very clear that the people of different countries are not just the object of policies; they are active agents of change and evolution.'[76] One challenge that persisted from Bill Clinton's time in office, however, was how to sell US foreign policy. In September 2010, Anne-Marie Slaughter recommended the use of the expression 'A New American Century' in a speech that Hillary was to make at the Council of Foreign Relations. 'I've been thinking about the need for a headline/bumper sticker for the speech. How about "A New American Century"[?] We cd take on the critics directly and right up front and make the argument this way.'[77] As in the 1990s, however, efforts to reduce US foreign policy to a bumper sticker slogan akin to 'Containment' proved fruitless.

Ultimately, the attempt to implement a smart-power approach to US foreign policy produced conflicting results. Success in engaging with Burma was offset by the nation's continued suppression of minority groups and human rights violations. Initial advances in relations with Russia under Medvedev were ultimately rendered irrelevant by the return to power of Vladimir Putin, who clearly adopted a hard-power approach to geopolitics. These efforts built on the work of her sixty-six predecessors, but the implementation of smart power as a driving force in US foreign policy will rightly be remembered as being the foundation of Hillary Clinton's time as Secretary of State.

HILLARYLAND GOES GLOBAL

Hillary Clinton's embrace of Joseph Nye's concepts was a reflection of the high premium that she placed on personal loyalty and on the advice and guidance she received from a small group of advisors. Some worked for her directly, while others, like Nye, maintained a professional distance but continued to feed her ideas. Some were recognised members of the inner circle, known as Hillaryland, which had been established in the 1990s while Hillary was First Lady. The name referred to both the physical office space that Hillary had utilised as well as the philosophical role that she occupied within her husband's administration. By the time Hillary became Secretary of State, the conceptual focus of Hillaryland moved to her seventh-floor suite of offices at the State Department.

Hillary Clinton retained the counsel of a small number of advisors and aides. She brought in Jake Sullivan as her deputy Chief of Staff before promoting him to direct the Policy Planning Staff following Anne-Marie Slaughter's departure in 2011. Her long-time aide Huma Abedin remained by her side, as did her Chief of Staff, Cheryl D. Mills, who had also worked with Hillary as far back as the White House years of the 1990s. She also called upon former members of her husband's administration for key posts as her emissaries to the world's flashpoints. Indeed, the extent to which Secretary of State Clinton continued to rely on former members of Bill Clinton's administration was revealed by the steady flow of emails from and about individuals including Richard Holbrooke, Mack McLarty, Sandy Berger, Anthony Lake, John Podesta and the apparently ubiquitous Sidney Blumenthal.

Richard Holbrooke, who masterminded the 1995 Dayton Peace
Accords that ended the Bosnian War and who could have been
Secretary of State had Hillary Clinton prevailed in the 2008
presidential election, was dispatched to oversee Afghanistan and
Pakistan. Former Senator George Mitchell, who had administered
the 1998 Good Friday Agreement that had brought relative peace
and harmony to the streets of Northern Ireland, was named Special
Envoy for Middle East Peace. Dennis Ross, who had been Middle
East Envoy for President Clinton, was appointed Special Advisor to
the Persian Gulf and Southwest Asia, although he quickly moved
to cover the Middle East at the National Security Council (NSC),
where his role brought him into conflict with Senator Mitchell.
These advisors, rising stars and old hands, provided Hillary with a
constant stream of information and enabled her to retain her roving
brief without getting bogged down in any single region or crisis.

Hillary had wanted to hire Sidney Blumenthal, the former Assistant and Senior Advisor to President Clinton, but was prevented
from doing so by the White House Chief of Staff, Rahm Emanuel,
who had also worked for President Clinton, on the basis of Blumenthal's opposition to Barack Obama during the 2008 campaign.
Instead, the Clinton Foundation placed Blumenthal on a retainer
of $10,000 a month, enabling him to routinely provide Secretary
Clinton with briefings and ad hoc advice on a wide variety of subjects. Blumenthal's role is particularly revealing, especially since the
release of Hillary Clinton's emails, which indicate that he appears
to have been paid to pass along press cuttings and gossipy assess-
ments of evolving political situations. He sent a string of emails

directly to Hillary during the course of the UK election in 2010 that revealed his strong affinity with the British Labour Party and clear disdain for the Conservatives, whom he dismissed as being 'contemptuous'. If the Conservatives came to power, Blumenthal advised, 'rather than eager to be Obama's poodle, Cameron would be superficially friendly and privately scornful. Class has a lot to do with the contempt. A Cameron government would be more aristocratic and even narrowly Etonian than any Conservative government in recent history.'[78] The blatant partisan nature of the communiqués is at odds with anything that Hillary would have received from her official State Department advisors.

On 27 June 2010, Blumenthal advised Hillary Clinton that 'in economic policy, the UK is no partner and no bridge to Europe', insisting that under the 'draconian Cameron government' the 'special relationship' was at risk, since 'at no other time since World War II have the US and UK governments been at such odds over international economics'.[79] The tone and content of Blumenthal's missives appear to justify the decision to block his appointment and betray the claims of political independence and clear political inclinations of the Clinton Foundation, which was paying Blumenthal to draft a constant stream of rather basic emails and forward press cuttings on which Hillary should, in theory, have been briefed as a matter of course by officials at the State Department.

Hillary Clinton's decision to appoint Holbrooke, Mitchell and Ross as her regional envoys initially appeared to be a smart move that conveyed the importance of these areas, while also enabling her to continue a bigger-picture approach and not get too focused on one geographical location, as had many of her predecessors. The usual bureaucratic tensions between the State Department and the NSC, however, continued unabated during Hillary Clinton's tenure as Secretary of State, as both entities and their respective leaders sought to influence policy and gain the all-important ear of the President. By deciding against appointing a strong National Security Advisor to coordinate policy, President Obama created a vacuum at the heart of his foreign policy team that led to unnecessary tensions. Having committed to a peace deal in the Middle East on his second day in office and having acquiesced with Hillary Clinton's request to appoint George Mitchell as envoy to the region, President Obama suddenly insisted publicly that Israel abandon its settlement-building to appease the Arab continent.

The foreign policy vacuum became apparent when President Obama met Israeli Prime Minister Netanyahu along with his Chief of Staff, Rahm Emanuel, and Senior Advisor, David Axelrod, neither of whom was a foreign policy expert but instead advised the President on domestic affairs, particularly with regard to polling and popularity. Absent from the Oval Office meeting were the National Security Advisor, the Secretary of State, the Secretary of Defense and the President's own envoy to the region.[80] The challenges in devising policy in the Middle East, when Senator Mitchell's remit at the State Department appeared to clash with that of Dennis Ross at the NSC, lead to personal and bureaucratic tensions and to both men's eventual departure from the administration as the quest for peace descended into bitter acrimony.

The tensions that finally forced Mitchell and Ross from the Obama administration were compounded by the situation regarding Richard Holbrooke. As perhaps the most gifted US diplomat of his generation, Holbrooke had routinely been denied the top job at the State Department on the basis of his temperament. In the words of Jef McAllister, White House correspondent for *Time* during Bill Clinton's administration, Holbrooke 'never got the top job because he remained a pain in the ass his whole life'.[81] Despite this reputation, Hillary had expended political capital to ensure his appointment within the Obama administration, where he was not beloved. As James Mann notes, Holbrooke was a contradictory figure: 'He was both a courtier to the old guard and careful challenger to it. He was intensely attracted to elites and the power they held, to fame and the journalists who could create it.'[82] Despite his success at Dayton, Holbrooke was advised in October 2008 that he would not be nominated as Secretary of State if Obama won. His cause had not been helped by his open role supporting Hillary during the campaign. He was believed to have lobbied the foreign policy community on her behalf, reminding them of her apparent inviolability and of the need to be on the winning team. His ambition was such that, when Hillary injured herself in June 2009, Colin Powell emailed her enquiring as to Holbrooke's possible involvement: 'Hillary, Is it true that Holbrooke tripped you? Just kidding. Get better fast, we need you running around.'[83]

While Obama needed Hillary on board, the same could not be said of her supporters, against whom resentments were apparent.[84] The White House refused to allow Hillary to name Richard

Holbrooke as her deputy and not all of her nominees were approved. After two frustrating years attempting to negotiate with Hamid Karzai in Afghanistan, senior White House officials began openly briefing against Holbrooke, forcing Hillary to intercede on his behalf and save his job. It was a short-lived exercise, however, as tragedy once more followed Hillary Clinton's political career. On 11 December 2010, Richard Holbrooke collapsed in her office and died two days later of a ruptured aorta.[85] Just as she had lost Vince Foster in the White House, now Hillary Clinton saw her friend and advisor collapse before her eyes in her own office.

Having called Hillary a 'monster' during the 2008 campaign, Samantha Power seemed an unlikely choice to serve under her at the State Department, but her inclusion in the Obama administration, first at the NSC and then as Ambassador to the United Nations, ensured that a hatchet was buried as Hillary continued to demonstrate her capacity to act as a team player, even if it meant working with people who had previously insulted her in print.[86] Power's inclusion in the administration, along with that of Susan Rice, ensured that women dominated the US foreign policy posts in the Obama White House. In addition to Hillary as Secretary of State (2009–13), Susan Rice served as Ambassador to the UN (2009–13) and then as National Security Advisor (2013–), Samantha Power worked on the NSC (2009–13) and then served as US Ambassador to the UN (2013–), while Anne-Marie Slaughter was Director of the Policy Planning Staff (2009–11).

Obama's approach of placing high-profile appointees in apparent conflict with one another was a strategy that had been adopted by US Presidents ranging from Abraham Lincoln to Franklin Roosevelt.

The 'Team of Rivals' approach was not one that always produced harmony, but it did ensure that the President received a wide range of opinions upon which to base decisions. It became accepted, however, that Obama was running a particularly centralised foreign policy operation, which was intriguing given his own total lack of experience in the area. His advisors, including Hillary Clinton, offered guidance, but Barack Obama made the final decision, often in small meetings with his inner circle, which excluded Cabinet members. These advisors, based primarily at the White House and the NSC, proved to be the main driving force behind the administration's foreign policy, demonstrating that proximity to power is itself power.

Hillary Clinton may not have ever been part of Obama's inner circle, but she met with the President once a week, as well as with the National Security Advisor and Secretary of Defense, ensuring that she had access and that her voice was heard. Yet she never fully emerged as the single, defining voice of authority on foreign policy within the administration. Instead, various colleagues, including Defense Secretary Gates and Vice-President Biden, contributed at various times on various issues, ensuring that no single individual overshadowed the President and certainly no one with a strong reputation in foreign policy. In Barack Obama's administration there was to be one single star: Barack Obama.

RESETTING RELATIONS

Despite the media attention on Hillary Clinton's embrace of new technology and her focus on interpersonal relationships between nations, traditional forms of diplomacy and bureaucratic interaction continued unabated during her time in office. A key goal was to re-establish strategic relationships that were believed to have been damaged in the previous eight years under George W. Bush. The primary focus of this effort was Russia. With Dmitry Medvedev rotating into power as Russian President during Vladimir Putin's brief, constitutionally mandated spell as Prime Minister, an effort was made to place US–Russian relations on a sounder footing than had been the case in the final years of the George W. Bush administration. As devised, in part, by the newly appointed US Ambassador to Moscow Michael McFaul, this was ostensibly about attempting to implement President Obama's desire for a new nuclear weapons reduction treaty.

Despite the serious nature of the reasoning involved, the move to restore cordial ties with Moscow will be remembered for a publicity stunt that went wrong. To announce the start of a new era in US–Russian relations, a press conference was held during which Hillary presented Russia's Foreign Minister, Sergey Lavrov, with a gift box containing a bright red button on a yellow base that had been removed from the whirlpool in the InterContinental Hotel in Geneva. It was emblazoned with the word *peregruzka*, believed by the State Department to be Russian for 'reset'. Unfortunately, as Lavrov pointed out to the attending world press, the correct Russian translation was *perezagruzka*. Rather than 'resetting' relations, the United States appeared intent on 'overcharging' the Russians.

Notwithstanding the gimmicky feel of the incident, the fact that the US State Department failed to provide the correct translation, and the manner in which the stunt was hastily arranged with components of a hotel spa, hardly conveyed the importance of the situation or the mutual need to normalise relations. As the focus of the 'reset' mission, it failed to reflect well on Hillary, notwithstanding her best efforts to laugh off the incident.

Despite this diplomatic *faux pas*, US–Russian relations appeared to stabilise for the first two years of Hillary Clinton's tenure. President Obama's dealings with his Russian counterpart appeared to be positive and produced results. There was an agreement regarding the stationing of missile defence installations and the signing of New START (Strategic Arms Reduction Treaty) in 2010, which reduced the number of strategic nuclear missile launchers by 50 per cent. Hillary Clinton's involvement and her personal relationship with Lavrov enabled cooperation across a range of areas, including the Arab Spring uprisings. Neither this, nor the Obama–Medvedev relationship, however, could counter Russia's own national interests or the political interests of Vladimir Putin. His return to power in 2012 signified the effective end of the 'reset' initiative and the start of a steady and persistent decline in US–Russian relations for the remainder of Hillary Clinton's time as Sectary of State.

Hillary's efforts on behalf of the Obama administration to improve US relations with its friends and allies, as well as her specific focus on resetting the relationship with Russia, were made far more difficult by the whistleblower mentality that developed during her time in office. The deluge of material that appeared on the WikiLeaks website in 2010 proved to be particularly challenging for Hillary since it contained vast numbers of diplomatic cables sent by State Department officials around the world, many of which included less-than-diplomatic language about foreign heads of state. In an email to his old boss, pollster Mark Penn made his view on the leaking of information quite clear:

> The administration's response seems quite weak to me. This is ... a wholesale capturing of the diplomatic material of the country. And if this is wikileaks can get, what can the Chinese or other able to secure? [*sic*] Just being seen as apologizing for the content is weak compared to reacting and acting to shore up the key principles behind security and aggressively dealing with the problem directly.[87]

The issue regarding the penetration of email accounts by foreign intelligence services was to be a problem that retuned to haunt Hillary in the coming years, as details of her own use of a private server emerged.

The damage from the WikiLeaks revelations was compounded shortly thereafter by the classified material unveiled by Edward Snowden. As a contractor at the US National Security Agency, Snowden gained access to material relating to a range of initiatives, including the government's surveillance programmes, as well as from foreign sources, including the UK and Australia, key members of the Five Eyes intelligence alliance.[88] Estimates of the amount of material that Snowden downloaded and subsequently passed on to the media range wildly, but appear to have easily exceeded a million documents. The release of the material was damaging enough, but this was exacerbated by Snowden's flight from the US

Justice Department that resulted in him claiming diplomatic immunity in Russia, a move that did little to improve tensions between the two nations.

THE PACIFIC PIVOT

A central concept to Hillary Clinton's time as Secretary of State was the pivot towards the Pacific region, an initiative driven by her department from the earliest days of the Obama administration. This was presented as a benign process of re-evaluating the nation's global focus away from Europe and the Atlantic that had dominated much, if not all of US foreign policy for the duration of the twentieth century. The initiative took the form of educational programmes and economic development across the Asia–Pacific region, but there were fewer soft-power elements to the process as the United States cemented defence alliances in the region. This included the establishment of the US–Australia Force Posture Agreement, under which the United States stationed 2,500 marines in Australia and made greater use of existing military establishments. It also included plans for joint training exercises and raised the potential for Australian participation in ballistic missile defence initiatives.

As Hillary wrote in *Foreign Policy*, the pivot to the Pacific would mean America 'strengthening bilateral security alliances; deepening our working relationships with emerging powers, including with China; engaging with regional multilateral institutions; expanding trade and investment; forging a broad-based military presence;

and advancing democracy and humån rights'.[89] Not so obvious, but worthy of consideration in the pivot, were Hillary Clinton's own roots as a Methodist and the importance of a sense of mission. She brought a determined drive to policy in the region, especially in Burma, where she made a concerted effort to bring around the military leadership and to engage with the formerly jailed dissident-turned-politician Aung San Suu Kyi.

This move and the attending military implications raised concerns on two continents: in Europe, long-time allies feared a reduced US engagement as the Cold War moved further into history and expressed both private and public fears that America's first non-white President was basing foreign policy on an anti-colonial strategy, while in Asia, China viewed the move as a deliberate attempt to halt and reverse what was viewed as Beijing's inexorable rise to both regional and international pre-eminence. Both the White House and Hillary Clinton's State Department were adamant that the pivot was not aimed at any one nation, or intended to signify a move away from any other region. Despite such assurances, suspicions lingered.

Missed by many in both Asia and Europe, however, was the extent to which Hillary Clinton's initiative reflected a previous attempt to execute a similar move during her husband's time as President. Bill Clinton failed to visit Europe during the first year of his presidency and when he did eventually cross the Atlantic it was to address NATO headquarters in January 1994, not to visit the individual European capitals and their leaders. Instead, he and his administration spent the first year focused on the Pacific Rim nations and on efforts to engage with China on human rights developments, initially tying Most Favoured Nation trading status to developments in this field. Then, as under Obama, fears were expressed in Europe that this new, young President, with no memory of the Second World War, was reneging on a commitment to the Continent and turning the United States into a Pacific, rather than an Atlantic, power. Such fears were unfounded as the Clinton administration's efforts proved far harder to implement than initially believed, ensuring that the White House eventually reverted to a more traditional Eurocentric approach. Similarly, Hillary Clinton's successor at the State Department, John Kerry, quietly moved to reassert a European-focused approach in Obama's second term, making his first overseas trip to London and adopting a more traditional approach to diplomacy.

MISSING MILIBAND

One individual with whom Hillary Clinton developed a warm working relationship during her time as Secretary of State was British Foreign Secretary David Miliband. Widely viewed as a future leader of the Labour Party and potential Prime Minister, Miliband was an heir to the Third Way concepts that Tony Blair and Bill Clinton had advocated in the 1990s and which Hillary continued to advocate. Unsurprisingly, therefore, a bond developed that extended beyond the usual diplomatic niceties as they recognised their shared political philosophies and potential for future national leadership with one another. These sentiments, however, disintegrated in the wake of the 2010 UK general election and the defeat of the Labour government. Fears over the result had been building for several weeks, as Hillary noted in an email dated 13 April: 'Just had drinks w Miliband who is still very worried. I have crossed fingers!'[90] In the days that followed the election, Hillary received a stream of emails from Sidney Blumenthal, who had flown to the UK to witness events first-hand. On 9 May, Blumenthal suggested to Hillary that an alliance between Labour and the Liberal Democrats would constitute 'a grand progressive alliance that would keep the Tories out of power forever'. He clearly feared, however, that this would not occur and that David Cameron was about to become Prime Minister and, as a result, 'I would doubt you'll see David [Miliband] again as Foreign Secretary.'[91]

William Hague was eventually named as David Miliband's successor, viewed by Blumenthal as being 'deeply anti-European' and someone he thought would 'be disingenuous' towards Hillary. Blumenthal warned Hillary Clinton that the new coalition government's plans 'would cause havoc with peace and economic recovery', and urged Hillary to move away from a relationship with London and to 'tilt publicly to Merkel on Europe for this reason among others'.[92] Despite the all-too-obvious partisan tone and content of these missives, Hillary urged Blumenthal to continue his input on the British election, advising him that she had shared his analysis with the former President: 'I shared your emails w Bill who thought they were "brilliant"! Keep 'em coming when you can.'[93]

On 13 May 2010, Blumenthal sent Hillary Clinton a memo addressing her meeting the next day with William Hague, which he had prepared following discussions with the recently ousted Secretary of State for Northern Ireland, Shaun Woodward. Having defected from the Tories to the Labour Party, Woodward was hardly a politically neutral source for Blumenthal. His memo suggests asking Hague, 'Does the new government understand the US interest in [Northern Ireland] and appreciate the fragility of the situation?' In addition, he warns that the new government will 'slash the deficit, cutting deeply into government programs. This really cannot be done without defense and foreign policy reductions.' Blumenthal recommended that Hillary 'seek claficiation [sic] on exactly whether and where these cuts be made. Will they affect Afghanistan policy and over what schedule? How will cuts in the foreign service affect British influence in other areas?' He concluded that the new British government was 'fundamentally at odds with itself' in language that betrayed his political sentiments.[94]

Having lost his position as Foreign Secretary following the 2010 election, David Miliband was expected by many to become the next leader of the Labour Party. His own brother successfully engineered his way to lead the party thanks to the support of the unions, thwarting David Miliband's political ambitions, in a result that Blumenthal referred to as being 'something of a regression'.[95] Hillary's closest aide, Huma Abedin, succinctly expressed the views of many in her email dated 25 September 2010: 'Wow.'[96]

Hillary remained in touch with David Miliband following his defeat and messaged his wife, sending good wishes. On 29 September 2010, he eventually messaged Hillary, noting that her recent successes had been 'one of the pleasures of the last few months to see you going from strength to strength'. Referring to his loss as party leader, he noted,

> Losing is tough. When you win the party members and MPs doubly so. (When it's your brother…). But I am so proud of the campaign we ran, the issues we raised etc. We got people to believe in a New Labour platform – and modernised the platform. I have announced today that I will stay in Parliament but not in shadow Cabinet. Thanks for all your encouragement over the last couple of years. I will let you know when I am in DC.[97]

Interestingly the effort to throw David Miliband a political lifeline began very quickly as Blumenthal advised Hillary that he had 'just had a conversation with Jonathan Powell. David Sainsbury (chief donor to the Labour Party, Shaun [Woodward]'s wife's cousin) wants to fund a new Third Way organization headed by David Miliband. David is up for it. Tony very keen. To discuss.'[98] Such manoeuvrings eventually resulted in David Miliband leaving the UK Parliament and becoming President and CEO of the International Rescue Committee, based in New York, in September 2013. Less than two years later, his brother Ed led the Labour Party to its worst defeat in thirty-two years and promptly resigned as party leader.

ARAB SPRING

During the George W. Bush administration the United States was roundly criticised for attempting to export democracy as part of the Freedom Agenda. Administration critics forgot, or perhaps were never aware of the fact, that the United States had long sought to promote and encourage the spread and defence of democracy. Woodrow Wilson justified US intervention in the First World War on the basis that the world needed to be made safe for democracy, and Bill Clinton had placed the promotion of democracy at the heart of his grand strategy initiative. George W. Bush's policy posited that introducing democracy to Iraq might act as a contagion, causing it to spread to neighbouring lands. The 'domino effect' of communism spreading from one nation to another was feared in the west during the Cold War; now such an effort was attempted with democracy. A theoretical commitment to such a concept, however, is very different from determining whether it can be successfully implemented, as the Arab Spring uprisings of 2011 perfectly demonstrate.

When democratic protests broke out in Tunisia, Egypt and Libya in 2011, it was thought that many former members of the Bush administration would be ruefully smiling in their retirement, as their long-derided plans appeared to be coming to fruition. They were, of course, no longer in power to help encourage these democratic protests, a task that fell to the administration that had gained office running against the foreign policy of George W. Bush. As Secretary of State, the challenge for dealing with these incidents fell heavily on Hillary Clinton. The uprisings raised a central dilemma in US foreign policy, however: as a nation born in revolution against perceived repression, the United States maintained its stance as being in favour of democracy and liberty, especially as it had only recently liberated Baghdad, partly in defence of these principles. As a major world power, with vested interests in key global regions, however, it also had reasons for maintaining the delicate balance of power and the status quo. The United States was eager to ensure that change, if and when it came, was managed and controlled with its own best, long-term interests in mind.

Hillary Clinton had spoken on this very issue at the Doha Forum for the Future in January 2011. She noted that across the Middle East, 'People have grown tired of corrupt institutions and a stagnant political order. They are demanding reform to make their governments more effective, more responsive, and more open ... in too many places, in too many ways, the region's foundations are sinking into the sand.'[99] Change was brewing, but few could imagine what form it would take, its direction or the speed at which it could move. It was clear, however, that the United States and Hillary Clinton recognised the dilemma before them:

> Those who cling to the status quo may be able to hold back the full impact of their countries' problems for a little while, but not forever. If leaders don't offer a positive vision and give young people meaningful ways to contribute, others will fill the vacuum. Extremist elements, terrorist groups, and others who would prey on desperation and poverty are already out there, appealing for allegiance and competing for influence.[100]

The contradictory nature of the United States on the world stage at this time is encapsulated in the conflict between its ideological desire to encourage the spread of democracy and its investment in and defence of existing power structures and bases around the world. As the Arab Spring uprisings demonstrated, such conflicts are far from theoretical and have real-world implications; advocating democracy while having a fundamental interest in the status quo were clearly not mutually supportive in this case. Overthrowing dictators who were contrary to the interests of the United States was one thing, as events in Iraq had demonstrated, but that had not committed the White House to the liberation of oppressed peoples around the globe.

The desire to support democracy and human rights in Egypt appeared to be the logical American position, especially in light of the Freedom Agenda of the previous eight years. The uprising was led, however, against a staunch American ally, Hosni Mubarak, whose support in the region had been a foundation of US foreign policy for decades and who was instrumental in maintaining Egyptian peace with Israel, dating back to the Camp David Accords of the Carter presidency. With popular uprisings against Mubarak's continued rule, the United States and Hillary Clinton's State Department were faced with a conflict between national security interests (which favoured his support) and a national commitment to democracy and liberty (which favoured his removal). Unsurprisingly, perhaps, given the stakes involved, the result was one of prevarication. That was enough, though, to signify a lack of commitment to the Mubarak regime, which ultimately lost the support of the White House and the Egyptian military, bringing to an end the Egyptian President's three decades in power.

An indication of how fast the situation in Egypt moved is revealed in a memo dated 20 April 2010, entitled 'Mrs Mubarak', in which Ambassador-at-Large for Global Women's Issues Melanne Verveer advised Hillary of her 'good visit' with the wife of the Egyptian leader, who 'very much wants you to come to Egypt for the major anti-trafficking event she is doing in December and sends you her regards'. Egypt, Verveer reported, was 'making good progress on women's issues: prosecuting child marriage cases, combating FGM and they're close to passing a tough anti-trafficking law. Mrs M is the guiding force.'[101]

Having apparently sided with the forces of democracy over the status quo, the Obama administration and Hillary Clinton's State Department quickly discovered the perils of freedom as Egyptians elected Mohamed Morsi of the Muslim Brotherhood, whose commitment to continued democracy and to long-standing agreements with the United States and Israel appeared less than total. This clearly presented a challenge to Hillary as Secretary of State. As Anne-Marie Slaughter notes, however, her smart-power strategy had advantages even here: 'Now we have contacts with women's groups, techies, and entrepreneurs through various programs. If diplomacy is building relationships that you can call on in a crisis, then she has developed the frame.'[102] The eventual overthrow of the Morsi government by the Egyptian military was hardly the democratic conclusion that anyone had hoped for and appeared to end any democratic aspirations, at least in the short term. Unfortunately, the situation soon became far worse for all concerned – including Hillary – in Libya.

LIBYA

Libya promised to be the ultimate expression of a smart-power approach to diplomacy and a ringing endorsement of Hillary Clinton's style of international relations during her time as Secretary of State. Unfortunately, any initial success has long since given way to anarchy, recrimination and loss of life. Rather than being an example of a positive, thoughtful act of US and international intervention, the case of Libya instead illustrates how the best of intentions can go horribly wrong, provoking unseen and unintended consequences with lingering implications.

Initially, the situation in Libya appeared clear-cut: a smart-power approach appeared to offer a solution as Colonel Gaddafi threatened reprisals against his countrymen who challenged his leadership in light of similar movements in Tunisia and Egypt. With the Obama White House determined to avoid being dragged into a conflict that teetered on the brink of a civil war but eager to be seen as a force for positive change in the world, Hillary Clinton initiated a plan to position the United States as an arbiter of progress and stability in Libya. She worked to secure Arab League backing for a UN-led no-fly zone and support for strikes on Libya led by the US with assistance from local forces, including Jordan, and she leveraged her personal relationship with Foreign Minister Lavrov to ensure Russia didn't veto a UN-mandated military intervention by US forces. By acting at the 'invitation' of the Arab League, the United States avoided the impression that it was reverting to Bush-era interventions in Arab lands with large oil reserves. Conversely, though, by stating its intention to 'lead from behind', the administration opened itself up to criticism for being too circumspect about its intent or role in the operation.

Regardless of the military approach, Hillary continued to work the smart-power approach, recruiting the Emir of Qatar, Sheikh Hamad bin Khalifa Al-Thani, to act as a go-between with various rebel groups. The rebels were provided with repairs to telecommunications networks as Hillary Clinton continued to adopt smart power and blend populist, practical and political elements to secure the administration's ambition of regime change in Libya. Just as in Iraq, however, the initial overthrow and death of the dictator did not result in the harmonious future that think-tank analysts had imagined. Instead, as Walter Russell Mead noted, 'Advocates of the Libya mission failed to take seriously one of the most important lessons of Iraq: When you overthrow a dictator in the Arab world, expect chaos and violence to follow.'[103] Mere anarchy could have been easily explained away as the unwelcome, inevitable result of a power vacuum following decades of despotic leadership. The attack on the US consulate in Benghazi on 11 September 2012, however, was a calamity for all concerned, and its implications continue to resonate. It cost the lives of a US Ambassador and three other Americans, forced President Obama to change his choice of Hillary's successor at the State Department in his second term, contributed to a decision not to intervene in Syria and continues to cast a shadow over Hillary Clinton's campaign for the presidency.

The death of Ambassador Stevens was the nadir of Hillary's tenure at the State Department and came with only months left on her watch; indeed, Washington, DC was already speculating about her replacement. President Obama's preferred choice was Dr Susan Rice, who was then serving as UN Ambassador to the United Nations and who had no role in the Benghazi debacle. She was dispatched to defend the administration on the American political talk shows on Sunday 16 September, just five days after the attack, partly as preparation for her eventual presentation as Obama's choice to replace Hillary if he won re-election. Her response to questioning, in which she denied that the attacks were planned and blamed them on a video depicting the prophet Muhammad, resulted in a backlash against her and the administration and forced her to withdraw from contention for Secretary of State.[104]

Hillary Clinton managed to avoid the grilling that Dr Rice received on the television talk shows, but could not avoid the United States Senate Foreign Relations Committee, which called her to testify in January 2013. Her testimony, delayed until after President Obama had been sworn in for a second term, had been postponed due to ill-health. Hillary had fainted shortly before was due to leave office and suffered a concussion in the ensuing fall. Doctors had subsequently discovered a blood clot, in a series of events that took Hillary several months to recover from. Her eventual testimony had the makings of a political circus as potential Republican presidential candidates, including Senator Rand Paul, took the opportunity to lambast their potential Democratic rival in 2016 for her role in the tragedy. Despite eight congressional investigations into the incident, none has so far found any evidence of criminal wrongdoing by any-one, least of all Hillary Clinton. The constant spectre of hearings and investigations continues to keep the suspicion of wrongdoing in the air, despite the inability of any hearings to successfully demonstrate criminality or flaws in Hillary Clinton's actions.

The failure to implement a viable democracy in Libya and the debacle in Benghazi made any US intervention in Syria even more unlikely than it had already been. Just as the deaths of US service personnel in Somalia in 1993 impacted on subsequent US policy towards Rwanda, so too did the events in Benghazi convince the administration that the American people and their representatives in Congress would not support any moves in Syria. Despite President Obama's repeated references to 'Red Lines' and the apparent use of chemical weapons by the Assad regime, no US military intervention was forthcoming during Hillary Clinton's time in office, while the people of Syria paid the ultimate price for a flawed initiative in Libya. An intervention would have run counter to everything for which the Obama administration had stood, as well as being against the wishes of his core supporters, who had opposed US military interventions and applauded his efforts to withdraw from foreign wars of intervention. The actions of the Assad regime also came at a precarious time for Obama, who was in the midst of his 2012 re-election campaign and was ill-disposed to take military action that had the potential to backfire as he prepared to debate Mitt Romney. Domestic politics and the tragedy in Benghazi ensured that not hard, soft nor smart power was to be used to aid the people of Syria from the abuses of their government.

KILLING BIN LADEN

Although the relations between the State Department and the NSC remained difficult during Hillary Clinton's tenure in office, relations with the Pentagon improved due to her excellent rapport with Defense Secretary Robert Gates and his successor Leon Panetta, who had previously worked as Bill Clinton's highly effective Chief of Staff. Gates, who had been appointed by George W. Bush and retained by Barack Obama, found a natural ally in Hillary, whose hawkish stance on national security was at odds with the often dove-like tendencies of previous Secretaries of State.

Leslie Gelb referred to the Clinton–Gates alliance as 'a phalanx', noting that Clinton and Gates 'are both center-right; they have their four feet firmly planted on that ground. And that is, they are not going to open themselves up to serious attack from the right, whether it's Iraq or Afghanistan or Iran or you name it.'[105] This ensured that, unlike during George W. Bush's first term, the State Department was not isolated in the development of policy and that, together, the State Department and the Pentagon could present a unified front in defiance of the NSC, which tended to be more concerned with the political implications of policy than may have been appropriate. Hillary Clinton and Robert Gates worked together on issues as diverse as Syria, Afghanistan and the ongoing struggle with political violence, with the phrase 'war on terror' having been banished from use by the White House early in Barack Obama's first term.

The terminology may have changed since George W. Bush was President, but the mission of the US intelligence services had not:

find and neutralise Osama bin Laden. Few doubted that the war in Iraq had diverted attention from this mission and as President Obama withdrew troops from that conflict he moved them into Afghanistan in a repeat of the surge that had been initiated in Iraq in 2007. Having avoided capture throughout the eight years of the Bush presidency, bin Laden remained the most wanted man alive, and his continued freedom was a constant source of conjecture; how could one man successfully evade capture for so long without someone in either the Pakistan or Afghanistan governments knowing where he was? The fear that American 'allies' were harbouring bin Laden had long been a concern in Washington, DC and had contributed to Richard Holbrooke's sense of frustration with the leadership in what he termed the 'AfPak' region. The 2011 discovery of bin Laden's compound, less than a mile from a Pakistani military academy in Abbottabad, confirmed the fears of many that the leadership in Islamabad had been turning a blind eye to the terrorist in their midst for several years.

The success of Operation Neptune Spear, which resulted in the death of bin Laden on 2 May 2011, had little to do with the State Department or Hillary Clinton, initiated as it was by the CIA and SEAL Team Six under the direct order of the Commander-in-Chief. As a member of the Obama administration, however, she had been intimately involved in the diplomatic efforts to locate and neutralise America's Public Enemy No. 1. The incident also demonstrated Hillary's discretion. Due to the historic nature of the mission, members of the foreign policy team were ordered not to discuss what was being initiated. When Barack Obama subsequently informed all living Presidents of the mission's success, he was startled to learn that Hillary had not already shared the news with her husband. Official photographs taken in the White House Situation Room reveal Hillary Clinton's active presence on the night of the raid that brought bin Laden to justice a decade after his organisation delivered death and destruction to her constituents in New York City. In so doing, Al Qaeda also changed the course of Hillary's life forever. The events that Hillary watched in real time from the Situation Room were the final shots in a cycle that had, to a certain extent, begun on 11 September 2001 and which had claimed her own initial presidential ambitions as one of its many casualties.

HILLARY CLINTON'S RECORD AS SECRETARY OF STATE

Winston Churchill remarked that history would reflect well upon him, because he intended to write it. Political memoirs have prevailed in recent years, despite contractions in the publishing market, as leaders, potential leaders and former leaders seek to convey their philosophies, rationalise their decisions and justify their actions. These publications confirm that history is never really settled and that political legacies are vital and worth fighting for. In the immediate aftermath of Hillary's departure from the State Department, a wide range of opinion was expressed regarding her time in office. In an interview with 60 *Minutes*, President Obama noted, 'I think Hillary will go down as one of the finest secretaries of state we've had.' She was perhaps the hardest-working and the most-travelled; she maintained daily schedules of more than eighteen hours and travelled almost 1 million miles on journeys to 112 countries. But does this remarkable outlay of energy and determination equate to greatness or success?

Hillary Clinton played a vital and highly visible role in efforts to successfully reset key relationships that had been damaged during the George W. Bush administration. Neither she nor President Obama, however, transformed US foreign policy or initiated sweeping changes to the national security architecture, global bodies or the community of nations. There was no 'Hillary Clinton Doctrine', and had such a doctrine been espoused during her time in office it would rightly have been afforded to her boss, President Obama. Her role as Secretary of State provided Hillary with a platform to establish solid foreign-policy credentials, but not the opportunity to dominate, control or overshadow her superior, the President of the United States. As had been the case in her previous role in the Senate, her celebrity status had got her the job, but grandstanding would have cost her the job. An underappreciated aspect of her time as Secretary of State, therefore, was her success in exploiting her status for the cause of the administration and the United States, but without appearing self-serving.

The steady stream of classified material that found its way into the hands of journalists and foreign governments did not make Hillary's job easier, nor did the comments of members of the military, such as General Stanley A. McChrystal, whose unguarded remarks to reporters became a challenge for the entire administration. In 2009,

McChrystal had referred to Vice-President Joe Biden's views on counterterrorism as 'shortsighted', that may result in 'Chaos-istan'. The remark earned a presidential rebuke aboard Air Force One. Six months later, McChrystal cooperated with Michael Hastings for a profile of US counterinsurgency policy in *Rolling Stone* magazine. The article revealed details of Obama's first meeting with McChrystal: '"It was a 10-minute photo op," says an advisor to McChrystal. "Obama clearly didn't know anything about him, who he was. Here's the guy who's going to run his fucking war, but he didn't seem very engaged. The Boss [McChrystal] was pretty disappointed."'

Hastings also revealed that 'Team McChrystal likes to talk shit about many of Obama's top people on the diplomatic side. One aide calls [James] Jim Jones, a retired four-star general and veteran of the Cold War, a "clown" who remains "stuck in 1985"'.[106] The article revealed that McChrystal was a staunch defender of Hillary Clinton due to her earlier support for his efforts but that he was particularly critical of Richard Holbrooke, stating that the general had stopped reading emails from the controversial presidential emissary to Afghanistan. The fallout from the McChrystal situation was followed at the State Department, as revealed by correspondence between Hillary Clinton's senior advisors. Philippe Reines noted in an email to Huma Abedin on 21 June 2010 that the forthcoming profile was to be explosive: 'It comes out later this week but what's leaked so far is definitely a doozie.' As an understatement, he concluded that it was 'unclear to me why anyone ever cooperates with *Rolling Stone*'.[107]

Suggestions that Hillary Clinton could or should have devised a new approach to US foreign policy during her tenure ignore the fact that Secretaries of State rarely devise new initiatives and even more rarely are credited with what occurs during their tenure. Few of Hillary Clinton's predecessors have placed their mark on global history. The office is an important, highly visible but ultimately subservient role in which the office-holder must do the bidding of the President in as effective a manner as possible, conveying the wishes and policies of the White House and ensuring that they credibly reflect the aspirations and intent of the administration. Barack Obama received the Nobel Peace Prize in his first year in office, in large part for not being George W. Bush. Whatever else Hillary was criticised for during her time as Secretary of State, no one accused her of chasing a Nobel Peace Prize to service her own political ambition. Brent Scowcroft, National Security Advisor to President George H. W. Bush, noted that Hillary Clinton had 'been a good Secretary of State. She is confident but not arrogant in her confidence, and quite agile.'[108] Hillary left office, however, before the fruits of the administration's secret negotiations in Cuba and Iran were revealed to the world. Whatever the long-term implications of these agreements, the decision to resume diplomatic ties with Cuba and the agreement with Iran over its nuclear aspirations will be at the centre of President Obama's foreign-policy legacy, and Hillary Clinton's departure from office prior to their unveiling reduces her ability to bask in any success that they may bring.

One of Hillary Clinton's smartest moves, which eventually failed to deliver on its early promise, has gone unheralded: her decision to appoint a series of global emissaries to regional hotspots, enabling her to roam the world as a global ambassador for the United States and not to get bogged down in one particular region. The genius of this decision was undermined by foreign players and elements within the Obama administration, notably the NSC, and did not receive Obama's wholehearted support. Indeed, a key challenge for Hillary was Barack Obama's inability to develop warm working relationships. This impacted on her ability to work with him directly, as well as her ability to work with other nations whose own leaders found it hard to bond with the President. Barack Obama's cool demeanour was also noticeable in his dealings with Congress, which again impacted on Hillary Clinton as Secretary of State as the President failed to develop strong working relations with the lawmakers from whom he needed support, not only domestically, but on key foreign-policy issues as well.

Hillary Clinton's unique status as former First Lady, former Senator, former presidential candidate and, vitally, as presumed future presidential candidate, greatly impacted on her actions as Secretary of State. Her status ensured that she was offered the position, but it also affected how she did the job and how the role was perceived. Her innate conservatism, all too often overlooked and unrecognised, was on display throughout her time in the role. There was no grandstanding and there were no dramatic gestures. Instead, she worked in a calm and collected manner to achieve her task of engaging with the world in a non-adversarial fashion, seeking to re-establish ties and mend fences that had been damaged or neglected in the previous eight years. Not all were impressed; in 2010, North Korea posted video clips on *YouTube* mocking Hillary as being a 'minister in a skirt' and branding Secretary of Defense Gates a 'war maniac'.[109]

In her efforts to re-engage with the world, however, Hillary was largely, though not universally, successful. The Pew Research Center indicated a marked rise in America's reputation during her time in office, particularly in Europe, suggesting that, along with President Obama, Hillary Clinton helped restore the nation's international standing. Conversely, America's reputation in the Middle East showed little improvement. Despite the vast financial resources and thousands of lives that the United States spent trying to stabilise the region, anti-Americanism in the Middle East remains rife. Only the Israeli public has a positive opinion of the United States, with 84 per cent in support of their ally. Two of the nations at the centre of the Arab Spring uprisings have particularly poor views of the United States, driven no doubt by the Obama administration's prevarication. Tunisians expressed a 47 per cent negative view of the US, along with a staggering 85 per cent of Egyptians. Even Jordanians, who have largely been removed from any direct conflict or uprisings, expressed 85 per cent disapproval of the United States when asked in 2014.[110]

Despite these setbacks, it is difficult to pin blame on Hillary Clinton or her department, although her opponents are currently engaged in attempts to do so because of her presidential ambitions. Hearings continue into the events in Benghazi, with political opponents determined to keep the tragedy in the public domain and tie Hillary directly to the first death of a serving American Ambassador since 1979. Having worked to implement a smart-power approach to foreign policy, the deaths in Benghazi and the collapse of the Libyan state represent a severe setback to Hillary Clinton's record in office and provide an opportunity for partisan political advantage.

The foreign policy that Hillary was called on to implement and promote, much like Bill Clinton's beforehand, was accused by critics of lacking direction. Just as John Lewis Gaddis called Bill Clinton's foreign policy 'ad hoc', former National Security Advisor Zbigniew Brzezinski criticised Obama's foreign policy for being 'improvisational'. However, as both know, all administrations are forced to respond to events. As Bill Clinton's former National Security Advisor Anthony Lake noted, 'Nobody in any government I am aware of, except perhaps in the Soviet Union or in Mao's China, says at a meeting, "OK, what did we say in the strategy document, therefore, here's what our policy is."'[111] Written foreign policy documents can only exist as a guideline for future action and in many cases 'there is no relationship between the document and policy'.[112] To presume that foreign policy documents are consulted in times of crisis is to misunderstand both the rationale for such reports and also the nature of government in such emergency situations. Grand strategy documents exist due to a legal requirement to report to Congress, as well as to provide the public with a sense of reassurance about the intent of an administration, but they can only ever be declarations of intent and should not necessarily be viewed as blueprints for future action.

In 2010, Stephen Krasner noted that 'most foreign policies most of the time have not been guided by grand strategy', and that most efforts to articulate a holistic vision have failed.[113] Official US foreign policy as printed, therefore, can only ever be theoretical, designed to indicate direction and principles. As former Director of the Policy Planning Staff, Morton Halperin noted, 'Nobody looks at them to clear up issues. Any concept that the policy influences events or people's reaction to them is just wrong.'[114]

Hillary Clinton's time as Secretary of State and the perceived success of her tenure resulted in a series of accolades, not least of which was the 2013 Chatham House Prize. Accepting the award, she said, 'America's leadership remains not only pre-eminent but necessary ... The world in which we live poses new challenges to all of us on an ongoing basis that require a level of strategic thinking and execution that starts, first and foremost, back in the democracies that we represent.'[115] It was a statement that perfectly captured Hillary Clinton's past, present and future – thinking strategically, but remembering that all politics is local and must be decided by the domestic electorate.

Reflecting on Hillary Clinton's time in office, Anne-Marie Slaughter noted that she 'took diplomacy directly to the people in ways that cannot produce a treaty or negotiated agreement, but that are essential to advancing America's interests over the longer term'.[116] Vitally, however, while she was visiting 112 countries and flying almost a million miles in efforts to advance the causes of the United States, President Obama remained in charge of all final decisions, being 'the decider', as his predecessor phrased it. This ensured that Hillary Clinton, as Secretary of State, implemented policy rather than instigated it, a fact of which her detractors may need to be reminded in 2016.

CONCLUSION

As a result of her temperament, political sensibilities and the remit under which she was operating, US foreign policy during Hillary Clinton's time as Secretary of State was restricted and constrained. It was geared towards ensuring that no more harm was done to America's international standing and reputation. President Obama's first term was geared towards halting the direction of US foreign policy as it had been enacted for the previous eight years and beginning the process of turning it around. By the end of Obama's first term and Hillary Clinton's tenure as Secretary of State, that process had been accomplished to an extent, enabling her successor, John Kerry, to adopt his own, more traditional, Eurocentric approach to foreign engagement.

Hillary clearly believes in a unique role for the United States in the world. Having served as First Lady (where she witnessed first-hand the pressures and the opportunities afforded the President of the United States), as a Senator on the Armed Services Committee (where she was exposed to the pressures on lawmakers to legislate with a global remit) and as Secretary of State (where she has been able to influence and implement policy), she has a had remarkable vantage point from which to devise her view of the world and the appropriate role that the United States should adopt. Her personal values, political philosophy and practical experience have convinced her that the United States has a powerful role to play in the world and that little can be gained from adopting a reactive, stay-at-home approach to global affairs.

Only time will tell if Hillary Clinton will be the first Secretary of State to become President since before the US Civil War, or if the Cabinet position marks the extent of her achievement in American political life. The fact remains that her tenure as Secretary of State will be remembered far better than most of the previous sixty-six occupants of the office. She will not be regarded as highly as Henry Kissinger, Dean Acheson, George Marshall or George Shultz, but neither will she become one of the many faceless, nameless, forgotten bureaucrats who have held the post. The history of Hillary Clinton's time at the State Department will undoubtedly be written in terms of what happens next in her career. If she secures the presidency, it will be regarded as a training ground for power and as an astute move on her part, as she follows in Thomas Jefferson's footsteps from the State Department to the White House. If, however, she fails in her effort to become the first female President, then her time as Secretary of State will almost certainly be one element that will be used to defeat her. It will be identified as a strategic blunder on her behalf and as a calculated manoeuvre by Barack Obama to sideline and derail the future aspirations of his most visible political adversary.

— CHAPTER 7 —

PHILANTHROPIST: LAYING FOUNDATIONS

Having announced early in her tenure that she only intended to serve one term as Secretary of State, there was always an air of expectation as to what Hillary Clinton would do after leaving office in January 2013. Working for Barack Obama precluded the opportunity of running for the presidency in 2012 and, with the US election timetable set in stone, any presidential ambitions needed to wait a further four years – an eternity in politics. Few doubted, however, that such a campaign would eventually be initiated; it was just a matter of when it would be announced. Until then, there were several years to spend preparing a second challenge for the presidency. Needless to say, if Hillary

Clinton's 2016 campaign fails, every moment of this prepara-
tory period will be scrutinised for potential errors of judgement
or lost opportunities.

With no government income to rely on, Hillary needed a job
and a focus for her energies and skills. She had already produced
one memoir, *Living History*, which had sold in high numbers and
earned her millions of dollars both in advances and in subsequent
royalties. Moreover, public interest was such that another book
covering her years at the State Department was a virtually guaranteed bestseller. Any such book, however, needed to walk a fine
line between revealing enough material to be of interest while not
betraying any sensitive information about an administration that
was still in office and about a President whose support Hillary
needed to rely on to fulfil her own presidential aspirations. It was
also clear that any new book would be compared to the previous bestseller in terms of content and sales. Where public interest
in *Living History* had, to an extent, been based on what Hillary
wrote about the events that led to her husband's impeachment,
no such salacious events would be addressed in any subsequent
book. With no personal scandal to address and the need to be coy
in regard to the administration she had only recently left (as well
as about her own future), any book would prove to be a challenge
to write, market and sell at a time of diminishing sales in the
industry as a whole.

With presidential ambitions to nurture, Hillary Clinton also
needed to maintain political relevance and a public profile. The
speaking circuit offered a route for her to do both while also earning

money to further aid a future campaign. Conveniently, there was a ready-made vehicle through which to do this: the Clinton Foundation. Coupled with the Clinton Global Initiative, the Clinton Foundation had demonstrated a remarkable capacity to raise and distribute funds to the disadvantaged. As a former Senator and Secretary of State with the support of her former-President husband, it made sense for Hillary to come on board and channel her own energies into the Clinton Foundation. However, Hillary's time at the foundation raised familiar questions regarding money, access, transparency and conflicts of interest. Such questions would have little relevance for a former office-holder, retired from public life and seeking to capitalise on her experience in the private sector. However, Hillary had clearly *not* retired and her time at the Clinton Foundation has proved to be a double-edged sword, as it generated both vast incomes and hard questions about her role and relationship with foreign governments. As with all stages of her life and career, therefore, 2013–15 proved to be a challenging, rewarding and difficult time for Hillary as she wrote, spoke and prepared for her second run for the presidency of the United States.

WHAT TO DO WITH FORMER (AND FUTURE?) PRESIDENTS?

A perennial question in Washington, DC has been what to do with former Presidents. In an age when people are living longer than ever, the time spent out of office can now far exceed the former chief executive's time in office. On occasion, some Presidents have continued to participate in the national political debate: William Howard Taft was named Chief Justice of the Supreme Court seven years after leaving the White House; John Quincy Adams served in Congress for nine terms following his single-term presidency; and Andrew Johnson had a short-lived tenure as a Senator five years after his time in the top job was over. These are the exception, however. Most former Presidents lead unremarkable lives after leaving office, content to play golf and, in recent years, earn a fortune from book deals and the speaking circuit. This question becomes all the more pressing when the President in question is relatively young. Often overlooked is that fact that Bill Clinton was the third-youngest President in US history, after Theodore Roosevelt and John F. Kennedy, and was only fifty-four when he left office in January 2001. Despite having campaigned in 1992 as a New Democrat to distinguish himself from perceived past Democratic failures, such as that of Jimmy Carter, Bill Clinton found himself turning to former Carter administration officials to fill his Cabinet, and it was to the Carter example that he looked for his post-presidential career.[117]

When Jimmy Carter left the White House after a single term in January 1981, he was perceived to have had a failed presidency. Despite the success of the Camp David Accords, inflation soared, unemployment rose, US hostages were held for over a year in Iran, the Russians invaded Afghanistan and a sense of malaise descended on the United States. Despite this, it has been generally accepted that Carter made a success of his post-presidency years by establishing the Carter Center in his native Georgia in 1982. The centre is located next to the Jimmy Carter Presidential

Library and operates as a non-profit, non-governmental organisation dedicated to alleviating human suffering and to promoting human rights, which Carter had previously championed as President of the United States. Working in over eighty countries, the success of the centre has been instrumental in rehabilitating the reputation of the former president and resulted in his being awarded the Nobel Peace Prize in 2002.

Bill Clinton left the White House with an approval rating of 68 per cent. Despite this, it was clear that his political and historical standing had been badly tarnished by the impeachment hearings that had dominated his second term in office. While this unfortunate situation had been successfully manipulated to assist Hillary's campaign for the Senate in 2000, it remained a blight on Bill Clinton's presidency that was impossible to erase; fairly or unfairly, he had become only the second President in the history of the country to be impeached. While nothing could now be done about the sins of the past, the Carter Center example provided Bill Clinton with a possible route to political and historical redemption. Therefore, along with establishing the William J. Clinton Presidential Library and Museum in Little Rock, Arkansas as home to the former administration's documents and artefacts, a forward-looking enterprise was created to channel the energies and political connections of the former President.

Originally known as the William J. Clinton Foundation, the centre was established in 2001 as a non-profit organisation based in New York and Little Rock. Building on the work done by President Clinton during his time in office, the foundation was created to address global issues of disease and economic inopportunity. Operating in the non-governmental, non-profit sector, it promotes and develops initiatives and humanitarian programmes. The organisation runs its own programmes through an expanding number of entities, operating under the umbrella of the Clinton Foundation. These include the No Ceilings Project, the Clinton Health Matters Initiative (CHMI), the Clinton Development Initiative (CDI), the Clinton Climate Initiative (CCI) and the Clinton Global Initiative (CGI). Through these entities the foundation has raised almost $2 billion from a variety of sources, including the financial sector and political donors, as well as international organisations and foreign governments. These projects have provided a much-needed platform for the former President's energies and skills and have, vitally, offered the possibility to build a lasting legacy of development and philanthropy to offset any lingering damage caused by the President's previous indiscretions.

Non-profit originations like the Clinton Foundation are not required under US law to disclose any information that might reveal the identities of their contributors. Had Bill Clinton's presidency marked the end of his family's political aspirations, the foundation's actions would doubtless have gone unnoticed by many. However, due to Hillary Clinton's role as Secretary of State and run for the presidency in 2016, questions have been raised about the Clinton Foundation's financial transparency. In 2008, when Hillary was nominated as Secretary of State, the Clinton Foundation released a list of global donors, including foreign governments and private organisations. At the same time, Bill Clinton agreed to curtail his activities, both in the name of transparency and the wish to avoid the appearance of impropriety. The foundation was subsequently renamed the Bill, Hillary and Chelsea Clinton Foundation in 2013, following the end of Hillary Clinton's time at the State Department, in a move that signified the start of a new era in her life, as well as the potentially dynastic approach to the future that the Clintons were embracing.

The Clinton Foundation, therefore, provided Hillary with a ready-made, natural base from which to operate following her departure from the Obama administration. Her time there, however, exacerbated the long-standing view that her greatest political asset, as well as her greatest political liability, remains her husband. His rise from Governor of Arkansas to President of the United States enabled Hillary to become First Lady and establish a national and international reputation for herself. His indiscretion in office arguably created the public sympathy for her that eased her election to the Senate in 2000. His vast list of political contacts was an asset during her initial campaign for the presidency in 2008, but his inability to take a backseat occasionally caused problems for her and cost her votes. At least part of the Democratic Party's hesitations concerning her candidacy in 2008 stemmed from issues of Clinton fatigue and the potential for further scandal surrounding the former President. Finally, Bill Clinton's tremendous efforts to establish and operate the Clinton Foundation provided her with a remarkable base from which to operate, but its remit, relations with foreign governments and moneymaking exercises ensured that there were always questions concerning potential conflicts

of interest and the vast sums charged by the former First Couple
for public speaking.

HARD CHOICES, EASY MONEY

Having written her first memoir in 2003, it was widely expected that
Hillary would produce a follow-up book detailing her time at the
State Department. Such a move was hardly exceptional and followed
recent publications from her predecessors Condoleezza Rice and
Madeleine Albright. Neither, however, had previously produced a
bestseller, nor were they expected to seek the presidency. For Rice
and Albright, such books were an effective conclusion to their public lives, detailing events as they saw them but not considering the
lasting implications of their work. Hillary, however, was in a very
different position. Her previous book *Living History* spent eighteen
weeks on the *New York Times* bestseller list, had been published in
thirty-six countries and had sold almost 4 million copies worldwide.
When it came out in the summer of 2003, nobody had been under
any illusion that it was intended to mark the end of her public life;
indeed, she had only recently been elected to the Senate. The very fact
that a second memoir was so widely anticipated fed into the broader
expectation of a 2016 campaign for the presidency. Hillary's second
memoir, therefore, would be read not merely as a reflection on her
career to date, but also for an indication as to what may lie ahead.

In April 2013, only two months after leaving the Obama administration, it was announced that Hillary had signed an agreement
with her long-standing publisher Simon & Schuster to produce a

second memoir detailing her time in the Cabinet. Written during the course of the following twelve months, *Hard Choices* was released in June 2014 to great expectation, broad media coverage and solid, if slightly underwhelming, sales. Hillary engaged in a marathon publicity tour to promote the book with events that felt more like political rallies than tame book signings. The first event in New York attracted over 1,000 people, many of whom waited in line to meet the author only to discover, somewhat disappointingly, that no dedications were permitted and only one word was to be written in any books purchased: 'Hillary'. This was to be a meticulous, automated process, with no time for conversation. Time and money dictated the flow of the book launch, which eventually took Hillary to several European capitals, including London, as the promotional tour gathered pace, stretching out over fifty days as she met world leaders, celebrities and the general public on two continents.

Reaction to the new book was mixed. Opponents suggested it had underperformed, while supporters claimed otherwise, highlighting its sales in relation to books by previous Secretaries of State and presidential candidates. It was yet another example of different rules applying to Hillary Clinton. For any another political memoir to debut at number one on the *New York Times* bestseller list and to remain there for three weeks would have been deemed a success. It was suggested, however, that this constituted a disappointment, especially when coupled with *Hard Choices* being dislodged from the number one position by *Blood Feud*, Edward Klein's exposé of the relationship between the Clinton and Obama families that sought to undermine the work that Hillary had done to mend fences with her former opponent. Regardless, the book sales and speaking fees enabled Hillary to earn $12 million in the sixteen months after she left the State Department, placing her in the top 1 per cent of American earners.

Writing her second memoir enabled Hillary Clinton to define both her time at the State Department and her relationship with her former competitor, Barack Obama, well ahead of the 2016 election campaign, and to ensure that both issues were discussed, debated and dealt with long before the first votes were cast. Writing in the *New York Times*, Peter Baker noted that Dean Acheson won a Pulitzer Prize for his account of his time as Secretary of State, *Present at the Creation*. Hillary, Baker concluded, 'seems to have a bigger prize in mind'.[118] The book was, in many ways, an early campaign publication detailing her preparedness for the presidency. It certainly defines the extent to which she travelled, the number of people she met and the hours she spent in meetings, in what is effectively a 600-page bid for power. As such, it parallels many of the characteristics of her husband's 2004 memoir, *My Life*, which was widely criticised for seeking to list everyone that he had met during his time in office, rather than to offer any insightful analysis or thoughts on the events that had transpired.

Both books ultimately suffered for the same reason: their final chapters could not be written, as the authors both had unfinished business in the public arena. Neither could they be as candid as other authors. Hillary Clinton's colleague from the Obama admin-istration, Robert Gates, was widely praised for his compelling and revealing memoir *Duty*, which pulled no punches when it came to reflecting on the challenges he faced while working at the White House. As with the previous books by Albright and Rice, however, no one expects Gates to return to office, enabling him to write a candid and forthright memoir. The Clintons, with their eyes on the future, were not at liberty to do the same.

LYING LOW, RAKING IT IN: THE CLINTONS AND CASH

The success of the Clinton Foundation and the public interest in the family brought about a financial and, consequentially, political transformation in the lives of the Clintons. When Bill Clinton first ran for the presidency in 1992, an early misperception was that he was just another wealthy politician, accustomed to a lavish lifestyle and out of touch with the lives of the average voter. This perception was, in part, based upon his education at Georgetown, Yale and Oxford, and a photograph of him meeting President Kennedy that implied an insider status. Yet nothing could have been further from the truth. Bill Clinton had been born on the wrong side of the tracks in a poor state and had succeeded in life due to his intelligence, benefiting greatly from the American education system. As such, the electorate initially misconstrued his hard work and determination to succeed until the reality was unveiled during the 1992 campaign. Indeed, Bill Clinton may have been the poorest American President in decades, with no private wealth upon which to rely. A further indignity was delivered when it was decided that Bill Clinton's successor as President would receive a

100 per cent pay rise, taking the presidential salary from $200,000
to $400,000 following the election of 2000. The Clintons' financial
situation was further hindered by the many legal challenges they
faced during their time in the White House and the attendant
legal fees, as well as the cost of Chelsea's education. It was this
combination of financial challenges that caused Hillary Clinton
to tell Diane Sawyer in 2014 that she and her husband left the
White House 'dead broke'.

Since January 2001, however, the former President and his family
have more than made up for any previous financial shortcomings.
Official tax returns reveal that the Clintons earned in excess of
$163 million between 2001 and 2012. This figure, however, does
not include undisclosed sources of income including investments,
book royalties and properties. In the years that Hillary was in the
Senate, the family earned almost $109 million, mostly from the
former President's engagements on the lecture circuit. Between
2001 and 2007, the Clintons donated more than 9 per cent of
their income, approximately $10 million, to charity and paid over
$33 million in income tax. As Secretary of State, Hillary earned
a total salary of $785,700. However, during her time at the State
Department, the Clintons earned over $53 million, again mainly
from the former President's speaking fees. Since leaving government service in 2013, Hillary has been able to contribute greatly
to the family finances, commanding speaking fees of $200,000 per
talk and earning an $8 million advance for *Hard Choices*, result-
ing in her earning $12 million in sixteen months after leaving
President Obama's administration.

The parallels with the scandals from the 1990s, therefore, are beguiling. Then, as now, Hillary Clinton's financial activities, enacted to secure her family's long-term security, have raised questions about her propriety and good judgement. In the 1980s, greed had famously been described as 'good' in the movie *Wall Street*. Decades later, however, such activity looked less than impressive coming from a politician who sought to position herself as a champion of the underclass. Instead, the impression was created that whenever Hillary took time away from government service it became an opportunity to cash in and make a fortune based on her experiences in office. Just as in the 1990s, the concern for Hillary Clinton's supporters is not that one allegation will destroy her career, but that the constant drip of allegations and hints of wrongdoing will prove impossible to adequately address and will cause the electorate to tire of her and the perpetual stream of unfounded allegations against her. By 2015, so many unfounded allegations had been made that Bill Clinton's former Campaign Director James Carville had christened the process 'spaghetti journalism' on the basis that eventually a story will be written that will stick, but until then more unfounded allegations will continue to be made.

Intriguingly, the charges against Hillary Clinton that focus on her time at the Clinton Foundation, as well as those that date back to her time as First Lady of Arkansas, all relate to the same subject: her apparent need to get rich quick. It is likely that this stems, in part, from her upbringing in a house dominated by a frugal father to whom life appeared to be an exercise in saving money. Having been raised to appreciate the importance of a dollar earned,

Hillary appears to have taken the lesson to heart and ensured that her family will never again be forced to shiver through a freezing winter with no heating.

Hillary's actions in this area stand in marked contrast to those of her husband, who generally appears to be less interested in the acquisition of wealth for its own sake. He has certainly earned a great fortune from a series of book deals and speaking fees, but somehow his efforts never appeared to be quite as self-serving or as mercantile. Fairly or not, Hillary's attempts to earn as much as possible during her time away from public office have long struck a nerve with her opponents and continue to cause her problems.

MORE HARM THAN GOOD?

While the Clintons have been able to benefit financially from their unique place in American political life, is it possible that it could come at a great political cost? The vast amount of money that has been earned and the allegations of a conflict of interest may prove to be detrimental to Hillary Clinton's 2016 campaign for the presidency or, at the very least, a distraction. As a candidate for the Democratic Party, which has traditionally aligned itself with unions and blue-collar voters, Hillary will be hard-pressed to demonise any Republican candidate as being out of touch with the electorate, as Mitt Romney was characterised in 2012. At a time of widening income inequality in the United States, Hillary Clinton's personal fortune risks becoming a problem, both within her own party and in the wider country. It has already attracted the attention of critics such as Peter Schweizer, whose book *Clinton Cash* sought to detail how the Clintons had enriched themselves. This is but one in a growing cottage industry of books eager to deliver a steady stream of salacious, often unfounded critiques of Hillary in a pattern of publication that can be traced back to the 1990s.

Despite the partisan nature of many of the attacks that have been levelled at both Bill and Hillary over the years, the role of the Clinton Foundation has raised serious challenges to their credibility and the spectre of a conflict of interest should she prevail in 2016. Questions linger over uranium deals, the Russian atomic energy agency Rosatom and donations to the Clinton Foundation to the tune of $31 million.[119] A major issue is the extent to which foreign nations may have sought to influence a future Hillary Clinton White House by donating to the family foundation. Despite the pledge by the Clinton Foundation not to accept donations from foreign governments while Hillary was Secretary of State, it continued to raise between $34 million and $68 million from over a dozen overseas sources with direct access to national governments in Saudi Arabia and Ukraine, to name but two examples. The United Arab Emirates, Saudi Arabia and Oman have all provided funds in the past, although once Hillary declared her decision to seek the presidency in 2016 the Clinton Foundation Board announced that it had narrowed future donations to six foreign countries: the Netherlands, Germany, Canada, Australia, the UK and Norway. While this list of countries might look benign enough, they all have their own national interests, which they will naturally wish to pursue with any future administration led by Hillary Clinton.

Potential conflicts of interest arise with the UK and Germany over the negotiation of the proposed Transatlantic Trade and Investment Partnership (TTIP) that would establish a free-trade zone between the European Union and the United States. Canada also has an interest in the development of the Keystone XL pipeline that Hillary may be required to decide upon as President of the United States.

Another issue is the extent to which Bill Clinton's speaking fees were impacted on Hillary Clinton's remit as Secretary of State. The former President's average fee had been $150,000, but during Hillary Clinton's time in the Obama administration he was paid $750,000 to address a telecommunications conference in China and $500,000 to address a Russian investment bank. The situation is compounded by the complex relationship between the Clintons' personal income and the fees that flow directly into the Clinton Foundation, often blurring the lines between the two. No single publication has ever delivered a knockout blow, but the constant attempt to undermine Hillary Clinton's credibility has already impacted on her polling numbers heading into the 2016 election. US First Amendment rights, however, ensure that the right of authors to attempt 'a death by a thousand cuts' will continue unabated.

To what extent does this hinder Hillary Clinton's chances in 2016? To supporters, the many questions are merely evidence of what she famously referred to as 'the vast right-wing conspiracy' that had been working against her husband (and herself) since he announced for President. To opponents, such issues confirm long-standing concerns about her suitability for office. The potential damage to Hillary Clinton's 2016 campaign, however, is the effect such continuing allegations may have on undecided voters, or those with no memory of Bill Clinton's time in office. Most elections are decided by a small number of undeclared, undecided voters, whose loyalty fluctuates from election to election. Hillary will need to convince them that such allegations are baseless if she hopes to be elected as the first female President of the United States. It would indeed be remarkable if a charitable foundation, established to channel the energies of America's third-youngest President and to aid women and children around the world through a series of development programmes, hindered Hillary Clinton's path to the presidency.

CONCLUSION

For most people, stepping down from a job that was fourth in line to the presidency of the United States at the age of sixty-five would mark a time to slow down, take things easy and retire. Most people, however, are not Hillary Clinton. Far from winding down, she wrote a second memoir detailing her years at the State Department, engaged in a hectic international tour to promote her new book, threw herself into a fundraising exercise for her family's foundation and became a grandmother. Her efforts to create a legacy from her time at the State Department, as well as a solid financial foundation from which to seek the White House in 2016, launched Hillary into a flurry of activity that included work on behalf of the Clinton Foundation and a series of highly paid talks on the lecture circuit. Not for the first time, Hillary found that there appeared to be one rule for her (requiring virtual financial piety) and another for everyone else (encouraging them to openly pursue the American dream).

If questions over the role of the Clinton Foundation have proven complicated to date due to the involvement of a former President and his politically active wife, then this will only be further complicated if Hillary becomes President of the United States in 2016. How the Clinton Foundation will be able to function without Bill or Hillary Clinton taking an active lead is a question that few can claim to answer. It is hard to imagine how the foundation could justify accepting any foreign donations due to the obvious potential for a conflict of interest, yet this constitutes the bulk of its income. Although the foundation has been built up over the past ten years, its future appears to be very much in the balance. The Clinton Foundation had been established as a vehicle of redemption, vindication and financial reward for Bill Clinton. The extent to which it may also prove to be the undoing of Hillary Clinton's political future remains unclear.

CHAPTER 8

THE CLINTON DYNASTY

As a nation, the United States is steeped in the belief that anyone can grow up to become President. Therefore, the concept of dynasties appears to be quintessentially un-American. Indeed, the US was, in part, founded in an attempt to escape the dynastic qualities that pervaded British political life and which kept power in the hands of the elite few, rather than the general masses. Yet, time and again, American dynasties have emerged to cast a hold on the imagination and voting intentions of the population. Over the history of the United States, a small number of families has held inordinate power at one time or another, representing both main national parties. From the Adams family in the early years of the Republic, through the Roosevelts, the Rockefellers and the

Kennedys, the United States has routinely produced families of great wealth that flourish for a season in public service. More recently, the Bush family has secured its place in the history of American political dynasties with three generations of elected leaders (Senator Prescott Bush, President George H. W. Bush and President George W. Bush). With the potential for a Hillary Clinton presidency, a new political dynasty appears possible, one that spans a husband and wife team, as well as a potential role for their daughter in the years to come. As Hillary campaigns for the presidency in 2016, she will also be campaigning for a legacy that will place the Clinton family in the rarefied atmosphere of the American political elite. Yet any Clinton dynasty would be distinct in several ways from those that have gone before and it is, therefore, interesting to consider the families that have dominated in the past in order to appreciate how and why Hillary Clinton's efforts in 2016 may set her family apart.

AMERICAN POLITICAL DYNASTIES

When the first shots were fired in the American War of Independence, the revolutionaries sought to establish a new system of government free from the perceived failings of the British Crown and its parliamentary system. Inherent in what was increasingly seen as a flawed governing body was the perpetual control of the masses by a small, elite group of families who held power from generation to generation, untroubled by changing political tides. This was not a situation unique to Great Britain; a similar scenario was in effect across the English Channel in France, where Thomas

Jefferson observed what he believed to be the 'scourge' of ancestral political rule inflicting a 'cursed existence' on the population. Writing in 1786, Jefferson advised George Washington that the introduction of such a system of 'hereditary aristocracy' to the United States would 'change the form of our Government from the best to the worst in the world'.

Shortly after Jefferson expressed his views, the hereditary ancestry was decapitated in France. Such a drastic measure was not enacted in the United Kingdom, however, where political dynasties continued to thrive and provide a rallying call against which to formulate a new American system of government under the US Constitution in 1787. Despite this, the very system of 'hereditary aristocracy' that Thomas Jefferson warned against was present from the very start of the American experience. The founding fathers, who have become synonymous with concepts of democracy and freedom, were the landholding elite of the time, replete with estates and great wealth, often slaveholding and eager to ensure that control of the new nation remained in the hands of similarly propertied men.[120] As originally drafted and ratified, the Constitution placed severe limits on political participation, restricting access to the ballot by preventing women, slaves and, in some states, free black citizens from voting. It took several amendments to the Constitution to overturn restrictions based on literacy tests, intellect, a poll tax, race and gender.

Even when elections took place, there were limits on their effect. As originally constituted, the only politicians for whom the population voted directly were members of the House of Representatives. The State Legislatures appointed Senators until 1913 and the presidency remains subject to the anachronism of the Electoral College, a system than can, and has, defied the popular will of the people on occasion.[121] Even the timing of elections and the differing duration of terms of office (two years in Congress, four years in the presidency, six years in the Senate), is a check on democracy designed to safeguard the status quo and prevent the domination of the US government in one electoral cycle.

The founding fathers actively sought to prevent the establishment of political parties, fearing that would undermine the new nation and lead to greater division. Their failure to do so was compounded by the rise of the first American political dynasty in the form of the Adams family, whose patriarch, John Adams, became the second President of the United States. In a quirk of fate, Adams, who lamented the deification of his fellow founding fathers, sired the first American political dynasty. His cousin, Samuel, served as Governor of Massachusetts and his son, John Quincy, became President of the United States in 1825, after having served as Ambassador to London and Secretary of State.[122] The election that brought Quincy Adams to the White House, however, was marred in controversy, as Andrew Jackson won the popular vote and the largest number of Electoral College votes, but not enough to secure the presidency. As a result, under the Twelfth Amendment, the House of Representatives named Adams as the sixth President, tainting his single term in office.

Across the country and throughout the history of the United States, hundreds of families have established local powerbases that have dominated for generations and formed an essential lock on power. These include the Daley family in Chicago, the Brown family in California, the Cabots in Massachusetts, the Goldwaters of Arizona, the Stevensons of Illinois and the Udalls of Arizona.[123] More recent examples include the Gore, Romney and Paul families.[124] However, it is the families who have achieved national prominence that attract most attention and interest with regard to concepts of an American political dynasty. Of these, three loom large: the Roosevelt, Kennedy and Bush families. Between them, these families have produced five American Presidents, four United States senators and four governors, as well as ambassadors to London and Japan and at least seven congressmen.[125] They have, however, also been involved in a number of tragic incidents that have tainted their family brand. These include the involvement of Neil Bush in the collapse of Silverado Saving and Loan in the 1980s, the death of Mary Jo Kopechne in a car driven by Edward Kennedy in 1969 and allegations of numerous affairs involving members of all three families. American political dynasties bring with them the benefit of significant name recognition and, in many cases, the memory of past glories and electoral success, but they are often accompanied by scandal, failure and allegations of corruption and collusion – characteristics that are all too familiar to the Clintons.

THE CLINTON DYNASTY

It is into this hallowed collection of the great, the good and the scandalous that many commentators are now attempting to place the Clinton family. What become immediately apparent, however,

are the differences that currently exist between the Clintons and the
other families that have constituted significant American political
dynasties. These differences not only highlight the power of a small
number of political families, but also demonstrate the rapid rise
of the Clinton family.

The significant families in American political life have three
things in common; great inherited wealth, electoral success and
generational endurance. The three elements are, to an extent, self-
reinforcing: wealth leads to influence and access, which leads to
political opportunity, which can lead to electoral success, which is
then utilised to create opportunities for successive generations of
family members who perpetuate the cycle of success. Money, success and access to power become an inheritance that is nurtured,
guarded and passed down from generation to generation. This has
been apparent in all successful political dynasties, and not only
those in the United States. The manner in which this inheritance
is predicated on an initial acquisition of wealth is a unifying factor: great wealth has led to great access, which has led to electoral
success, which has led to political influence and dominance. Joseph
P. Kennedy, for example, made and secured a fast fortune that
granted him access to Franklin D. Roosevelt, enabling him to secure
an ambassadorship and to carve out a place for himself, his sons
and his family in the American political system that continued
throughout much of the twentieth century. His influence endures
today, with his granddaughter serving as US Ambassador to Japan
and his great-grandson serving in Congress.

Significantly, however, the Clinton family has not followed

this path to a potential dynasty. The wealth and access to power did not come prior to electoral success, but because of it. Indeed, the concept of a Clinton dynasty is remarkable considering Bill Clinton's origins and financial status upon taking office in January 1993. Bill Clinton was not born to wealth; instead, he was born on the wrong side of the tracks, in Hope, Arkansas, a dirt-poor town in a dirt-poor state. Only his intellect and hard work secured him places at the nation's most prestigious schools and then at Oxford University as a Rhodes Scholar. Although Hillary Clinton was born to more middle-class status than her husband, there was nothing elite or particularly affluent about the circumstances of her birth or upraising. Both benefited greatly from the American educational system but neither was wealthy in comparison to established political dynasties or, indeed, to many other Americans. Throughout their years in Arkansas, Hillary was the main source of income for the family in her role at the Rose Law Firm, while her husband drew his government pay cheque as Governor. The Governor's mansion had been their only home in Arkansas. Unlike the Bush family retreat at Kennebunkport, the Kennedy compound at Hyannis Port or the ranches of previous Presidents such as Lyndon Johnson or George W. Bush, there was no Clinton family home to which they could retreat.

This was, perhaps, an indication of the great divide between the Clintons and other dynasties prior to Bill Clinton leaving office. He had become President on a $200,000 salary but had no family money, while Hillary Clinton had quit the law firm to be First Lady. They continued to live in government housing (the White

House) and much, if not all of their funds was consumed in covering the cost of Chelsea's education and in legal fees associated with the various accusations levelled at them. As a result, when they left the White House the Clintons were not only broke, but heavily in debt – hardly an auspicious position from which to build a dynastic political legacy.

Where the Clintons have been particularly successful is in maximising their experience to address the financial constraints that they faced in 2001. Through a series of astute ventures and negotiations they have secured not only their financial futures but also a political dynasty, which are not unrelated. The Clintons have both benefited from the public interest in their lives and their willingness to provide their own candid accounts of their experience. Bill Clinton received the world's largest ever advance for a book when the Knopf Publishing Group paid him $15 million for his memoirs, *My Life*, published in June 2004. Three years later, the same company released *Giving: How Each of Us Can Change the World*, detailing good causes and ways to get involved. Bill Clinton earned $6.3 million from this book and donated $1 million to charity. The two books earned him over $30 million. Hillary was paid an $8 million advance for her first memoir, *Living History*, which eventually earned her over $10 million. Her second memoir was accompanied by unconfirmed suggestions that she had been paid an advance of $14 million. The income from royalties has been compounded by fees accrued on the lecture circuit. Bill Clinton has earned $104.9 million from 542 speeches between 2001 and 2013. Since leaving the State Department Hillary Clinton has secured dozens of similar speaking engagements, charging upwards of $200,000 for an appearance. Both are represented by the Harry Walker Agency, which has devised a rigid contract that prevents the distribution of remarks or footage of their speeches and usually ensures that they are closed to the media. Unsurprisingly, the income stream from book deals and public speaking has enabled Bill and Hillary Clinton to live a dynastic lifestyle unimaginable to most Americans, with houses in New York and Washington, DC.

CHELSEA RISING?

For a political family to truly be considered a dynasty, however, it must be multi-generational. For the Clintons to qualify, therefore, the expectation is that Chelsea Clinton will step up in the years ahead and serve in an increasingly vital capacity. She has already spent her entire life in the public spotlight, brandishing flags at her father's campaign rallies when she was still a toddler, waving nervously at Michael Jackson at her father's first presidential inaugural gala, guiding her parents to Marine One following her father's confession of an affair with Monica Lewinsky and campaigning for her mother in the Senate race of 2000 and then the presidential campaign of 2008. As a member of the millennial generation, Chelsea has a capacity to reach an entire demographic that has no living memory of the first Clinton presidency but also cannot remember a time when the family wasn't in the news.

There can be little doubt that Chelsea Clinton sees a role for herself in elected office, and she has recently confirmed as much, ensuring that 2016 is a pivotal year for her, as well as for her mother. A successful bid for the White House will place Chelsea in the unique position of being the first First Daughter in two non-consecutive presidencies. To assist her mother in her presidential aspirations, Chelsea Clinton has spoken on university campuses in a deliberate attempt to connect with a younger audience. This was a process that began in 2007, when she was brought in to speak for Hillary Clinton in a variety of locations. Eight years later, Chelsea has married, had a daughter, worked (briefly) for *NBC* television and has written a book. She has also joined the Clinton Foundation as a full-time board member, which has been reflected in the new name for the organisation: the Bill, Hillary and Chelsea Clinton Foundation. One of her first decisions was to have the foundation audited, drawing on her brief experience working for McKinsey & Company in New York. The shake-up led to changes at many levels within the foundation as several long-time allies of the President had their remits reduced and Donna E. Shalala was hired as the new CEO.

Chelsea Clinton's role at the foundation will undoubtedly expose her to accusations similar to those that have routinely been levelled at her mother, namely of relationships with foreign governments and the fees charged for speaking appearances. These questions will emerge if Chelsea Clinton ever enters a political contest or takes a position in any future administration. In addition, of course, there is the final challenge that Chelsea Clinton faces: the charge of nepotism. She has been named to the board of directors and has been granted what one might call a disproportionate say in the running of a \$2 billion enterprise having little to no experience.

This is not the first time that the charge has been made. In 2011, she was hired by *NBC* on a salary of $600,000, despite having no media experience and having been deliberately shielded from the press by her parents. It was a decision with few supporters and did not endure; the highlight of her time there amounted to her surreal interview with the computer-generated mascot of an insurance company, the GEICO Gecko.

Having left the world of television to join the Clinton Foundation, the expectation is that both Chelsea and her father will play significant roles in Hillary Clinton's 2016 campaign. Learning from the mistakes of 2008, and in an effort to build on his speech at the 2012 Democratic National Convention that set pundits writing about Bill Clinton as 'the greatest communicator', the former President will be used to attract key voting groups and pull in influential help. Chelsea Clinton is likewise being utilised to focus on younger audiences. The challenge here, however, is to avoid previous accusations from the 2008 campaign by David Schuster of *MSNBC* that the Clintons were 'pimping out' their only child. The charge has now become multi-generational, since Hillary is making repeated references to her new role as a grandmother, ensuring that Chelsea Clinton's infant daughter Charlotte is being politicised before she can even walk or talk.[126]

If Hillary Clinton prevails in the 2016 election, Chelsea Clinton is expected to take on a fairly robust, high-level role at the White House, possibly in strategic management. In so doing, she has the potential to become a key, if informal, aide to her mother, continuing a role that has developed during the campaign. Legislation prevents her from being named to any paid government position in her mother's administration, but she could well be appointed to an advisory position or head up a specific research committee, as Hillary herself did on healthcare back in the early 1990s. Whatever her exact position, Chelsea Clinton has the potential to fill a role unlike anyone since Robert Kennedy, who advised his brother between 1961 and 1963. Doing so may potentially prevent her mother from falling victim to the classic case of groupthink, whereby the very advisors designed to ensure their continued relevance cause leaders to become disconnected from reality. As so often happens in politics, proximity to power breeds arrogance, along with a defensive unwillingness to speak truth to power. This leads to a cocoon effect, whereby the candidate becomes shielded from reality and harsh truths by advisors, whose sole ambition is to serve and see their client elected, but whose actions often prevent this from happening. Chelsea Clinton, like Robert Kennedy before her, has both unfettered access and the ability to deliver the unvarnished truth. This could be her most important role in any future Hillary Clinton administration, the success of which would exacerbate expectations about an eventual role in elected politics for Chelsea, establishing what could then be a true American political dynasty.[127]

CONCLUSION

Despite the apparent intent of America's founding fathers, US history is replete with political dynasties, both locally and nationally, with powerful families routinely exerting unprecedented influence over the direction of policy. The extent to which the Clinton family can be said to fit into this pattern is yet to be decided. Certainly, Bill and Hillary Clinton dominated the political scene in Arkansas in the 1980s and attempted to project this to a national level in the 1990s. The extent to which this succeeded politically is clearly debatable. What is indisputable, however, is that the family has produced a State Governor, a President of the United States, a Senator, a Secretary of State and a serious candidate for the United States presidency in 2016. This alone is enough to make the Clintons a serious contender for inclusion in any list of powerful American political families.

However, the true political power in the Clinton family has so far only been held by one generation, and never at the same time; as Bill Clinton's time in office ended, Hillary Clinton's journey was just beginning. Yet, not for the first time, it is possible to see how the Clintons are making their own rules and redefining what a dynasty may look like. Simply because Bill Clinton is no longer in elected office does not mean he no longer yields political influence. His role at the Clinton Foundation has granted him a tremendous platform from which to influence global development and raise awareness of issues. He was called on by President Obama to aid in the 2012 election campaign, doubtless earning a valuable political IOU in the process. The wealth that Bill and Hillary Clinton have amassed ensures that they will remain a dominant force in American politics for the rest of their lives and will provide a springboard for Chelsea Clinton to enter public life, free from the need to worry about having to earn a salary.

Although the concept of a political dynasty appears on the surface to be contrary to the American Dream, few voters appear too
upset at the thought of another Clinton sitting in the Oval Office.
Neither does Hillary Clinton's campaign seem too concerned about
the dynastic aspects involved, choosing to launch the 2016 bid on
Roosevelt Island in New York City, with all the obvious connotations
involved. Whatever other challenges Hillary Clinton may face as
she bids to become the first female President of the United States,
charges of dynasty-building appear to be the least of her concerns.

— CHAPTER 9 —

THE LAST CAMPAIGN

On 12 April 2015, Hillary Clinton announced her intention to again seek the Democratic Party's nomination for the presidency of the United States. Following eight years as First Lady of the United States, eight years as a United States Senator and four years as Secretary of State, the announcement marked Hillary Clinton's final roll of the dice: at sixty-seven years old, she has reached a point of no return. The 2016 campaign will either result in Hillary becoming the first female President of the United States or it will undoubtedly mark the end of her political career. Victory is not assured. She must first secure the Democratic Party's nomination and then defeat her Republican opponent in the general election in November 2016. To do both, Hillary will need to address a series of formidable obstacles, including her age, her gender, her past, her critics, the changing nature of American politics, her party, her husband, her role in the Obama administration, her 2008 campaign and her own personal weaknesses.

The previous chapters have laid out the route by which Hillary arrived at her decision to seek the Democratic Party's nomination for the White House in 2016. They have revealed a series of character traits, political commitments and diplomatic, as well as political initiatives that have both helped and hindered her career. To appreciate the true impact of these elements, however, it is necessary to draw them together to consider how they will affect Hillary Clinton's 2016 campaign for the presidency and to assess what has been learned from her previous endeavours. We may also wish to consider the traits that are essential for a successful presidential candidate and ask whether Hillary fulfils these criteria, as well as the political context in which she begins her historic campaign for the presidency. This chapter considers the state of the Union, the state of the candidate, the state of the world and the state of her opposition in 2016, arguing that each of these will have an important role to play in deciding whether Hillary Rodham Clinton will take the oath of office on 20 January 2017 as the forty-fifth President of the United States.

THE STATE OF THE UNION: 2015

The United States that Hillary Clinton seeks to lead in 2016 looks very different from the one she initially sought to govern in 2008. The country is no longer in an economic downturn, its military is no longer actively engaged in Iraq or Afghanistan, it is no longer led by an administration that appeared to thrive on being universally unpopular overseas and it has made great strides in terms of social inclusion. Despite these factors, however, all is not well with the American body politic. The racial divide that many expected to be addressed by Barack Obama as the first African-American President has not healed; economic disparity continues to widen as the number of Americans on food stamps has hit a historic high, up from 17 million in 2000 to 46 million in 2015, costing $76.1 billion a year.[128] Internationally, US interests are being challenged daily by rising world and regional powers. The concept of American decline appears to have become an accepted reality in many circles, coupled with a grudging acceptance of an inevitable Chinese ascendency.

Despite a national sense of pessimism, the economic figures for 2015 are a considerable improvement from 2008. The US Bureau of Labor reported that the national unemployment rate in the United States decreased to a seven-year low of 5.3 per cent in June 2015, a figure beneath the average unemployment rate of 5.83 per cent between 1948 and 2015. In another sign of increasing national prosperity, average wages in the United States hit an all-time high of $10.55 per hour in January 2015. Another sign of the improved market conditions was the increase in the birth rate among American women, which rose 1 per cent, the first increase since the start of the recession in 2007.

The United States is no longer on the verge of an economic precipice, but racial tensions have risen to the fore as the race riots in Missouri and Maryland demonstrate. The nation is no longer actively engaged in Iraq or Afghanistan, but the threat posed by Islamic extremists presents a clear and present danger to American interests and there is no tangible policy in place with which to address it. Osama bin Laden may have been neutralised and the apparent threat from Al Qaeda significantly diminished, but the threat of political violence in the form of extremism has not ended, but has morphed into something different and potentially more destabilising. This is the state of the Union on the eve of the 2016 presidential election.

THE ANNOUNCEMENT

Long before it was announced, it was widely assumed that Hillary Clinton would seek the presidency in 2016. Since an official announcement would have triggered federal regulations surrounding campaign finances, it was not made until relatively late in the day. Nothing, however, could disguise the steady stream of high-ranking Democrats who began to move quietly from the White House to think tanks such as the Center for American Progress and other bodies closely tied to the Clinton Foundation. Hillary didn't need to announce a decision; the cash was already rolling into the 'Ready for Hillary' Super PAC campaign that had been established in her name, if not necessarily with her tacit approval. An evolution in campaign fundraising that came about due to judicial decisions in 2010, these 'independent-expenditure only' Super Political Action Committees can raise and spend unlimited funds on behalf of, but must be autonomous from, political candidates and parties. In retrospect, it appeared that Hillary Clinton had never stopped running. The perpetual campaign concept, so embraced by her husband's administration, had been adopted, nurtured and implemented by Hillary Clinton to such an extent that attempting to distinguish between 'doing' and 'seeking to do' became an unenviable task for observers. Finally, however, the speculation ended on 12 April 2015, as Hillary officially announced her intention to seek the presidency of the United States.

Clearly, if Hillary Clinton is to win the presidency, it is crucial that she learn from the mistakes of the past. Nowhere was the determination to do so more apparent than in the launch of her 2016 campaign. In 2008, Hillary announced her intention to run with a video that focused solely on her, speaking directly to the camera, stridently telling America that she was running and that she intended to win. The video launch had one star, one message and one focus: Hillary Clinton. Eight years later, everything had changed. The two-minute campaign launch video features a series of individuals, all of whom are getting ready to do something new in their lives: retire, start a business, start work, go back to work, get married. It is a variation on Ronald Reagan's highly successful 'Morning in America' commercial from 1984, updated for a millennial generation to whom interracial dating and same-sex partnerships are taken for granted. Only towards the end, ninety seconds into the two-minute film, does Hillary appear to announce that she is 'getting ready to do something too'. Standing on a street outside a regular American home, she announces simply, 'I'm running for President.' The tone is far more accessible, designed to present a softer image of the candidate and how she intends to campaign in the year ahead. 'Everyday Americans need a champion. And I want to be that champion,' Hillary announces. 'So I'm hitting the road to earn your vote – because it's your time. And I hope you'll join me on this journey.'

The use of the launch video, released via social media, reflected the changing nature of American elections as well as the preferences of the candidate. Hillary Clinton made a conscious effort to engage on Twitter and encouraged the State Department to use the platform as a tool of soft and smart power during her time as Secretary of State. Now, as a candidate for the presidency, she can use the internet to get her message across to her supporters and the media without the need to conduct press conferences. Social media, therefore, partly enables Hillary to cut out the middle man and connect directly to the voters, circumventing the need for difficult questions. It is also an astute way of connecting with a much younger age group and with demographics that don't watch television news.

The video launch was immediately followed by a road trip to Iowa and New Hampshire, during which Hillary Clinton ditched the media, the trappings of power and celebrity that had accompanied her for over twenty-five years, and disappeared from sight as she engaged with voters and residents in the first states to vote in 2016. The only imagery to emerge came from store surveillance cameras that caught her and her aides ordering fast food in a Chipotle drive-through. Everything about Hillary Clinton's efforts to engage in Iowa is in contrast to her apparent distance in 2008, when she was initially focused on securing re-election to the Senate. The events that Hillary has been attending are noticeably different from those in 2008, too, in a concerted effort to engage directly with the voters in a classic case of retail politics. Gone are the impersonal rallies with attendees numbering in the thousands. In their place are visits to Community Colleges to meet with students and academics, during which she pledges her support to make such institutions free for students. Instead of arriving at such events by helicopter ('The Hill-o-copter') and Gulfstream jet as she did in 2008, Hillary has been utilising the 'Scooby' van to convey a down-to-earth approach to campaigning. As with so much to do with US politics, however, the 'Scooby' van is something of a conceit. It looks like the vehicle from *Scooby-Doo* (hence the name), but it is actually a $60,000 Secret Service vehicle, fitted with a television, sound system, sofa and swivel chairs. Like it or not, as a former First Lady, US Senator and Secretary of State, Hillary Clinton is afforded full Secret Service protection, so the idea that she could, even if she wished to, escape that protective bubble is unrealistic.

This marked an effective 'soft launch' for the campaign, which enabled Hillary Clinton to formally declare her candidacy, end months of uncertainty and begin the official drive for the White House. To mark the end of this initial phase, her team staged a large outdoor rally on 13 June 2015. Following an internal debate over the location of the event, the decision was made to use Roosevelt Island in New York, the state Hillary Clinton had represented in the Senate for eight years. This was something of a bizarre choice for several reasons. Firstly, the logistics were difficult. Roosevelt

Island is a small sliver of land in the East River between Manhattan and Queens, and getting to it is not particularly easy. It is served by a single line on the New York Metro, but is usually reached by a Cable Car, known to visitors of Universal Studios' Kongfrontation ride and for its appearance in the 2002 film *Spiderman*. It is not, therefore, a logical place to stage a large outdoor rally that thousands of supporters were expected to attend. This was compounded by the decision to hold the event on Roosevelt Island Day, an annual celebration that draws vast crowds and which has nothing to do with politics or presidential campaigns. The timing and logistics, therefore, were unfortunate, especially as the speech had originally been scheduled for May. It was also a strange choice because of the name of the island at which the event was held. Considering the concerns surrounding the concept of a Clinton dynasty, holding the event at Four Freedoms Park on Roosevelt Island reinforced memories of a previous dynastic clan and appeared to encourage, rather than diminish such comparisons.

Hillary Clinton's speech was delivered as expected, without great oratorical fireworks and without mistakes. It had been drafted and redrafted by the same group of advisors that had contributed in 2008, plus some new colleagues who had previously worked for Barack Obama. As a result, the speech felt less impassioned than perhaps it could or should have been. The images from the event came across as steady and efficient, if not quite as dynamic as Ronald Reagan's 1980 launch with the Statue of Liberty as a backdrop. What was immediately apparent, however, was that this was not a speech that Hillary could have given eight years previously. It was laced with humour and policy ideas, and referenced both her gender and her résumé. 'America can't succeed unless you succeed,' she told the crowd. 'Here, on Roosevelt Island, I believe we have a continuing rendezvous with destiny ... I'm running to make our economy work for you and for every American.' Hillary Clinton was determined to make her speech resonate on several levels, reminding listeners, 'I've stood up to adversaries like Putin and reinforced allies like Israel. I was in the Situation Room on the day we got bin Laden. But, I know – I know we have to be smart as well as strong,' in a reference to her embrace of smart power as Secretary of State.

It was in its embrace of gender role models that the campaign speech really resonated for many, however, as Hillary Clinton credited her mother with inspiring her and instilling the determination and drive that were required for the campaign ahead: 'My mother taught me that everybody needs a chance and a champion. She knew what it was like not to have either one,' she insisted, in a line that would certainly not have been used in 2008 when Hillary was attempting to be more robust than her male challengers. The decision to weave her personal narrative into her campaign speech was a clear sign that Hillary's campaign team had considered where mistakes had been made in 2008 and was attempting to rectify them, making the candidate more human and accessible. That line of thinking also extends to the use of humour. Faced with daily speculation regarding her past activities, Hillary Clinton appears content to use humour as a shield: 'Along the way – I'll just let you in on this little secret – I won't get everything right. Lord knows I've made my share of mistakes. Well, there's no shortage of people pointing them out!' Even her specific use of language ('I'll just let you in on this little secret') draws in an audience for a moment of intimacy, a technique which was not utilised in 2008. The speech enabled Hillary to emerge on the campaign as a three-dimensional candidate, replete with policies and humour, blending geopolitics and gender issues: 'All our Presidents come into office looking so vigorous. And then we watch their hair grow greyer and greyer,' she told the gathered crowd. 'Well, I may not be the youngest candidate in this race, but I will be the youngest woman President in the history of the United States! And the first grandmother as well. And one additional advantage: You won't see my hair turn white in the White House. I've been colouring it for years!'

All things considered, therefore, this was far from the usual, formal start to a presidential campaign. Instead of a vast rally and a policy-laden speech, there had been a low-key announcement posted on the internet and an off-camera trip to engage with the electorate. Only two months later, on 13 June, did the spectacular kick-off rally occur, by which time Hillary had already spent vital time in the battleground states of Iowa and New Hampshire. In 2008, the message had been that Hillary Clinton was *tough* enough to be Commander-in-Chief. Now, in 2016, the message has changed to convey the fact that she is *compassionate* enough to care about and improve the lives of ordinary Americans. Vitally, she is also raising her gender at every opportunity. Finally, reverting back to a message not dissimilar to her husband's 1992 campaign, Hillary is stressing economic issues such as the need to revive the ailing American middle class. Over two decades after Bill Clinton won the presidency, it's still 'the economy, stupid' that could win the White House for the Clinton campaign.

HILLARYLAND 2016

With Hillary Clinton's 2016 campaign officially announced, her team could finally open its campaign headquarters located across two floors in Pierrepont Plaza in Brooklyn Heights, a hip district of New York deliberately designed to be less corporate and more in touch with the electorate than Manhattan. Despite the focus on this complex, however, the campaign also retained office space in Manhattan to ensure that there was a base of operations for Hillary to meet and greet without having to trek all the way out to Brooklyn. Therefore there was a public-facing HQ and a more private operation, a move that was pragmatic but which raised questions about sincerity and image.

Irrespective of office locations, Hillary Clinton's years of experience and international reputation have enabled her to draw on a wide range of highly skilled, experienced and dedicated professionals to work on her 2016 campaign for the White House. Drawn to her team from a variety of backgrounds and for a variety of reasons, all seek to place Hillary Clinton in the Oval Office and secure key roles for themselves in her future administration. Her team has been derived from former members of Barack Obama's administration, former advisors to President Bill Clinton and loyal members of Hillaryland in an effort to create a dream team of consultants and, crucially, to avoid the mistakes of 2008.

The management of a national campaign is vital, providing as it does a sense of tone, direction and strategy. To that end, John Podesta has been appointed campaign chairman and perfectly blends experience from both the Clinton and Obama administrations. He served as Bill Clinton's Chief of Staff from 1998 to 2001 before establishing the Center for American Progress think tank. He subsequently led Barack Obama's transition team in 2008 and later served as Counselor to President Obama before stepping down ahead of his appointment to Hillary Clinton's campaign. At sixty-six, he is one of the older members of the team and almost twice as old as the campaign manager, Robby Mook, who will be looking to replicate the success he had in getting long-time Clinton confidant Terry McAuliffe elected as Governor of Virginia in 2013. Mook is a contrast to James Carville, Bill Clinton's campaign manager, who was loud, brash and outgoing. Mook is far more measured and less likely to appear on television, preferring instead to crunch data. As a former member of Hillary's 2008 campaign, Mook can help her to replicate wins in Nevada, Indiana and Ohio, but also to consider where things went wrong and to rectify these errors.

Interestingly, Hillary has made a conscious decision to recruit Barack Obama's top pollsters, whose job it is to test voter intent and response to policy initiatives. Her use of Mark Penn, who had previously served as her husband's pollster, in 2008 was seen to have been a grievous mistake, so her recruitment of Joel Benenson, who did much to help Obama beat her in 2008, speaks volumes to the need to bring together members of the former opposing camps. As Hillary Clinton's chief strategist and pollster, Benenson will work alongside former Obama strategists David Binder and John Anzalone to help hone her message, especially in the vital early states of Iowa and New Hampshire.

Of crucial importance will be Hillary Clinton's ability to craft her message and communicate it to the American people. In the past, she has been accused of lacking her husband's renowned soft skills in this area, so she has recruited former White House Communications Director Jennifer Palmieri to oversee these efforts. Palmieri, like Podesta, blends experience from both the Clinton and Obama camps, having worked at the Center for American Progress and at the Clinton White House in the 1990s. She will be assisted by Jim Margolis, Obama's senior media advisor in 2012, and by Mandy Grunwald, who has ties with the Clintons going back to 1992. The communications team has been completed with Kristina Schake, Michelle Obama's former aide, joining as Deputy Communications Director, and Nick Merrill, who has worked with Hillary since she arrived at the State Department in 2009, as Travelling Press Secretary.

A very small number of people are guaranteed to be in Hillary's immediate orbit. These include Huma Abedin (perhaps her most trusted and influential aide and vice chairwoman of the campaign), Cheryl Mills (who was general counsel to Hillary's 2008 campaign and worked previously at the White House, the State Department and subsequently at the Clinton Foundation), and Jake Sullivan (Deputy Policy Director on Hillary's 2008 presidential campaign and a key member of her team at the State Department). Sullivan is playing a major role as her key foreign policy advisor on the campaign and is virtually guaranteed to be appointed National Security Advisor if Hillary is elected President.

Joining Sullivan in Hillary Clinton's policy team is former senior fellow at the Center for American Progress (CAP) Maya Harris, who has a background in human rights, and Hillary's former legislative director Ann O'Leary, who focuses on early childhood education. The input from CAP cannot be underestimated, as it also contributed Tony Carrk from its Action Fund to serve as Hillary Clinton's campaign research director, and its president, Neera Tanden, remains a constant source of advice and policy input. CAP has rapidly emerged to be for Hillary what the Project for the New American Century was for George W. Bush in 2000: a vital intellectual hub of ideas and willing advisors, politically attuned to the needs and aspirations of the candidate.

The members of Hillaryland in 2016 will need to focus heavily on rectifying two areas where Hillary needs to learn as much as possible from the mistakes of 2008: the use of social media and fundraising. To that end, the campaign has recruited former Google executive Stephanie Hannon as Chief Technology Officer and former State Department and Clinton Foundation aide Katie Dowd as Digital Director, along with Teddy Goff and Andrew Bleeker, both of whom were instrumental in devising Obama's digital operation. Hillary has had the advantage of two Super PACs dedicated to her cause. For two years, the Ready for Hillary Super PAC raised funds and interest for a potential campaign. Its founder, Adam Parkhomenko, has been appointed to direct grassroots support for the campaign to replicate the success that Barack Obama had in 2008 in generating vast sums from multiple small donations. Jim Messina, who worked for both Barack Obama and David Cameron, is now running the Priorities USA Action Super PAC, along with Buffy Wicks, who is dedicated to financing a victory for Hillary in 2016 that is likely to exceed $2.5 billion, the most expensive presidential campaign ever mounted.

In deliberately seeking to draw together a diverse group of advisors for her campaign, Hillary Clinton has tapped into three vital power bases: former members of Barack Obama's team, former members of her husband's team and her own loyal advisors, who have either worked for her personally, at the Clinton Foundation, or at the Center for American Progress. In contrast to the in-fighting that marred the 2008 campaign, there has been a concerted effort to build what Robby Mook referred to in a launch weekend mission statement as a 'unified family'. This sense of unity has been coupled with a differing focus. In 2008, Hillary was the focal point of her campaign; this time there has been a deliberate bid to make the new campaign about the American people and the challenges facing the nation. This has been done in an attempt to refute allegations that were rife in 2008 that Hillary expected to be appointed as the Democratic Party candidate without a challenge. The 2008 launch, with its rather brash declaration by Hillary Clinton ('I'm in, and I'm in it to win') struck some as a sign of hubris. Of course, it was also a declaration of intent and purpose; Hillary was not merely seeking attention or hoping to be considered as a vice-presidential candidate in 2008, and a similar statement from a male candidate would undoubtedly have been perceived very differently.

Not for the first time, different rules were applied to Hillary Clinton's candidacy. Nothing is being left to chance for the 2016 campaign, with no words left open to misinterpretation. As the launch memo stated, the campaign 'is not about Hillary and not about us – it's about the everyday Americans who are trying to build a better life for themselves and their families'. To achieve this, she has built a team with a track record of success and a single ambition: electing Hillary Clinton President of the United States in 2016.

CAN SHE WIN?

Having announced her candidacy, Hillary Clinton basked in the approval of 81 per cent of Democrats who told a *CBS News* poll that they would consider voting for her that spring. Simply having almost universal name recognition, however, will not mean that the party nomination is a guarantee, or that the presidency could be considered 'in the bag'. Hillary has tremendous advantages heading into the 2016 election: she has no financial burdens and enters the race with a vast treasure chest to help secure the nomination; her years of experience have created a huge network of supporters across the country, eager to work to secure her victory, and she has 99 per cent name recognition and a husband who remains wildly popular both in the country at large and within the Democratic Party. The strength of her candidacy has forced a number of potential candidates to avoid the 2016 race altogether, suggesting that she will be a giant surrounded by pygmies in the primary season. If, as expected, she secures the Democratic Party's nomination, she will face a Republican opponent who will have had to overcome a deeply divisive primary season against sixteen other challengers. Any Republican candidate will also need to convince voters that 2016 is not the time to make history and elect the first female President, which will be a central theme of Hillary Clinton's campaign.

For all of her formidable strengths, however, Hillary brings with her a series of issues that must be addressed and overcome for her to be victorious in 2016, relating to her character, her career and her politics. How she addresses each of them will determine whether she enters the history books as the first female President or merely as a contender for the greatest electoral prize available. As in 2008, the case can be made that the election of 2016 is Hillary Clinton's to lose. As was shown before, victory is by no means guaranteed and the greatest challenge to a Hillary Clinton presidency, as with her husband's administration, is most likely to come from the classic Clinton Achilles heel: themselves.

AGE, HEALTH AND GENDER

The Clintons have always presented themselves as a progressive force for generational change. However, Hillary has been in Washington, DC since the election of 1992 and, if elected in November 2016, will be sixty-nine when she takes the oath of office in January 2017, making her America's second-oldest President. The baby boomer generation that Hillary Clinton represents is now retiring, as the millennial generation comes to the fore. An entire generation of voters, therefore, have no living memory of Washington, DC prior to Hillary serving as either Senator or First Lady. In the last months of her tenure as Secretary of State, Hillary suffered a number of ailments that resulted in her being hospitalised. It is vital that her campaign finds a way to diminish attention on her age and any health issues. The simplest way to do so is to run a positive campaign that generates stories about the candidate's vitality and vigour while avoiding any health relapses.

It was apparent that Hillary did not want to play the gender card in the 2008 campaign and instead sought to portray herself as being as tough and capable as any of her male opponents. In seeking to pass the commander-in-chief test, however, Hillary appeared to be content to jettison her femininity and unique appeal to 51 per cent of Americans. Instead, in 2008, the historic candidacy of Barack Obama successfully appealed to the African-American community that accounted for 14 per cent of US citizens. It appears clear that in 2016 Hillary Clinton will not allow herself to be outmanoeuvred again. In this regard, it appears that her new approach began on the last day of her 2008 campaign, as she conceded to Obama while referencing the 'glass ceiling' in her appeal to her fellow American women.

On that occasion she was campaigning against an opponent whose own minority status also marked him for distinction, and, while Barack Obama did not openly campaign as 'the black candidate', his race could not be ignored or diminished. Indeed, just as John F. Kennedy utilised anti-Catholic bigotry to his advantage in 1960, so was Obama's campaign able to carefully ensure that issues of race and the historic opportunity to elect the first non-white candidate to the presidency were never too far from the surface. It appears to be a lesson that Hillary Clinton's campaign has learned heading into 2016: not only has she repeatedly stressed her new role as a grandmother but her campaign has also unleashed a barrage of vintage photographs from Hillary's past, in an effort to portray her as a normal American woman, rather than as a high-powered, globetrotting diplomat.

Hillary appears far more content to exploit the gender issue if it will help secure victory in 2016. In addressing issues regarding age, health and gender, Hillary has wisely drawn on a past master to utilise a gentle line of humour. In 1984, a poor performance in his first debate with Walter Mondale raised concerns about President Reagan's health at the end of his first term in office. Responding directly to a question in the subsequent debate, Reagan humorously insisted that he was not prepared to take political advantage of his opponent's youth and inexperience, thereby ending the argument. During her rally at Four Freedoms Park in June 2015, Hillary told the audience she would be 'the youngest woman President in the history of the United States'. Such an approach helps bring levity to the campaign and humanises Hillary in a way that few other methods can ever truly hope to achieve.

The campaign has also been helped in this regard by the most natural and yet unpredictable of circumstances: the marriage and motherhood of Hillary Clinton's only daughter, Chelsea. The third member of the Clinton family has grown up in public, having emerged on the national stage with her parents in 1992 as a twelve-year-old. Through eight tumultuous years in the White House,

Chelsea Clinton was seen to develop into a poised and confident young woman, who all agreed was a blessing to her parents and who, on occasion, was the emotional bridge between them. The twelve-year-old girl has grown to be a married 35-year-old woman who gave birth to a daughter, Charlotte, in 2014. Irrespective of what this meant for Chelsea Clinton, the implications for Hillary became immediately apparent. The arrival of a grandchild served to humanise and soften what was seen as Hillary's rather harsh and prickly exterior and perfectly enabled her to reposition herself not merely as a highly efficient manager of public life, but also as a loving and caring matriarch not only to her family, but to the American family.

Her new role has been used to subtly remind voters of Hillary Clinton's career-long advocacy on behalf of both women's and children's rights, all with a perfect and dutiful prop: her own granddaughter. The role of grandmother provides the capacity to flesh out a whole new persona for Hillary – a softer image that can be conveyed simply and directly, requiring little by way of explanation. In an election in which the Latino vote will be of great importance, this new role could pay electoral dividends. Since Hillary has no obvious connection with the Latino community, positioning herself as a matriarch may strike many in the community as particularly appealing. Her appeal will be heightened if she names a Latino as vice-presidential candidate, warding off the obvious appeal of Marco Rubio or the Spanish-speaking Jeb Bush.

Indeed, it is against her Republican opposition that Hillary Clinton's new grandmotherly status has the potential to be most important. Long before the general election and before she has secured her party's nomination, Hillary Clinton's campaign high-lighted the voting record of leading Republicans on women's issues, including Jeb Bush's 1994 comment that 'women on welfare should get their life together and find a husband'.[129] Little wonder perhaps that Jess McIntosh of EMILY's List, a political action committee established to elect pro-choice female candidates to office, insisted that Republicans have been 'tone-deaf on women's issues'.[130] Considering the twenty-point gender gap from which Barack Obama benefited in 2012, positioning Hillary as a compassionate, caregiving grandmother to the nation is one that could well propel her to the White House in 2016.

HER PAST, HER HUSBAND AND HER PARTY

Most candidates for public office lack extensive name recognition. This is not Hillary Clinton's problem: it emerged in 2015 that Hillary had 99 per cent name recognition among voters. Perhaps the most remarkable aspect to the number was not that it was so high, but rather the fact that 1 per cent of Americans apparently claimed not to recognise her. With a population of 321 million, that implies that over 3 million Americans do not know who Hillary Clinton is. However, while her name brings huge positives to her campaign, it carries daunting negatives due to past scandals that might detract from her message on the campaign trail. Her past, her husband and her political party all present formidable challenges.

In any election, candidates talk up their achievements, while their opponents highlight incidents for which they must be held

accountable. So it is with Hillary Clinton, whose attempt to highlight her tenure as Secretary of State has been met with accusations
regarding events in Benghazi. Her Republican opponents have
attempted to embarrass her in front of congressional hearings in
a replay of similar efforts in the 1990s. In these sessions she has
retained her composure, aiding her campaign for the presidency.
During her 2013 appearance before the Senate Foreign Relations
Committee hearings into the Benghazi tragedy, Hillary displayed
her dismay at the line of questioning by Wisconsin Republican
Senator Ron Johnson: 'With all due respect, the fact is, we had
four dead Americans! Was it because of a protest or was it because
of guys out for a walk one night who decided they'd go kill some
Americans? What difference at this point does it make?'[131] It was,
perhaps, the most forthright public display of anger and annoyance
in her public career and one that will undoubtedly be utilised against
her by a Republican opponent if she emerges as the Democratic
Party's candidate in 2016.

Another obvious point of attack against Hillary Clinton will
focus on her husband and the Clinton family foundation. Bill Clinton was woefully underutilised in the election of 2000, in a move
that contributed to the Democratic defeat that year. In 2008, he
was too high profile at times, which undoubtedly contributed to
Hillary Clinton's defeat. Clearly, the question of how best to use
Bill Clinton on the campaign trail needs to be adequately dealt
with in order to prevent the problems that emerged in 2008 when
he inadvertently dug the campaign into difficulty by ruminating
on its racial aspects and doing much to undermine his otherwise

exemplary record on race relations in the United States. As a former President, Bill Clinton remains a huge draw for events and fund-raising, an asset that Hillary Clinton's campaign needs to exploit wisely and creatively to ensure that he does not emerge once more as both his wife's greatest liability and her greatest asset.

In fact, Bill Clinton could return to haunt his wife's campaign without saying or doing anything in 2015. Instead, his own words from 1992 could be used against her. As a candidate for President, Bill Clinton made a persuasive argument for generational change, insisting that, at sixty-eight, George Herbert Walker Bush was too old to lead a young country. With his wife poised to become America's second-oldest President, a number of Republican candidates, particularly Senator Marco Rubio, are well placed to use Bill Clinton's words from 1992 against Hillary in 2016 and to ask the logical question: 'If your husband was right then, why is he wrong now?' Time and again, therefore, Hillary Clinton's campaign will undoubtedly find itself faced with the dilemma that is Bill Clinton: without him, Hillary would not be in a position to run for President, but he constantly throws up issues that risk damaging her candidacy. Having spent her life running around attempting to tidy up politically after her husband, it will be a tragedy of grand proportions if his actions were to cost her the presidency at the final hurdle.

The leadership of the Democratic Party is known to share such fears and remains sceptical of Hillary Clinton's campaign as a result. Despite her concerted efforts to win them over during her time in the Senate, the senior leadership felt compelled to look elsewhere for a new candidate in 2008, eventually settling on Barack Obama. Fears of Clinton fatigue and the ever-present risk of new scandals convinced the likes of Charles Schumer and Harry Reid to recruit Obama as a fresh-faced candidate, free from the allegations that seemed, rightly or wrongly, to constantly swirl around Hillary Clinton.[132] Neither is the Democratic Party necessarily convinced by Hillary Clinton's liberal credentials. For many in her party, the New Democrat approach that she and her husband adopted in the 1990s was as unpopular as the New Labour project was with socialists in the UK; it felt like a betrayal of the party principles in a (successful) bid to gain power.

Having been out of power for twelve years in 1992, the Democratic Party was inclined to accept such an approach. In 2016, however, having been in power for the last eight years, this is no longer the case, and explains, in part, why many members of the Democratic Party hanker after a candidate further to the left of the political spectrum. Senator Elizabeth Warren, who made her name by attacking Wall Street, was openly courted but declined to run. Incredibly, the self-described socialist Senator from Vermont, Bernie Sanders, whom no one expected to be any threat to Hillary, initially pulled ahead of her in key battleground states and drew tens of thousands to rallies across the country advocating an approach very different from that offered by the Clinton campaign. Although he is unlikely to win the nomination, his efforts have drawn Hillary to the left of the political spectrum in order to gain her party's nomination, thereby making it difficult to realign herself with the political centre ground if she were to find herself running in the general election in the autumn.

AMERICA'S CHANGING DEMOGRAPHICS

The United States of America is a country in flux: the Caucasian birth rate is declining rapidly and the Asian/Latino birth rate is doubling in a pattern that is having a profound impact not only culturally and socially, but also politically. An appeal to white, middle-class voters is no longer sufficient to secure the presidency, as Mitt Romney discovered in 2012 when he won 59 per cent of the white vote and still lost to Barack Obama.

Barack Obama was re-elected in 2012 because, in addition to securing 41 per cent of the white vote, he also won the support of the Asian, Latino and African-American communities. These groups are, therefore, becoming increasingly important, and this is evident in the campaigns that are being waged and the tactics that are being utilised, particularly in the southern states with a high Latino population. The US Census Bureau estimates that, as of 1 July 2013, there were roughly 54 million Latinos living in the United States, representing approximately 17 per cent of the total US population. This makes people of Latino origin the nation's largest ethnic or racial minority, with Mexicans accounting for the largest proportion at 64 per cent. The US Latino population for 2060 is estimated to reach 128.8 million, constituting approximately 31 per cent of the US population by that date. In 2012, Latinos constituted 23.3 per cent of all elementary and high school students but only 6.8 per cent of college students. As of July 2013, the state with the largest Latino population was California (14.7 million), a vital state in the presidential election with fifty-five Electoral College votes. New Mexico, the state with the highest percentage of Latino population (47.3 per cent), could also prove important, offering five Electoral College votes that may well prove decisive in a tight election.

From these figures, it is clear to see why candidates are actively seeking the Latino vote and making concerted attempts to appear in tune with the needs of the Latino population. Back in 2000, George W. Bush was already delivering campaign adverts in Spanish. In 2016, Jeb Bush, who speaks fluent Spanish and has a Mexican wife, was expected to be Hillary Clinton's most formidable opponent. Also running is Senator Marco Rubio from Florida, who has Cuban heritage, speaks fluent Spanish and is pursuing the Latino vote. To counter these challenges, Hillary needs to openly court the Latino community. She cannot do so through any appeals to her own past or culture, but she may well do so by exploiting events that occurred during her time in office and by her choice of Vice-President. Although the diplomatic breakthrough that has occurred between Cuba and the United States occurred after Hillary left the Obama administration, it is a process that began during her tenure as Secretary of State and is, therefore, one that she can credibly claim some credit for in an effort to endear herself to those members of the Latino community who had campaigned for the normalisation of relations. Finally, if Hillary selects a Latino running mate, such as Obama's Housing and Urban Development Secretary Julián Castro, she may well be able to lock up the presidency with an appeal to women, African-Americans, Latinos and 50 per cent of the white male vote. Such a core group would be virtually insurmountable for a Republican due to the demographics at play in the United States in 2016.

To prevail in 2016, Hillary Clinton will need to continue the Democratic Party's lock on a range of minority groups and mobilise the female vote in the manner that Barack Obama marshalled the African-American vote in 2008. In her efforts to do so, Hillary has several advantages. Firstly, Toni Morrison referred to Bill Clinton as 'the first black President' years before Barack Obama took the stage due to his work with the African-American community and apparent cultural similarity with the community. He was, according to Morrison, 'blacker than any actual black person who could ever be elected in our children's lifetime. After all, Clinton displays almost every trope of blackness: single-parent household, born poor, working-class, saxophone-playing, McDonald's-and-junk-food-loving boy from Arkansas.'[133] Being able to draw on her husband and President Obama to help court the African-American community will be a vital asset for Hillary in 2016, especially in key states such as South Carolina, which will play a vital role in determining who secures the Democratic Party's nomination. President Obama can be expected to campaign heavily in the general election, particularly in the African-American community. It is unlikely that the community will be as energised as it was in 2008, but if Obama can convince them to vote in numbers comparable to 2012, then this, combined with Hillary's potential appeal to the female vote, should provide a lock on the White House.

ELECTORAL HISTORY

Hillary Clinton is seeking to follow a two-term President of her own party, a feat that has not often succeeded in American political history. Usually, the nominee seeking to replace the incumbent from their own party is the sitting Vice-President. Only George H. W. Bush achieved this in the modern era, winning election in 1988 but subsequently losing in his bid for a second term to Bill Clinton. The last time it had been achieved was by Martin Van Buren in 1836 and in the entire history of the United States only Thomas Jefferson served two full terms as President after having previously served as Vice-President. Of course, Hillary has not served as Vice-President and will be able to place some distance between herself and Barack Obama. She will need his support, however, if she is to win over key sectors of the electorate, so she will have to walk a fine line between embracing the Obama administration and stressing its successes, while also positioning herself as her own person and not merely seeking to complete Obama's (or her husband's) third term. Serving as Secretary of State has also not helped Hillary Clinton's historical odds of becoming President, as no former holder of that office has become President since James Buchanan before the US Civil War.

The worry for Hillary Clinton, therefore, must be in being viewed as a competent manager but not necessarily as a leader. In theory, her experience makes her an ideal candidate for the highest office, but the ability to step out of the shadow of a President has been hard to achieve and competence at the Cabinet level does not necessarily translate into the kind of leadership that is necessary at the head of government. Very few American Vice-Presidents have been able to make the transition, and in the UK Gordon Brown recently demonstrated that no matter how much the second-in-command wants to run the country, the results are not always to anyone's liking.

THE ELECTION PROCESS

Despite these challenges, the 2016 presidential election remains Hillary Clinton's to lose. For that to happen, someone must beat her, and this could happen at one of two stages: the primaries or the general election. The first battle that Hillary needs to win is for the right to represent the Democratic Party in the general election to be held on 8 November 2016. To do so, Hillary needs to prevail in the primary elections and caucuses that will be held in every state between January and June in 2016. In that process, she will face challengers from within her own party, all of whom are equally determined to win the nomination. While Hillary Clinton will face competition in the Democratic primaries, there is no young, dynamic candidate to challenge for the right to represent her party as there was in 2008. Instead, she initially faced a challenge from Senator Bernie Sanders of Vermont, former Governor of Maryland Martin O'Malley, former Senator Jim Webb of Virginia and former Governor of Rhode Island Lincoln Chafee. In July 2015, a Monmouth University poll showed Webb and O'Malley polling at 1 per cent, with no support at all for Chafee. Sanders garnered 17 per cent support, 15 per cent were undecided and Hillary was far ahead on 51 per cent.[134]

Such figures give a clear indication of Hillary Clinton's commanding lead in a national poll. A Suffolk University poll conducted in August 2015 gave Hillary a 34-point lead over Sanders in the vital state of Iowa, leading 54 per cent to 20 per cent. In New Hampshire, on the other hand, a state Hillary won in 2008, she trailed Sanders by seven points in a Public Policy Polling survey also conducted in August.[135] To lose New Hampshire would be embarrassing for Hillary, but not terminal, especially when the direction of the race is considered. As a local candidate, the Vermont Senator is likely to exceed expectations in New England, but then run into problems that will benefit Hillary Clinton. Even if the vote in Iowa and New Hampshire is closer than Hillary may like, as soon as the race heads south and west the demographics swing in her favour, particularly in South Carolina, where African-Americans constitute the majority of Democratic Party voters. It is important to consider the limited traction that Hillary Clinton's opponents have within the black community, a factor that looks set to play a key role in her eventual success.

Senator Sanders has championed campaign finance reform and constraining Wall Street, not social or racial policies. He also represents a state with a 95 per cent white population and an African-American population of just 1.2 per cent. Former Maryland Governor Martin O'Malley has historically struggled to secure the African-American vote and rioting in Baltimore, where his tough anti-crime measures were seen to be particularly unpopular, has not helped his standing in the community. Former Senator Jim Webb dropped out of the race in October 2015, long before his conservative voting record and stance in regard to the Confederate flag in the wake of the murders at the Emanuel African Methodist

Episcopal Church on 17 June 2015 impacted on his ability to win the African-American vote. Lincoln Chafee quickly followed Senator Webb in departing the race, greatly enhancing Hillary Clinton's chances of securing the nomination.

A win in Iowa and a strong showing in South Carolina would establish Hillary as the front runner, almost irrespective of results in New Hampshire, and enable her to go into the Super Tuesday primaries on 1 March confident of a strong showing that could effectively end the race in her favour. Her campaign has identified the Super Tuesday elections as an effective 'firewall' designed to deliver a knockout blow to any competition.

If this strategy fails and Hillary Clinton's campaign falters, many who had been persuaded to avoid seeking the nomination may be tempted to reconsider their positions. Many on the left of the Democratic Party, for example, had courted Senator Elizabeth Warren and had begun to raise funds and awareness on her behalf, but all in vain. Most dangerous for Hillary, however, could have been the current Vice-President, Joe Biden. As President Obama's deputy, Biden should have been the presumptive nominee for the Democratic Party. The fact that he was not reveals the strength of Hillary Clinton's perceived inevitability during Obama's second term in office. It was thought that Biden might have been tempted to try for the nomination if Hillary stumbled or performed poorly in early debates, but this did not occur. To have been a serious candidate, Biden would have formed an exploratory committee during Obama's second term and would have been making regular trips to the early voting states of Iowa and New Hampshire.

The fact that he did not speaks to his lack of serious intent, despite occasional statements to the contrary. The death of his son, Beau, in May 2015 also appeared to rule out a late run. Having sought the presidency in 1988 and in 2008, a third lacklustre bid would undoubtedly have contributed to a deeply unhappy year for Biden and served only to divide the Democratic Party. His 21 October 2015 decision not to seek the presidency bolstered Hillary Clinton's chances and also removed a dilemma for President Obama over whom to support. For the second time in eight years, therefore, a two-term presidency will expire without its Vice-President seeking election in his own right.[136]

It must be remembered that even if she secures the Democratic Party's nomination, Hillary Clinton will face a Republican opponent in November 2016 eager to secure the White House after eight years of the Obama administration. A Democratic Party victory, therefore, irrespective of who their candidate is, cannot be taken for granted. Whatever levels of energy exist for Hillary Clinton's candidacy within the Democratic Party, her candidacy will also energise the Republican Party base with a 'Stop Hillary' agenda. As soon as Hillary announced her candidacy, Jeb Bush, who at that point was not a candidate, immediately released a statement that may well be a blueprint for any future attacks on her record, referring to the 'Obama–Clinton foreign policy that has damaged relationships with [America's] allies and emboldened [America's] enemies.'

Jeb Bush, however, is only one of the candidates seeking the Republican Party nomination in 2016. The sheer number of candidates ensures that the Republicans will spend more time attacking each other and take longer to arrive at a nominee than the Democrats. Assuming Hillary secures the Democratic Party's nomination, the Republican Party's in-fighting will be to her advantage. The Republican field will dwindle rapidly as money flows to the successful candidates and drains from those who have not been able to emerge from the crowd. Rick Perry and Scott Walker dropped out in September 2015; Bobby Jindal quit the race in November; former Senator Rick Santorum and former Governor George Pataki are likely to be among the next casualties as the leading contenders emerge throughout the primary season.

Of the leading Republican candidates, several pose interesting challenges for Hillary Clinton to overcome in a general election. The initial front runner, former Floridian Governor Jeb Bush, has excellent name recognition and has raised a vast war chest to fight in the primary elections. He has, however, struggled to position himself in regard to his former President brother. Jeb Bush has appeared to be campaigning like a tortoise so far, and, while the primary season can be likened to a marathon not a sprint, his lack of energy and drive is noticeable in contrast to his competitors. In a general election against Hillary he would need to explain why it was time to elect the third President Bush and not the first female President. He would, however, be able to win the state of Florida, and he has a Mexican wife with whom he could woo Latino voters, which could complicate Hillary Clinton's journey to the White House.

Jeb Bush's ability to win the Republican Party's nomination, however, is complicated by Senator Marco Rubio, who is also from

Florida, has Cuban heritage and, unlike Bush, is young (forty-four) and dynamic. He emerged unscathed and with plaudits from the initial Republican debates and has the advantage of age and heritage on his side in any potential line-up against Hillary. If he can emerge from a leading field of Republican candidates as the voice of reason and energy, he will be a formidable candidate in a general election and could leverage the Latino vote in a similar manner to Obama's appeal to African-Americans. Were he to name Governor John Kasich of Ohio as his running mate, the Republicans could have a strong claim on the Electoral College votes of Florida and Ohio, a serious impediment to Hillary's ability to win the presidency.

Several other Republicans are running who do not represent the mainstream of the Party, including Senator Ted Cruz of Texas and Senator Rand Paul of Kentucky. Despite their firebrand approach to politics and determination to change the system, history is against their gaining the nomination and thereby challenging Hillary in the general election. Traditionally, the Republican Party nominee has been the candidate with the leading pedigree, who appears to have deserved it and has not traditionally looked to radically change the system, a quintessentially un-conservative approach that tends to scare off primary voters. One of the fascinating dilemmas that the Republican Party faces is that while moderate conservatives are more likely to draw support from independent voters in a general election and thereby potentially beat Hillary, they are unlikely to win the nomination. Chris Christie of New Jersey, for example, is a Republican Governor in a state that has often voted Democratic, which is indicative of his ability to appeal to a broad section of society. Yet this ensures that he is not trusted by the right of the Republican Party or by those who believe his work with President Obama during Hurricane Sandy in 2012 helped to defeat Mitt Romney.

The great unknown, of course, is Donald Trump. With no experience in political office, his candidacy should be a joke, but it has become clear that it is not. Heading into 2016, he leads all national polls and is ahead in Iowa, New Hampshire and South Carolina by anything up to twenty points. All election 'experts' maintain that he cannot win the Republican Party nomination, but few are prepared to explain why not. Trump has the money, at least $2 billion, to self-finance his primary campaign, as well as the name recognition and the media attention necessary to prevail. Even his attacks on immigrants and on media figures such as Megyn Kelly of Fox News have so far failed to dent his figures. If anything, they appear to have helped his cause. His Republican challengers have hesitated to openly attack him for fear of unleashing the avalanche of abuse that has previously been delivered on his critics. As the primaries approach, however, Trump's fellow contenders have realised they have no choice but to challenge his stance on a range of issues. As a recently registered member of the Republican Party who had previously been a registered Democrat, attempts will be made to identify him as a RINO (Republican in Name Only), although so far such attempts have failed to resonate.

The great fear for the Republican Party, however, is not necessarily that Donald Trump wins the nomination, but rather that he does not and then fails to endorse the eventual candidate.

The Republican nightmare scenario is that Trump self-finances an independent run for the White House. Were he to do so, the general consensus is that he will split the Republican vote and hand the White House to the Democratic candidate. This concern is not without precedent. In 1992, another extraordinarily wealthy American businessman with no experience of political office took the presidential campaign by storm. Ross Perot was initially more popular than both the incumbent (George H. W. Bush) and the Democratic candidate (Bill Clinton) and eventually gained 19 per cent of the vote in the general election. The result was that Bill Clinton was elected President of the United States with 43 per cent of the popular vote as the Republican vote splintered.

ELECTORAL MATHEMATICS

For all of the talk about personality, politics and policy, however, the US presidential election is all about electoral mathematics. 270 is the magic number; indeed, it is the only number that counts. All considerations must be geared towards securing the 270 Electoral College votes that are needed to win the White House. The popular vote would be nice, but it is the Electoral College that decides the election, as Al Gore discovered in 2000. Each state awards a number of electors depending on its population. California, with the largest population, awards the most delegates (fifty-five) and is a state that Hillary Clinton, as a Democrat, is expected to win.

Any electoral calculation, however, needs to address Ohio and Florida, major challenges for Hillary considering the prevailing white, male, working-class vote in Ohio and the presence of two formidable Floridian opponents from the Republican Party in the form of Senator Marco Rubio and former Governor Jeb Bush. If either man secures the Republican Party nomination, Hillary Clinton's capacity to win their home state would be virtually impossible, making victory that much more difficult. However, the Democrats have won five of the last seven elections and secured the popular vote in five of the last six, ensuring that Republicans have only won the popular vote in a one presidential election since 1988.

Despite having been First Lady of Arkansas for twelve years, Hillary is likely to find that the somewhat difficult relationship she had with the state will continue into Polling Day in 2016. This time, however, it will not be personal; it will be strictly political. The Arkansas of the Clinton years is long gone. The state's two seats in the Senate, its four house members, the Governor and the state legislature are now solidly Republican, a sweep that occurred during Barack Obama's two terms as President. Janine Parry, a political science professor at the University of Arkansas, noted, 'Arkansas is overwhelmingly white and rural, and Barack Obama is neither of those things. He's just foreign to folks here, and they just can't identify. And that's particularly in a state where people are used to being able to identify with candidates.'[137] In 2016, the state is closer to Mike Huckabee than Hillary Clinton, ensuring that in a recent poll of Arkansas voters she only received 33 per cent against an unnamed Republican candidate who polled 50 per cent.

Hillary Clinton, therefore, will need to retain the overwhelming ethnic minority support that secured Barack Obama's two terms in the White House and build upon the large female vote that she secured in the 2008 primaries. Such a combination of Latinos, African-Americans and women, as well as the usual percentage of white men who are expected to vote Democrat, should be sufficient to enable Hillary to capture the White House in 2016.

SELF-SERVER?

Hillary Clinton's route to victory, therefore, is relatively routine: secure her base support of female voters, couple it with the strong support from the African-American community, pitch to the Latino community with a vice-presidential candidate drawn from their number and hold on to a strong share of the white male vote. So what could go wrong?

Hillary's greatest political manoeuvre will be to persuade voters of the legitimacy of her own separate claim to the White House. Her opponents will accuse her of defending the status quo and Republicans may well draw on Bill Clinton's own speeches from 1992 in which he called for generational change and ask why his comments don't still apply in 2016. They will raise the scandals of the 1990s, play on the prospect of Clinton fatigue and attempt to tie her to the Obama administration's social programmes and healthcare policies. Finally, critics will raise her role as Secretary of State in relation to the Benghazi incident. With polls suggesting that the American public continues to have doubts about Hillary Clinton's honesty, her opponents will do all they can to perpetuate such concerns.

Despite her best efforts, Hillary appears unable to escape the constant spectre of scandal. Throughout her career she has been plagued by allegations either relating to her own behaviour or that of her husband. As she makes her final effort to secure her place in history, this pattern shows no sign of abating. The latest issue concerns her use of a private server to manage her emails while serving as Secretary of State. It has emerged that during this time she used her @clintonemail.com address, and often sent messages under her Secret Service codename, 'Evergreen'. Rather than using a server based in Washington, Hillary used one that was located in her family home in Chappaqua, New York, paying a State Department official to maintain it. When she left the Obama administration, management of the server was taken over by a small company named Platter River Networks, who insisted that all emails were moved to a new server and subsequently removed by Hillary Clinton's legal advisors.

To many, this may sound like a technicality and not worth focusing upon. However, under US law, the writings and official records, including emails, of office holders, including Secretaries of State, are federal property and constitute part of the administration's record in office under the Federal Records Act. As such, they must be preserved and the individual office holder does not retain rights over them, nor over the remit to delete or destroy such records. After leaving office it emerged that over 30,000 of her emails had been summarily deleted and were beyond the reach of anyone interested in understanding the daily record of America's sixty-seventh Secretary of State and her relationship with her family's foundation or foreign governments.

Several factors emerge from the release of Hillary Clinton's emails that has been mandated throughout 2015. The first is how mundane a great many of the exchanges are, with questions about flight times, meeting schedules and the designated times to leave the office dominating most of the exchanges. In one email, Hillary makes a request for skimmed milk and for specific teacups to use in her office.[138] Secondly, it is clear how few people have direct access to the Secretary of State. Despite the vast number of people trying to reach Hillary, most, if not all, are routed through a number of gatekeepers, including Jake Sullivan, Cheryl Mills and Huma Abedin. Thirdly, it is apparent how many of the emails she received were merely highlighting press stories, demonstrating the extent to which the US government appears dependent on the media as a source of open intelligence despite the vast sums spent on intelligence agencies. Fourthly, readers can see how gossipy many of the emails are, as details are passed forward or are requested about how individuals are, or are being perceived in the never-ending power play of international politics. Of particular note was an email exchange in which the wife of the former British Prime Minister sought to get the Secretary of State in touch with the Crown Prince of Qatar, although Cherie Blair managed to misspell the name of America's top diplomat, referring to her as 'Hilary'.[139]

Not all of the emails released, however, relate to matters of state. In December 2010 an email exchange occurred between Chief of Staff Cheryl Mills and Clinton's lawyer David Kendall regarding a story in the *Washington Post* detailing a bank robbery in Virginia in which the perpetrator had worn a rubber Hillary Clinton mask. Hillary 'does, uh, have an alibi, I presume?' Kendall asks. 'One never knows...' Mills replies. Subsequently forwarded to the Secretary of State, Hillary replies:

> Should I be flattered? Even a little bit? And, as for my alibi, well, let's just say it depends on the snow and the secret service. So, subject to cross for sure. Do you think there could be copycats? Do you think the guy chose that mask or just picked up the nearest one? Please keep me informed as the case unfolds.[140]

The remarkable parallel with President Nixon is hard to escape. As his presidency disintegrated, Nixon attempted to hide his secret tapes from the world and appears to have deliberately deleted an eighteen-minute section of one particularly damning recording. Likewise, a great many of the emails released by the State Department are totally redacted, particularly those that relate to Russia or its emissaries. One of the staff members who was required to listen to these recordings was a young Hillary Rodham, who later noted, 'You could hear Nixon talk and then you'd hear very faintly the sound of a taped prior conversation ... and you'd hear [the President] say, "What I meant when I said that was..." It was surreal, unbelievable.'[141] Forty years later, Hillary finds her own efforts to destroy official government communications coming under increasing scrutiny and investigation by the FBI, in a probe that could do much to derail her campaign and cause others to enter the race if her polling numbers deteriorate.

Alas, the predicament that Hillary finds herself in has parallels not only with the Nixon presidency, but also with that of her husband. At the climax of the impeachment process, Bill Clinton was forced to address the nation and admit to his 'inappropriate' relationship with Miss Lewinsky. The consensus, however, was that he had not been contrite or apologetic enough in his remarks and as a result he spent several subsequent speeches making a series of attempts to apologise for his actions, before finally striking the correct tone. In her public comments and in-depth interviews on the email server debacle, Hillary found herself in a similar situation, initially refusing to apologise on the basis that she believed that no laws had been broken. She then attempted to use humour to brush off the incident, before finally offering a full and frank apology for the situation and for the unnecessary distraction that it had caused.

CAMPAIGN ISSUES: THE ECONOMY / FOREIGN AFFAIRS

Beyond any issues regarding her use of a private email system, two main areas of policy have the ability to damage Hillary Clinton's campaign for the presidency: the economy and foreign affairs. Neither is necessarily within the domain of the Obama administration to control and they remain, therefore, something of an unknown quantity. As the former British Prime Minister Harold Macmillan once noted, 'events, dear boy, events' remain the biggest potential threat to any politician's future, and Hillary Clinton is no exception.

Heading into the 2016 presidential election, the US economy appears to be on track. Interest rates have been kept at a record low, unemployment is down from its previous levels and there appears to be a new buoyancy in the market. Clearly this could change in an instant and events on the Chinese stock market demonstrate the fragility of the global economic situation. However, as long as the US economy remains strong, Hillary can embrace it and talk about the need to safeguard an economic recovery while doing more to help those who have so far been left behind. She can also claim to have been involved in the policies of the 1990s that brought the longest era of growth in US history and an unemployment rate that fell as low as 3.8 per cent, as the economy expanded at 4.5 per cent. Whatever else happened during the Clinton administration, the economy performed superbly. Welfare was reformed, the Head Start programme was expanded, the North American Free Trade Agreement was implemented to increase trade with Mexico and Canada, and participation increased in the Earned Income Tax Credit for less well-off Americans. Despite Republican suggestions that Bill Clinton benefited from fortunate timing, they opposed his economic measures, with not a single Republican voting in favour of his Omnibus Budget Reconciliation Act of 1993, which was designed to reduce the deficit. By tapping into memories of the economic boom of the 1990s, Hillary should be able to offset any negative connotations associated with the deregulation of the era that may have contributed to the subsequent downturn in the market.

Hillary Clinton finds herself in a similar situation regarding foreign policy. Heading into 2016 there is minimal US foreign intervention, the Obama presidency being about scaling down, not ramping up, US interventions. Hillary appears to be in favour of a more robust foreign policy than Barack Obama, but neither she nor her husband has ever been accused of being armchair generals eager to send America's young men and women around the world to die unnecessarily at their behest. Prudent intervention and the use of soft and smart power have been the Clinton calling cards in foreign affairs, in contrast to the more muscular approach adopted both in theory and in fact by Republican Presidents and candidates.

None of the Republican Party candidates has any experience in foreign affairs, but this may not necessarily be to their detriment. In the United States, economic issues tend to prevail in elections. If the international scene remains calm, the Republicans' lack of foreign policy experience may be seen as irrelevant by a domestically focused electorate. Likewise, it is not impossible that Hillary Clinton's record as Secretary of State could be manipulated against her by an opponent with no track record of their own to distort. Hillary will be placed in a difficult position of seeking to maximise the positives from her time as Secretary of State, distancing herself from any negatives, while also distinguishing herself from both Barack Obama and Bill Clinton.

Finally, it must never be forgotten that only American citizens vote in American elections, meaning that irrespective of how popular any candidate is overseas, it is the domestic electorate that will determine their fate; the views of foreigners do not count on election day. That being said, if the foreign environment remains calm and constant, Hillary will be well placed to lay claim to be an architect of the modern world after her time as Secretary of State and to assume control as President of the United States in January 2017.

WHO IS HILLARY RODHAM CLINTON?

Perhaps the greatest hurdle that Hillary Clinton needs to address involves perceptions of herself. During her time in the public eye, perhaps only Madonna has routinely reinvented herself and reintroduced herself to the American public more than Hillary Clinton. As she announced her campaign for the presidency in 2015, the *New York Times Magazine* ran a cover story asking, 'How will America's most famous woman reintroduce herself?' Indeed, one of Hillary Clinton's greatest challenges in 2016 is overcoming a sense of Clinton fatigue and assumptions about who she is and what she stands for.

A campaign memo from 1992 concluded, 'Voters need to meet the real Hillary Clinton. They have a distorted, limited and overly political impression of her.'[142] Twenty-four years later, little has changed and a serious challenge for Hillary lies in her likeability. To too many Americans she remains a cold, distant figure, aloof from the mainstream. American voters have demonstrated a propensity for voting for a candidate that they would like to have a beer with, not necessarily the one who would make the best leader. On that basis, Hillary will have a battle on her hands as she strives to come across as a warm and engaging individual. In 2008, she deliberately ran a gender-neutral campaign, barely acknowledging her role as a woman and dismissing any trace of femininity. That has changed in 2016 as she has made repeated reference to her new status as a grandmother, but her campaign has been far from warm and fuzzy. In her determination to be taken seriously, she risks alienating voters who want to know the human side of their candidates. As Sally Bedell Smith noted, 'To be girlish would seem frivolous ... That disadvantage meant [Hillary] could not indulge in the kinds of behaviour that humanised her husband. She had no choice but to appear publically buttoned-up, which made her less likeable.'[143]

Hillary has been known to address her personal preferences, but the feeling has always been that it is something she is loath to do and only does when she is seeking to ingratiate herself for a reason, such as on her book tour in 2014 when she revealed her love of swimming and *Dancing With the Stars* and described her ideal day to Diane Sawyer. Hillary has discussed her taste in music in the past, identifying bands from her youth such as the Rolling Stones, the Who, the Doors and the Beatles, as well as various classical composers, but there is no attempt to make a leap and connect this to a new generation, joking instead that these bands are far older than many who will be voting in 2016, which further alienates her from her constituents. The release of Hillary Clinton's State Department emails betray something of the rarefied atmosphere of her circle, including members of rock royalty: 'Dearest Hillary, Happy Birthday – we're sad to have missed the other night, but arrived late from the west coast. We are in NY for a month ... if you and Bill are upstate and have time for a catch up, let us know.

Love Bono & Ali.'[144] Clearly the lead singer of U2 has come a long way from his humble roots to be on first-name terms with the former President (in a breach of accepted protocol) and the current Secretary of State.

Demonstrating a less well-known side to her daily routine, the released emails revealed Hillary's yoga workouts and her TV viewing habits. In one she asks her aide Monica Hanley, 'Can you give me times for two TV shows: *Parks and Recreation* and *The Good Wife?*'[145] She has revealed that she no longer drinks coffee or diet drinks, but instead drinks as much water as she can. Her close friends have spoken of her sense of humour, and this comes across on occasion, though infrequently. Instead, 'Hillary is more inclined to react to humour than to instigate it, but when she does her instinct is toward drollness. She handles solitude comfortably, often preferring it to uninspired company.'[146] She is, by temperament, therefore, not a natural politician.

Hillary Clinton's taste in films may be discerned from a very reverential email sent to her office by movie mogul Harvey Weinstein:

> I don't know if movie producers are still worthy in your world, but next time you're in NYC I'd love to see you. I have such fond memories of you guys watching *Shakespeare in Love*. I made another movie you might like about the ascendancy of King George after Edward abdicated, it's called *Kings Speech* … It's a fun movie that is much in the tradition of *Shakespeare in Love*, again I think you would both like it (and Hillary would approve because it's PG-13 with not too many swear words).[147]

The rather highbrow film choices serve to remove her from main-stream audiences and her seeming disdain for vulgarity again appears to reveal far more conservative characteristics than many necessarily expect from her.

In 2014, the *New York Times* interviewed her about her favourite books. She mentioned that she was reading, or preparing to read, *The Goldfinch* by Donna Tartt, *Mom & Me & Mom* by Maya Angelou and *Missing You* by Harlan Coben. She also noted that she read a series of mainstream authors including Walter Isaacson, John Le Carré, John Grisham, Hilary Mantel, Toni Morrison and Alice Walker. She listed e. e. cummings, T. S. Eliot, Seamus Heaney and W. B. Yeats as her favourite poets. She believed that all students should read *Pride and Prejudice* by Jane Austen, *Out of Africa* by Isak Dinesen and *Schindler's List* by Thomas Keneally, while conceding that cooking, decorating, diet/self-help and gardening books were her guilty pleasures. She also noted the importance of the Bible, which remained 'the biggest influence' on her thinking. In 2011, Hillary provided a rather different list of favourite books to Oprah Winfrey. These included Henri J. M. Nouwen's *The Return of the Prodigal Son*, *The Color Purple* by Alice Walker, *Little Women* by Louisa May Alcott, *The Clan of the Cave Bear* by Jean M. Auel, *West with the Night* by Beryl Markham, *The Joy Luck Club* by Amy Tan and *The Poisonwood Bible* by Barbara King-solver. Accordingly, it is difficult to ascertain exactly where Hillary Clinton's literary tastes lie, but they appear to be rather main-stream and fundamentally conservative, betraying her upbringing in middle-class Illinois.

CONCLUSION

After a lifetime in politics, Hillary Clinton finds herself at the threshold of greatness. The White House beckons, yet still the American people are uncertain what to make of her. Her steadfast determination through much of her life to appear tough and resilient has ensured that she has also remained removed from the lives of the American electorate. There is no doubt that she has, therefore, been subject to a cruel double standard. As Mickey Kantor, a former member of her husband's Cabinet, noted, 'Men can show emotion more, but for women in politics it has a more pernicious effect … Emotions are seen as weakness, a signal that a woman is not in control.'[148] Little, it seems, has been as important to Hillary as portraying a sense of control, either real or imagined, throughout the course of her life. All things considered, this is perhaps not surprising. Raised by a cold and distant father and married to the world's most famous unfaithful husband, it is little wonder that Hillary appears to have created a seemingly perfect public persona that few can penetrate.

As a candidate for the presidency of the United States, however, Hillary Clinton will be required to engage in the politics of personality, as voters have repeatedly demonstrated a propensity to select a candidate that they feel most comfortable with, irrespective of specific policy pledges. When Hillary has revealed her humanity, she has endeared herself to the public and they have responded warmly. To prevail in 2016, she needs to ensure that this is a regular occurrence and not something that happens only in times of crisis. Despite concerns over her personality and recurring questions regarding her use of private email accounts, the economy, the international environment and, vitally, the demographics of the United States in 2016 all favour Hillary Clinton. The stars have not quite aligned just yet, but they appear to be as well set as they will ever be for her to emerge victorious.

CAN HILLARY CLINTON WIN IN 2016?

Hillary Diane Rodham Clinton has come a long way from her childhood in the Republican stronghold of Park Ridge, Illinois. She has already achieved much, holding elected office and representing both her adopted state of Arkansas and her country as First Lady and as Secretary of State. She has travelled the world and has been heckled and praised in equal measure. She has written books that have earned her millions of dollars and has become a role model for millions around the world.

By any measure, therefore, Hillary Clinton has already lived an extraordinary life. Many would doubtless have expected her to now be reflecting on a life well lived, preparing to enjoy retirement with her granddaughter, Charlotte, and to travel the world as an elder stateswoman, basking in the adulation that followed a sterling career. Hillary, however, has no intention of resting on such laurels. She fully realises her opportunity to make history by becoming the first female President of the United States and that 2016 is the last opportunity to make this dream a reality. Unlike eight years ago, she does not face a younger, equally epoch-making candidate to deny her the nomination of the Democratic Party. At the very least, therefore, she appears set to make history by becoming the first woman to head a national ticket in the United States.

If she secures the Democratic Party's nomination, can she win the presidency? The cold hard electoral mathematics suggest that she can. The Republicans have only won the popular vote in a presidential election once since 1988. The Democrats, in contrast, have secured the popular vote in five of the last six elections and won five of the last seven presidential contests. The national demographics appear to point to a Democratic victory irrespective of the party candidate. With Hillary Clinton's unique appeal, such a result appears all the more likely. Securing the female vote and the active support of the Jewish, Latino and African-American communities, while also maintaining an expected level of support among white voters, would give her sufficient support to win the White House.

Any electoral calculations, however, need to address the state-by-state approach that the United States adopts on election day. There is no national poll, but rather fifty individual polls that will determine a victor. As Al Gore discovered, it is possible to be the most popular presidential candidate in twelve years and still lose the presidency due to the Electoral College. Therefore, it is vital for any winning candidate to secure Ohio and Florida, a major challenge for Hillary considering the prevailing white, male, working-class vote in Ohio and the presence of two formidable Floridian opponents from the Republican Party, Senator Marco Rubio and former Governor Jeb Bush. If either secures the Republican Party nomination, Hillary Clinton's ability to win their home state would be ruined, making victory much more difficult, but not impossible.

A key determining factor will be Hillary Clinton's continuing capacity to adapt and change. In 2008, she was determined to run on the basis of being the best-qualified candidate and was adamant that gender play no part in her campaign. 'I am not running as a woman,' she told supporters at the Iowa State Fair in July 2007, 'I am running because I believe I am the best-qualified and experienced person.'[149] Her focus was on strength and foreign policy. It was clear that her campaign took far too long to recognise that it had missed an opportunity to make Hillary Clinton's candidacy about more than her. In the 2016 race, foreign policy has rarely been mentioned as Hillary has repositioned herself as a grandmother, happy to address gender issues and determined to focus on domestic affairs that matter to the American electorate. By campaigning as a woman, Hillary can challenge the United States to remove the final block on the White House: the gender bar. She arguably began this race just as she ended the last one, with a nod towards the 18 million cracks that she put in the glass ceiling. That glass ceiling needs to be shattered once and for all for Hillary Clinton to claim her place in history. She must also heed advice that is as pertinent in 2016 as it was when it was written in 1992: 'While voters genu-inely admire Hillary Clinton's intelligence and tenacity, they are uncomfortable with these traits in a woman. She needs to project a softer side – some humor, some informality.'[150]

Another key difference in 2016 is Hillary Clinton's ability and willingness to strike back. In 2008, Obama's opponents struggled to know how to respond to his attacks. That is not the case in 2016. Hillary still believes that a concentred effort exists to undermine the work that she and her husband have engaged in throughout their political lives. As she noted in her memoir *Living History*, 'I do believe that there was, and still is, an interlocking network of groups and individuals,' who use money and influence to fight the liberal agenda and who engage in 'the politics of personal destruction'.[151] Her concerns about this will be confirmed by the continuing calls for yet more hearings on Benghazi, designed to ensure that media attention remains on unfounded allegations and not on her cam-paign message. 'In a nutshell, Benghazi's not a scandal. It's a hoax,' observed David Brock.[152] With a vast war chest and a far smarter use of social media than in 2008, Hillary Clinton's campaign is clearly going to be ready for the incoming fire it expects to take and will need to be ready to hit back to prevent rumours from festering and so becoming accepted facts.

Hillary Clinton has successfully maximised the financial oppor-tunities that have accompanied her celebrity and political power in the United States. Not for the first time, perceptions about her family's finances have the potential to upset a presidential bid. In 1992, Bill Clinton initially struggled to convey an accurate image of his humble origins and rise from virtual poverty in Arkansas. In a quirk of fate, his time at Georgetown University, Yale Law School and Oxford, coupled with his 1963 meeting with President Kennedy, convinced the public that he was another wealthy, out-of-touch politician who had little in common with the average voter. Twenty-four years later, Hillary finds herself in a similar situation. Her highly publicised lecture fees and book royalties have elevated her income and personal net worth into the stratosphere, beyond the wildest imagination of most Americans. Her wealth is compounded by the amount of time she has spent in the public arena. When Bill Clinton first appeared on the national stage in 1992, he was relatively unknown and could introduce himself to the American public, to whom he was virtually a blank canvas. In the subsequent quarter-century, however, the Clintons have rarely been out of the American eye, complicating efforts to present a 'new' Hillary Clinton to voters in 2016. Indeed, Hillary has been omnipresent since 1992, through eight years of her husband's administration, eight years in the Senate, a presidential campaign in 2008 and four high-profile years as Secretary of State. First-time voters in 2016 will have never known an American political landscape that didn't include Hillary Clinton in one role or another, as she has become part of the establishment. Such a situation presents a challenge to her campaign, which is eager to portray her as a progressive candidate for change.

This is already a difficult proposition for two reasons. Firstly, she is seeking to follow Barack Obama, a fellow Democrat and her former boss, whom she eventually endorsed when her own presidential aspirations ended in 2008. Her future is tied to his administration, so she cannot be seen to run away from his record in office, since it is linked inexorably to her own political past. This reduces her ability to promote herself as an agent of change, which will be far easier for any Republican challenger to advocate in 2016. The second factor is Hillary Clinton's age. If elected, she will be sixty-nine on inauguration day 2017 and become the second-oldest President in American history; only Ronald Reagan will have been older. This again presents challenges as to how to present Hillary to the American electorate, which is often swayed by calls for generational change, as it was in 1992 when a 46-year-old Bill Clinton beat the 68-year-old George H. W. Bush. It may be, however, that fate, fertility and the third generation of the Clinton family have provided a secret weapon that assists Hillary Clinton with all of these potential hurdles. A grandchild and America's changing demographics appear set to place Hillary Clinton in the White House and fulfil her place in American political history as the first female President of the United States.

ACKNOWLEDGEMENTS

This book was written during the long hot summer of 2015, which was, alas, a time of great personal upheaval. As people moved in and out of my life, the book remained a constant, and a pleasure to work on. Even though only my name appears on the cover, this project has been a true collaboration and I am profoundly grateful to Iain Dale, Olivia Beattie, Ashley Biles, Sam Deacon, Victoria Godden and the team at Biteback for having the faith to get the book to market in what could only be called a Herculean effort. You would not be reading this book at all without the direct impact of my commissioning editor, Caroline Wintersgill, whom I worked with on my previous book, *Clinton's Grand Strategy*, and with whom I am delighted to continue to work at Biteback.

I am grateful for the support I have received from Richmond University in London, and in particular to my friends and partners in the pursuit of academic excellence: Professor Michael Keating, Dr Martin D. Brown, Dr Eunice Goes and Dr Chris Wylde. Thanks are also due to Dr Clare Loughlin-Chow for her constant support over the years, as well as to Professor Alex Seago, to whom I shall always be grateful for giving me my first full-time academic position. I'd also like to note my appreciation to the late Julia Jeannet, whose friendship and support in the first years of my time at Richmond were of great help and whose passing was a great personal loss. Thanks also to the many wonderful students who have kept me so engaged over the past several years and of whom I am so very proud. In particular, thanks to Patricia Schouker for her constant stream of insights and observations from Washington, DC, to Alia Mohammed for her encouragement from within the Obama administration and to Olivia Westbrook-Seward for her support and feedback.

Within the wider academic community I am most grateful to Dr Joanne Paul, who proofread the manuscript, and Dr Diana Bozhilova, both at the New College of the Humanities, for their gracious support and encouragement, as well as to Dr Lindsey Fitzharris (aka *The Chirurgeon's Apprentice*), Dr Michelle Bentley at Royal Holloway, Professor Robert Singh at Birkbeck College, Dr John Bew at King's, Professor Philip Davies at the Eccles Centre and Professor John Dumbrell at Durham. Thanks also for the support that this project and my wider research has received from the Salzburg Seminar American Studies Association, in particular Marty Gecek, Ron Clifton and Professor Cornelis 'Kees' van Minnen of

Ghent University's Roosevelt Study Center. Thanks also to J. David Morgan and Clodach Harrington of the American Politics Group for their kind invitation to discuss my continuing research at the 2015 colloquium at the American embassy in London.

On a personal note, I must thank my wonderful mum, Pauleen, who instilled in me a love of the written word from an early age. She nurtured my reading, helped my writing and was unflinching in her support of me throughout the years. She was the best mum I could have asked for and the dementia that robbed her of her later years was a particularly cruel way to lose her. A note of appreciation also to Liz Roper, whose warmth and friendship have been a blessing over the years. A true fighter, loving mother and adoring wife, she is the epitome of grace and humour and a wonderful friend who, along with the unique Pat Whale, formed a blessed trinity with my mum at family dinner parties in the 1980s.

I gladly tip my hat to the musical genius that is Michael L. Roberts, whose friendship and exquisite music have been a highlight of an altogether appalling twelve months, as well as to Gary James for doing what he can with my limited capacity to get something sonorous out of my beloved Telecasters. Rock on, Gary! Thanks also to my legal eagles, Rob Jones and John Doherty, for regular liquid support and for reminding me that money is only money and that it can't fundamentally make people any happier. Thanks also to Kimberley Pearce at Bliss, for working wonders to make me look as presentable as possible in recent years.

Thanks to my many friends in the media, in particular Joanna Bostock and Riem Higazi at Radio FM4 in Austria, as well as to the teams at Sky News and Monocle 24, especially Andrew Mueller, for continuing to draw upon my offerings on US politics. I'm grateful to my growing numbers of Twitter followers and contacts on other social network sites who have been so very supportive of my work. Thanks to Brian Fallon, the Gaslight Anthem, the Horrible Crowes and Taylor Swift for providing the soundtrack to which this work was completed, fuelled by copious amounts of Ben & Jerry's chocolate cookie-core ice cream and black coffee, at my home office on Epsom Downs.

Not all relationships, however, are so easy to reflect upon. As the song goes, 'The price of the memory is the memory of the sorrow it brings.' Achievement cannot apparently come without great loss and the past year has witnessed far too many losses to dwell upon. Whatever success has been achieved was not meant to come at such great cost and is sadly diminished as a result.

However, life moves on and to that end I am most grateful to two remarkable women I have encountered during the production of this book. Anderson Hillen Ferguson managed to keep me sane in the first months of 2015 when everything else was falling apart. A constant source of encouragement, enthusiasm and emotional support, she has been a true lifesaver and has my eternal gratitude. Finally, my great thanks to Sarah Fowler: in the summer of 2014 Sarah volunteered to be my research assistant and in that capacity she has read and re-read this manuscript and contributed greatly to the finished prose. Sarah has proven to be a remarkable assistant on this project and has a promising career ahead of her. She is an exceptional young lady who epitomises Hemingway's definition of courage as being 'grace under pressure'. It takes no courage to do what causes no distress; to do what causes personal distress on a daily basis and to persevere is the very definition of courage. At a time of great personal anguish Sarah has been a great motivation and a harbour in a tempest. For that I am grateful, and gladly dedicate this work to her.

JAMES D. BOYS
Epsom Downs
Summer 2015

BIBLIOGRAPHY

Documents / Speeches

A full record of Hillary Clinton's legislative accomplishments can be found at https://www.congress.gov/member/hillary-clinton/C001041

Materials from Hillary Clinton's time as Secretary of State can be accessed at the State Department website: http://www.state.gov/secretary/ 20092013clinton/

Diane Blair's papers are available at the University of Arkansas's Special Collections Library in Fayetteville. A selection is available at the Free Beacon website: http://freebeacon.com/politics/the-hillary-papers/

An archive of Hillary Clinton's speeches since leaving the State Department is available at: http://hillaryspeeches.com

Previously declassified materials relating to Hillary Clinton from her time as First Lady are being released on a rolling basis and can be accessed via the Clinton Library website: http://www.clintonlibrary.gov/previouslyrestricteddocs.html

Hillary Clinton's emails as Secretary of State are being released on a rolling

basis and can be accessed via the State Department at: https://foia.state.gov/
search/results.aspx?collection=Clinton_Email

The Public Presidential Papers of Bill Clinton are available as part of the
Presidential Papers series, maintained by the US Government Printing Service:
http://www.gpo.gov/fdsys/browse/collection.action? collectionCode=PPP

The Presidential Papers of US administrations dating back to Hoover can be
accessed via the University of Michigan Digital Library: http://quod.lib.umich.
edu/p/ppotpus/

A range of presidential materials is available at the Clinton Presidential Library
website: http://www.clintonlibrary.gov/

Books/Reports/Papers

Albright, Madeleine. *Madam Secretary* (New York: Miramax Books, 2003)

Aldrich, Gary. *Unlimited Access* (Washington, DC: Regnery Publishing, 1998)

Alinsky, Saul. *Rules for Radicals: A Practical Primer for Realistic Radicals*
(New York: Random House, 1971)

Allen, Brooke. *Moral Minority* (Chicago: Ivan R. Dee Publisher, 2006)

Allen, Charles F. and Jonathan Portis. *The Comeback Kid: The Life and Career of
Bill Clinton* (New York: Birch Lane Press, 1992)

Allen, Jonathan and Amie Parnes. *HRC: State Secrets and the Rebirth of Hillary
Clinton* (New York: Hutchinson, 2014)

Ashmore, Harry. *Arkansas: A Bicentennial History* (New York: W. W. Norton,
1978)

Baker, Peter. 'Calculated Risks: Hillary Rodham Clinton's "Hard Choices"',
New York Times, 6 July 2014

Balz, Dan and Haynes Johnson. *The Battle for America: The Story of an Extraordinary Election* (London: Penguin Books, 2009)

Becker, Jo and Mike McIntire. 'The Clintons, The Russians and Uranium', *New
York Times*, 24 April 2015

Bedell Smith, Sally. *For the Love of Politics: The Clintons in the White House*
(New York: Aurum Press, 2008)

Berek, Richard L. 'Judge Withdraws From Clinton List For Justice Post', *New
York Times*, 6 February 1993

Bernstein, Carl. *A Woman In Charge: The Life of Hillary Rodham Clinton* (New York: Alfred A. Knopf, 2007)

Beschloss, Michael and Strobe Talbott. *At the Highest Levels: The Inside Story of the End of the Cold War* (Boston, MA: Little, Brown, 1993)

Blumenthal, Sidney. *The Clinton Wars* (New York: Farrar, Straus & Giroux, 2003)

Boys, James D. 'What's So Extraordinary About Rendition?' *The International Journal of Human Rights* 15, Issue 4, May 2011, pp 589–604

———. 'A Lost Opportunity: The Flawed Implementation of Assertive Multilateralism (1991–93)', *European Journal of American Studies* 7, No. 1, December 2012, pp 2–14

———. 'Exploiting Inherited Wars of Choice: Obama's Use of Nixonian Methods to Secure the Presidency', *American Politics Research* 42, No. 5, September 2014, pp 815–40

———. *Clinton's Grand Strategy: US Foreign Policy in a Post-Cold War World* (London: Bloomsbury, 2015)

———. 'The Presidential Manipulation of Inherited Wars of Choice: Barack Obama's Use of Nixonian Methods as Commander in Chief', *Congress & the Presidency* 42, No. 3, October 2015, pp 264–86

Branch, Taylor. *The Clinton Tapes: Wrestling History with the President* (New York: Simon & Schuster, 2009)

Brock, David. *The Seduction of Hillary Rodham* (New York: The Free Press, 1996)

———. *Blinded by the Right* (New York: Crown, 2002)

Bruck, Connie. 'Hillary the Pol', *New Yorker*, 30 May 1994

Brummett, John. *Highwire: From the Back Roads to the Beltway – The Education of Bill Clinton* (New York: Hyperion Books, 1994)

Calabresi, Massimo. 'Hillary Clinton and the Rise of Smart Power', *Time*, Vol. 178, No. 18, 7 November 2011, pp 18–25

Campbell, Colin and Bert A. Rockman (eds). *The Bush Presidency: First Appraisals* (Chatham, NJ: Chatham House, 1991)

Carpozi, George, Jr. *Clinton Confidential: The Climb to Power* (Del Mar, CA: Emery Dalton Books, 1995)

Carson, Clayborne (ed.). *The Papers of Martin Luther King, Jr. Vol. VI: Advocate of the Social Gospel September 1948 – March 1963* (Berkley, CA: University of California Press, 2007)

Carville, James and Mary Matalin. *All's Fair* (New York: Simon & Schuster, 1995)

Chernow, Ron. *Alexander Hamilton* (New York: Penguin, 2004)

Clarke, Richard A. *Against All Enemies: Inside America's War on Terror* (New York: Free Press, 2004)

Cleave, Maureen. 'How Does A Beatle Live? John Lennon Lives Like This', *Evening Standard*, 4 March 1966

Clinton, Hillary Rodham. *Hard Choices* (New York: Simon & Schuster, 2014)

————. America's Pacific Century', Op-Ed, *Foreign Policy*, 11 October 2011

————. *Living History* (New York: Simon & Schuster, 2003)

————. *Dear Socks, Dear Buddy* (New York: Simon & Schuster, 1998)

————. *It Takes a Village, and Other Lessons Children Teach Us* (New York: Simon & Schuster, 1996)

Cole, Steve. *Ghost Wars: The Secret History of the CIA, Afghanistan, and bin Laden, from the Soviet Invasion to September 10, 2001* (New York: Penguin Press, 2004)

Conason, Joe. *The Hunting of the President* (New York: St. Martin's Press, 2000)

————. 'The Third Term: The Dawning of a Different Sort of Post-Presidency', *Esquire*, December 2005

Cunningham, Noble E. Jr. *In Pursuit of Reason: The Life of Thomas Jefferson* (New York: Ballantine Books, 1987)

Drew, Elizabeth. *On the Edge: The Clinton Presidency* (New York: Simon & Schuster, 1994)

Dumas, Ernest (ed.). *The Clintons of Arkansas* (Fayetteville: University of Arkansas Press, 1993)

Ellis, Joseph J. *American Sphinx* (New York: Vintage Books, 1996)

————. *American Creation* (New York: Alfred A. Knopf, 2007)

Esler, Gavin. *The United States of Anger: The People and the American Dream* (London: Michael Joseph Ltd, 1997)

Flinn, Susan K. *Speaking of Hillary: A Reader's Guide to the Most Controversial Woman in America* (Ashland, Ore: White Cloud Press, 2000)

Fortini, Amanda. 'The Feminist Reawakening: Hillary Clinton and the Fourth Wave', *New York Magazine*, 21 April 2008

Friedman, Thomas L. 'Clinton Backs Raid but Muses About a New Start', *New York Times*, 14 January 1993

Fulbright, J. William. *The Arrogance of Power* (New York: Random House, 1967)

Gallen, David. *Bill Clinton as They Know Him* (New York: Gallen Publishing, 1994)

Gates, Robert M. *Duty: Memoirs of a Secretary at War* (New York: Alfred A. Knopf, 2014)

Gergen, David. *Eyewitness to Power* (New York: Simon & Schuster, 2001)

Ghattas, Kim. *The Secretary* (New York: Time Books, 2013)

Gitlin, Todd. *The Sixties: Years of Hope, Days of Rage* (New York: Bantam, 1987)

Glasser, Susan B. 'Was Hillary Clinton a Good Secretary of State? And Does it Matter?', *Politico*, 8 December 2013

Goldenberg, Suzanne. *Madam President* (London: Guardian Books, 2007)

Griffin, Michael. 'Smith Rips Bush's "Find A Husband" Tip For Women On Welfare', *Orlando Sentinel*, 7 September 1994

Green, Joshua. 'The Front-Runner's Fall', *The Atlantic Monthly*, September 2008

Halley, Patrick S. *On the Road with Hillary* (New York: Viking, 2002)

Hamilton, Nigel. *Bill Clinton: An American Journey* (New York: Random House, 2003)

Hartmann, Margaret. 'Hillary Admits Her Comments About Wealth Were "Inartful"', *New York Magazine*, 26 June 2014

Hastings, Michael. 'The Runaway General', *Rolling Stone*, 22 June 2010. Available at http://www.rollingstone.com/politics/news/the-runaway-general-20100622. Accessed 20 October 2015

Healy, Patrick D. 'Senator Clinton Calls for Withdrawal from Iraq to Begin in 2006', *New York Times*, 30 November 2005

Heilemann, John and Mark Halperin, *Game Change* (New York: HarperCollins, 2010)

Henriksen, Thomas H. *Clinton's Foreign Policy in Somalia, Bosnia, Haiti and North Korea* (Stanford, CA: Stanford University Press, 1996)

Hirsh, Michael. 'The Clinton Legacy: How Will History Judge the Soft-Power Secretary of State?' *Foreign Affairs*, Vol. 92, No. 3, May/June 2013, pp 82–91

———. 'The Talent Primary', *Newsweek* 150, Issue 12, 17 September 2007

Hirshman, Linda. '16 Ways of Looking At A Female Voter', *New York Times Magazine*, 2 February 2008

Isikoff, Michael. *Uncovering Clinton: A Reporter's Story* (New York: Crown, 1999)

Jackson, Robert L. 'Pace of Clinton Appointments not E-G-Gs-actly Swift',
      Los Angeles Times, 12 May 1993

Johnson, Rachel. *The Oxford Myth* (London: Weidenfeld Nicholson, 1988)

Karini, Annie. 'This time, Hillary Clinton embraces "gender card"', *Politico*,
      21 July 2015

Kelley, Virginia. *Leading with My Heart* (New York: Simon & Schuster, 1994)

Klein, Edward. *Blood Feud* (Washington, DC: Regnery Publishing, 2014)

Klein, Joe. 'The State of Hillary', *Time*, Vol. 174, No. 19, 16 November 2009,
      pp 16–25

————. *The Natural: The Misunderstood Presidency of Bill Clinton* (New York:
      Doubleday, 2002)

Krasner, Stephen D. 'An Orienting Principle for Foreign Policy', *Policy Review*,
      October 2010, No. 163, pp 3–5

Landler, Mark. 'Scare Adds to Fears That Clinton's Work Has Taken Toll', *New
      York Times*, 4 January 2013

Leibovich, Mark. 'Being Hillary', *New York Times Magazine*, 19 July 2015,
      pp 32–7, 52, 55

Levin, Robert E. *Clinton: The Inside Story* (New York: S. P. I. Books, 1992)

Limbacher, Carl. *Hillary's Scheme* (New York: Crown Forum, 2003)

Lizza, Ryan. 'The Iron Lady: The Clinton Campaign Returns From the Dead,
      Again', *New Yorker*, 17 March 2008

Luce, Edward and Daniel Dombey, 'US Foreign Policy: Waiting on a Sun
      King', *Financial Times*, 30 March 2010

Mann, James. *The Obamians* (New York: Viking, 2012)

Maraniss, David. *First in His Class* (New York: Simon & Schuster, 1995)

Margolick, David. 'Blair's Big Gamble', *Vanity Fair*, No. 514, June 2003

McCullough, David. *Truman* (New York: Simon & Schuster, 1992)

————. *John Adams* (New York: Simon & Schuster, 2001)

————. *1776* (New York: Simon & Schuster, 2005)

Mead, Walter Russell. 'Was Hillary Clinton a Good Secretary of State?'
      Washington Post, 30 May 2014

Milton, Joyce. *The First Partner* (New York: William Morrow, 1999)

Moore, Jim. *Clinton: Young Man in a Hurry* (Fort Worth: The Summit Group,
      1992)

Morris, Dick. *Behind the Oval Office* (New York: Random House, 1997)

————. *Off with Their Heads* (New York: Regan Books, 2003)

Morris, Roger. *Partners in Power: The Clintons and Their America* (New York: Henry Holt, 1996)

Morrison, Toni. 'Talk of the Town: Comment', *New Yorker*, 5 October 1998, pp 32–3

Morton, Andrew. *Monica's Story* (New York: St. Martin's Press, 1999)

Nelson, Rex. *The Hillary Factor* (New York: Gallen Publishing, 1993)

Newton-Small, Jay. 'How Clinton Lost Her Invincibility', *Time*, 23 December 2007.

Nye, Joseph. 'Get Smart: Combining Hard and Soft Power', *Foreign Affairs*, July/August 2009, pp 160–63

Oakley, Meredith L. *On the Make: The Rise of Bill Clinton* (Washington, DC: Regnery Publishing, 1994)

Olson, Barbara. *Hell to Pay* (Washington, DC: Regnery Publishing, 1994)

Osborne, Claire G. *The Unique Voice of Hillary Rodham Clinton* (New York: Avon Books, 1997)

Packer, George. 'The Choice', *The New Yorker*, 28 January 2008

Pear, Robert. 'A Go-Slow Plan on Health Gains Support in Congress', *New York Times*, 5 May 1994

Peretz, Evgenia. 'How Chelsea Clinton Took Charge of Clintonworld', *Vanity Fair*, September 2015

Radcliffe, Donnie. *Hillary Rodham Clinton: A First Lady for Our Time* (New York: Warner Books, 1993)

Rauch, Jonathan. *Demosclerosis* (New York: Random House, 1994)

Reeves, Richard. *President Kennedy: Profile of Power* (New York: Simon & Schuster, 1993)

Remnick, David. *The Bridge: The Life and Rise of Barack Obama* (London: Picador, 2010)

Renwick, Robin. *Ready for Hillary?* (London: Biteback Publishing, 2014)

Sang-hun, Choe. 'North Korea Takes to Twitter and YouTube', *New York Times*, 16 August 2010

Sanger, David E. *The Inheritance: The World Obama Confronts and the Challenges to American Power* (New York: Harmony Books, 2009)

Senior, Jennifer. 'The Once and Future President Clinton', *New York Magazine*, 21 February 2005

————. 'The Politics of Personality Destruction', *New York Magazine*, 11 June 2007

Sheehy, Gail. *Hillary's Choice* (New York: Random House, 1999)

————. 'What Hillary Wants', *Vanity Fair*, May 1992

Smith, Ben, Jen DiMascio and Laura Rozen, 'The Gates–Clinton Axis', *Politico*, 24 May 2010

Stephanopoulos, George. *All Too Human* (New York: Little, Brown, 1999)

Stewart, James B. *Blood Sport: The President and His Adversaries* (New York: Simon & Schuster, 1996)

Sullivan, Andrew. 'Goodbye To All That: Why Obama Matters', *The Atlantic Monthly*, December 2007

Walker, Martin. *The President They Deserve* (London: Fourth Estate, 1996)

Warner, Judith. *Hillary Clinton: The Inside Story* (New York: Penguin Publishing, 1993)

Willis, Gary. 'Reagan Country', *New York Times Magazine*, 11 August 1996

Woodward, Bob. *The Agenda: Inside the Clinton White House* (New York: Simon & Schuster 1994)

————. *Shadow: Five Presidents and the Legacy of Watergate* (New York: Simon & Schuster, 1999)

————. *Plan of Attack* (New York: Simon & Schuster, 2004)

ENDNOTES

1   David Brock, *The Seduction of Hillary Rodham* (New York: The Free Press, 1996), p. xi.
2   Hillary D. Rodham, 1969 Commencement Speech, Wellesley College, Massachusetts. Available in full at http://www.wellesley.edu/events/commencement/archives/1969commencement/studentspeech.
3   Kenneth Reece quoted in Judith Warner, *Hillary Clinton: The Inside Story* (New York: Penguin Publishing, 1993), p. 25.
4   Hillary Clinton quoted in 'Transcript of Interview with Hillary Clinton', *New York Times*, 6 July 2007. Available at http://www.nytimes.com/2007/07/06/us/politics/07clinton-text.html?pagewanted=print&_r=0
5   David Margolick, 'Blair's Big Gamble', *Vanity Fair*, Issue 514, June 2003. Available at http://www.vanityfair.com/news/2003/06/blair-200306
6   John Lennon quoted in Maureen Cleave, 'How Does A Beatle Live? John Lennon Lives Like This', *Evening Standard*, 4 March 1966.
7   Dr Martin Luther King, Jr, 'Communism's Challenge to Christianity', Sermon Outline, 9 August 1953. Reprinted in Clayborne Carson (ed.), *The Papers of Martin Luther King, Jr. Vol. VI: Advocate of the Social Gospel September 1948 – March 1963* (Berkley, CA: University of California Press, 2007), pp 146–50.
8   Hillary Clinton later wrote her thesis on Alinsky at Wellesley College.
9   Hillary Clinton, *Living History* (New York: Simon & Schuster, 2003), p. 23.

10   Hillary Rodham letter to John Peavoy, 13 April 1967. Quoted in Gail Sheehy, *Hillary's Choice* (New York: Random House, 1999), pp 47–53.

11   Hillary Rodham's senior thesis quoted in David Remnick, *The Bridge: The Life and Rise of Barack Obama* (London: Picador, 2010), p. 130.

12   Hillary Clinton, *Living History*, p. 40.

13   David Maraniss, *First In His Class* (New York: Simon & Schuster, 1995), p. 336.

14   Diane Blair, 'Of Darkness and of Light', in Ernest Dumas (ed.) *The Clintons of Arkansas* (Fayetteville: University of Arkansas Press, 1993), p. 63.

15   Ibid., p. 64.

16   Hillary Clinton quoted in Charles E. Allen and Jonathan Portis, *The Comeback Kid: The Life and Career of Bill Clinton* (New York: Birch Lane Press, 1992), p. 211.

17   Connie Bruck, 'Hillary the Pol', *New Yorker*, 30 May 1994.

18   See Suzanne Goldberg, *Madam President* (London: Guardian Books, 2007), p. 74.

19   Connie Bruck, 'Hillary the Pol', *New Yorker*, 30 May 1994.

20   Dinae Blair quoted in Carl Bernstein, *A Woman In Charge: The Life of Hillary Rodham Clinton* (New York: Alfred A. Knopf, 2007), p. 187.

21   Hillary Clinton, *Living History*, p. 93.

22   Dick Morris quoted in Maraniss, *First in His Class*, p. 407.

23   If Bill Clinton had been elected president in the 1988 election, he would have been forty-two years and 154 days old on inauguration day 1989, younger than Theodore Roosevelt by 168 days and younger than John F. Kennedy by one year and eighty-two days.

24   Memo from Celinda Lake and Stan Greenberg to the Clinton Campaign, Re: Research on Hillary Clinton, 12 May 1992, Diane Blair Papers, University of Arkansas, Fayetteville, Arkansas.

25   Gary Willis, 'Reagan Country', *New York Times Magazine*, 11 August 1996.

26   Larry Berman and Bruce W. Jentleson, 'Bush and the Post-Cold War World: New Challenges for American Leadership', in Colin Campbell and Bert A. Rockman (eds), *The Bush Presidency: First Appraisals* (Chatham, NJ: Chatham House, 1991), pp 93–128.

27   Quoted in Michael Beschloss and Strobe Talbott, *At the Highest Levels: The Inside Story of the End of the Cold War* (Boston, MA: Little, Brown, 1993), p. 434.

28   Gavin Esler, *The United States of Anger: The People and the American Dream* (London: Michael Joseph Ltd, 1997), p. 7.

29   Truman's involvement in the 1952 election is contradictory. He was not bound by the twenty-second Amendment to the Constitution that prevented Presidents from seeking a third term in office and his name was on the

New Hampshire Primary, which he lost to Estes Kefauver. However, in his memoir he insisted that he had no intention of running in 1952 and David McCullough's masterful text *Truman* reveals that the president announced this to his staff six months beforehand.

30 Hillary Clinton quoted in James L. 'Skip' Rutherford, 'Then We Serve', in Dumas (ed.), *The Clintons of Arkansas*, p. 146.

31 Bill Clinton remarks from Illinois Democratic Party candidates' debate, 15 March 1992, quoted in Martin Walker, *Clinton: The President They Deserve* (London: Fourth Estate, 1996), p. 130.

32 Transcript of Bill and Hillary Clinton interview with Steve Kroft on *60 Minutes*, CBS Television, 26 January 1992. Available at http://www.washingtonpost.com/wp-srv/politics/special/clinton/stories/flowers012792.htm. Accessed 15 July 2015.

33 Steve Kroft quoted in Gail Sheehy, *Hillary's Choice* (New York: Random House, 1999), p. 200.

34 Hillary Clinton quoted in Margaret Hartmann, 'Hillary Admits Her Comments About Wealth Were "Inartful"', *New York Magazine*, 26 June 2014.

35 Memo from Celinda Lake and Stan Greenberg to the Clinton Campaign, Re: Research on Hillary Clinton, 12 May 1992, Diane Blair Papers.

36 Bill Clinton quoted in Gail Sheehy, 'What Hillary Wants', *Vanity Fair*, May 1992.

37 Diane Blair, transcript of conversation with Hillary Clinton, 19 May 1993, Diane Blair Papers.

38 Hillary Clinton quoted in Taylor Branch, *The Clinton Tapes* (New York: Simon & Schuster, 2009), p. 343.

39 Jonathan Rauch, *Demosclerosis* (New York: Random House, 1994).

40 Robert L. Jackson, 'Pace of Clinton Appointments not E-G-Gs-actly Swift', *Los Angeles Times*, 12 May 1993.

41 David Gergen, *Eyewitness to Power* (New York: Simon & Schuster, 2001), p. 258.

42 Joe Klein, *The Natural: The Misunderstood Presidency of Bill Clinton* (New York: Doubleday, 2002), p. 47.

43 Richard L. Berek, 'Judge Withdraws From Clinton List For Justice Post', *New York Times*, 6 February 1993.

44 Memo from Celinda Lake and Stan Greenberg to the Clinton campaign, Re: Research on Hillary Clinton, 12 May 1992, Diane Blair Papers.

45 Diane Blair, transcript of conversation with Hillary Clinton, 1 February 1993, Diane Blair Papers.

46 Connie Bruck, 'Hillary the Pol', *New Yorker*, 30 May 1994.

47 Daniel Patrick Moynihan quoted in Robert Pear, 'A Go-Slow Plan on Health Gains Support in Congress', *New York Times*, 5 May 1994.

48   Robert Packwood quoted in 'Hearing Before the Committee on Finance United States Senate' (Washington, DC: US Government Printing Office, 4 May 1994), p. 16.

49   Hillary Clinton, *Living History*, p. 248.

50   Madeleine Albright, *Madam Secretary* (New York: Miramax Books, 2003), p. 340.

51   For more on this see James D. Boys, *Clinton's Grand Strategy: US Foreign Policy in a Post Cold War World* (London: Bloomsbury, 2015).

52   Diane Blair, transcript of conversation with Hillary Clinton, 9 September 1998, Diane Blair Papers.

53   Hillary Clinton interviewed by Mat Lauer, *Today*, NBC, 27 January 1998.

54   Diane Blair, transcript of conversation with Hillary Clinton, 9 September 1998, Diane Blair Papers.

55   Ibid.

56   Ibid., 3/4 February 1993.

57   Hillary Clinton, *Living History*, p. 506.

58   For full details of Hillary Clinton's legislative efforts in the United States Senate, visit www.congress.gov.

59   Lindsey Graham, 'Hillary Rodham Clinton', *Time*, 8 May 2006.

60   Hillary Clinton quoted in *Congressional Record*, 12 September 2001, pp 168–70.

61   Bill Clinton quoted in Thomas L. Friedman, 'Clinton Backs Raid but Muses About a New Start', *New York Times*, 14 January 1993.

62   Hillary Clinton quoted in Patrick D. Healy, 'Senator Clinton Calls for Withdrawal from Iraq to Begin in 2006', *New York Times*, 30 November 2005.

63   Robert M. Gates, *Duty: Memoirs of a Secretary at War* (New York: Alfred A. Knopf, 2014), p. 376.

64   David Remnick, *The Bridge*, p. 400.

65   Jay Newton-Small, 'How Clinton Lost Her Invincibility', *Time*, 23 December 2007.

66   Hillary Clinton quoted in John Heilemann and Mark Halperin, *Game Change* (New York: HarperCollins, 2010), p. 183.

67   See James D. Boys, *Clinton's Grand Strategy: US Foreign Policy in a Post-Cold War World* (London: Bloomsbury, 2015)

68   Unclassified US Department of State Case No. F-2014-20439 Doc. No. C05762290, 'No WH mtg', 12 June 2009. Released 30 June 2015.

69   Joseph Nye, 'Get Smart: Combining Hard and Soft Power', *Foreign Affairs*, July/August 2009, pp 160–63.

70   Unclassified US Department of State Case No. F-2014-20439 Doc. No. C05775537, 'Re: Update on your trip to Doha', 26 April 2010. Released 31 August 2015.

71 For more on the Nixon–Obama analogy see James D. Boys, 'Exploiting Inherited Wars of Choice: Obama's Use of Nixonian Methods to Secure the Presidency', *American Politics Research*, September 2014, Vol. 42, No. 5, pp 815–40. See also James D. Boys. 'The Presidential Manipulation of Inherited Wars of Choice: Barack Obama's Use of Nixonian Methods as Commander-In-Chief', *Congress & the Presidency* 42, No. 3, October 2015, pp 264–86.

72 Unclassified US Department of State Case No. F-2014-20439 Doc. No. C05774478, 'Yo-Yo Ma', 23 October 2010. Released 31 August 2015.

73 Unclassified US Department of State Case No. F-2014-20439 Doc. No. C05769909, 'Re: I-Pad Questions', 24 July 2010. Released 31 August 2015.

74 Unclassified US Department of State Case No. F-2014-20439 Doc. No. C0576288, 'Re: can you hang up the fax line, they will call again and try fax', 23 December 2009. Released 30 June 2015.

75 Unclassified US Department of State Case No. F-2014-20439 Doc. No. C05774081, '1st known case of a successful social media campaign in Syria', 24 September 2010. Released 31 August 2015.

76 Anne-Marie Slaughter quoted in Susan B. Glasser, 'Was Hillary Clinton a Good Secretary of State? And Does it Matter?' *Politico*, 8 December 2013.

77 Unclassified US Department of State Case No. F-2014-20439 Doc. No. C05771289, 'For the CFR speech: A New American Century', 4 September 2010. Released 31 August 2015.

78 Unclassified US Department of State Case No. F-2014-20439 Doc. No. C0576615, 'Re: New memo. Decline and fall, etc. Cheers, Sid', 26 November 2009. Released 31 August 2015.

79 Unclassified US Department of State Case No. F-2014-20439 Doc. No. C0577O101: 'Memo on UK politics/budget/economy Sid', 27 June 2010. Released 31 August 2015.

80 Edward Luce and Daniel Dombey, 'US Foreign Policy: Waiting on a Sun King', *Financial Times*, 30 March 2010.

81 Author's interview with J. F. O. McAllister (*Time* State Department correspondent 1989–95, White House correspondent 1995–97, Washington Deputy Bureau Chief 1998–99), 28 February 2014.

82 James Man, *The Obamians* (New York: Viking, 2012), p. 20.

83 Unclassified US Department of State Case No. F-2014-20439 Doc. No. C0576243, 'Aw Shucks', 19 June 2009. Released 30 June 2015.

84 Michael Hirsh, 'The Talent Primary', *Newsweek* 150, Issue 12, 17 September 2007, p. 36.

85 James Mann, *The Obamians*, pp 229–40.

86 '"Hillary Clinton's a monster": Obama aide blurts out attack in Scotsman interview', *The Scotsman.com*. http://www.scotsman.com/news/hillary-clinton-s-a-monster-obama-aide-blurts-out-attack-in-scotsman-interview-1-1158300

87 Unclassified US Department of State Case No. F-2014-20439 Doc. No. C05771923, 'WikiLeaks', 28 November 2010. Released 31 August 2015.

88 The Five Eyes group consists of the United States, the United Kingdom, Australia, Canada and New Zealand. The group work together under the auspices of the UKUSA Agreement to share Signals Intelligence.

89 Hillary Rodham Clinton, 'America's Pacific Century', Op-Ed, *Foreign Policy*, 11 October 2011.

90 Unclassified US Department of State Case No. F-2014-20439 Doc. No. C05768307, 'Re: H: If this poll holds, Labour has a majority. 1st debate thu. Sid', 13 April 2010. Released 31 August 2015.

91 Unclassified US Department of State Case No. F-2014-20439 Doc. No. C05770267, 'H: Sunday am report UK. I return later today to DC. Sid', 9 May 2010. Released 31 August 2015.

92 Ibid.

93 Ibid.

94 Unclassified US Department of State Case No. F-2014-20439 Doc. No. C05774888, 'H: IMPORTANT. Memo for Hague meeting. Sid', 13 May 2010. Released 31 August 2015.

95 Unclassified US Department of State Case No. F-2014-20439 Doc. No. C05774171, 'Subject: H: Labour Party leadership vote... Sid', 25 September 2010. Released 31 August 2015.

96 Unclassified US Department of State Case No. F-2014-20439 Doc. No. C05774171, 'Fw: (AP) – Ed Miliband is new UK Labour Party leader', 25 September 2015. Released 31 August 2015.

97 Unclassified US Department of State Case No. F-2014-20439 Doc. No. C05775219, 'From David Miliband', 29 September 2010. Released 31 August 2015.

98 Unclassified US Department of State Case No. F-2014-20439 Doc. No. C05772695, 'H: when you have time... Sid', 11 October 2010. Released 31 August 2015.

99 Hillary Clinton, 'Remarks at Forum for the Future', Doha, Qatar, 13 January 2011.

100 Ibid.

101 Unclassified US Department of State Case No. F-2014-20439 Doc. No. C05768650, 'Mrs Mubarak', 20 April 2010. Released 31 August 2015.

102 Anne-Marie Slaughter quoted in Michael Hirsh, 'The Clinton Legacy: How Will History Judge the Soft-Power Secretary of State?', *Foreign Affairs*, May/June 2013, Vol. 92, No. 3, pp 82–91.

103 Walter Russell Mead, 'Was Hillary Clinton a Good Secretary of State?', *Washington Post*, 30 May 2014.

104 Dr Susan Rice remained as UN ambassador for the initial duration of Obama's second term until she was appointed National Security Advisor in July 2013, a post that did not require Senate approval.

105 Ben Smith, Jen DiMascio and Laura Rozen, 'The Gates–Clinton Axis', *Politico*, 24 May 2010, http://www.politico.com/news/stories/0510/37672.html.

106 Michael Hastings, 'The Runaway General', *Rolling Stone*, 22 June 2010. Available at http://www.rollingstone.com/politics/news/the-runaway-general-20100622. Accessed 20 October 2015.

107 Unclassified US Department of State Case No. F-2014-20439 Doc. No. C05769909, 'Re: Rolling Stone', 21 June 2010. Released 31 August 2015.

108 Brent Scowcroft quoted in Massimo Calabresi, 'Hillary Clinton and the Rise of Smart Power', *Time*, 7 November 2011, Vol. 178, No. 18, p. 24.

109 Choe Sang-hun, 'North Korea Takes to Twitter and YouTube', *New York Times*, 16 August 2010.

110 Pew Research Center, *Global Opposition to US Surveillance and Drones, but Limited Harm to America's Image*, http://www.pewglobal.org/2014/07/14/chapter-1-the-american-brand/

111 Author's interview with Anthony Lake (Assistant to the President for National Security Affairs 1993–97), 14 September 2004.

112 Thomas H. Henriksen, *Clinton's Foreign Policy in Somalia, Bosnia, Haiti and North Korea* (Stanford, CA: Stanford University Press, 1996), p. 39.

113 Stephen D. Krasner, 'An Orienting Principle for Foreign Policy', *Policy Review*, October 2010, No. 163, pp 3–5.

114 Author's interview with Morton Halperin (Consultant to the Secretary of Defense and the Under Secretary of Defense for Policy 1993; Special Assistant to the President and Senior Director for Democracy at the National Security Council 1994–96; Director of the Policy Planning Staff 1998–2001), 22 June 2004.

115 Hillary Clinton in conversation with Dr Robin Niblett, Chatham House Prize 2013, 11 October 2013.

116 Susan B. Glasser, 'Was Hillary Clinton a Good Secretary of State?'

117 For more on Bill Clinton's determination to establish himself as a New Democrat see James D. Boys, *Clinton's Grand Strategy* (London: Bloomsbury, 2015)

118 Peter Baker, 'Calculated Risks: Hillary Rodham Clinton's "Hard Choices"', *New York Times*, 6 July 2014.

119 Jo Becker and Mike McIntire, 'The Clintons, The Russians and Uranium', *New York Times*, 24 April 2015.

120 For more on the founding era and the principles that defined the United
     States see Brooke Allen, *Moral Minority* (Chicago: Ivan R. Dee Publisher,
     2006); Joseph J. Ellis, *American Creation* (New York: Alfred A. Knopf, 2007);
     David McCullough, *1776* (New York: Simon & Schuster, 2005); Noble E.
     Cunningham, Jr, *In Pursuit of Reason: The Life of Thomas Jefferson* (New
     York: Ballantine Books, 1987); David McCullough, *John Adams* (New York:
     Simon & Schuster, 2001); Ron Chernow, *Alexander Hamilton* (New York:
     Penguin, 2004); and Joseph J. Ellis, *American Sphinx* (New York: Vintage
     Books, 1996).

121 As it did in the election of 2000, to Al Gore's chagrin.

122 This is the same Sam Adams that the rather excellent beer is named for.

123 The Daley family dominated Chicago politics with Richard J. Daley and his
     son Richard M. Daley, serving as mayor from 1955–76 and from 1997–2000
     respectively. Richard J. Daley's son William served as Commerce Secretary
     in the administration of Bill Clinton from 1997 to 2000. The Brown family
     in California have been influential at a gubernatorial level with Edmund
     'Pat' Brown serving as governor from 1959 to 1967 and his son Edmund 'Jerry'
     Brown serving as governor from 1975 to 1983 and from 2011 to the present
     day. The Cabots dominated Massachusetts politics until being eclipsed by
     the Kennedys, when JFK defeated Henry Cabot Lodge in the Senate race of
     1952. The Stevenson family was particularly influential in Illinois, with four
     generations representing the state and the nation at the highest levels. The
     Udall family of Arizona have held office since the nineteenth century and
     have members in the United States Senate as of 2015.

124 Al Gore Sr was a United States Senator; his son Al Gore Jr was a Senator,
     Vice-President and defeated presidential candidate in the 2000 election.
     George Romney was Governor of Michigan; his son Mitt was Governor of
     Massachusetts and the defeated presidential candidate in the 2012 election.
     Ron Paul was a member of Congress from 1979 to 1985 and from 1997 to the
     present and sought the presidency in 1988, 2008 and 2012. His son, Rand, is
     a US Senator and a presidential candidate in 2016.

125 George H. W. Bush (Ambassador to the UN, Representative to China,
     Director of the CIA, Vice-President 1981–89, President 1989–93), George
     W. Bush (Governor of Texas 1995–2001, President 2001–09), Theodore
     Roosevelt (Governor of New York, Vice-President, President 1901–09),
     Franklin Roosevelt, (Governor of New York, President 1933–45), Joseph P.
     Kennedy (Ambassador to London), John F. Kennedy (Congressman 1947–53,
     Senator 1953–61, President 1961–63), Robert F. Kennedy (Attorney General
     1961–64, US Senator 1964–68), Edward Kennedy (US Senator), Patrick J.
     Kennedy (Congress), Joseph P. Kennedy II (Congress), Joseph P. Kennedy
     III (Congress), Caroline Kennedy (Ambassador to Japan 2013–).

126 Chelsea Clinton's daughter, Charlotte Clinton Mezvinsky, was born on 26 September 2014, seven months prior to Hillary Clinton's announcement that she would seek the presidency for a second time.

127 See Evgenia Peretz, 'How Chelsea Clinton Took Charge of Clintonworld', *Vanity Fair*, September 2015.

128 Supplemental Nutrition Assistance Program (Food Stamp) data provided by US Department of Agriculture.

129 Michael Griffin, 'Smith Rips Bush's "Find A Husband" Tip For Women On Welfare', *Orlando Sentinel*, 7 September 1994.

130 Annie Karini, 'This time, Hillary Clinton embraces "gender card"', *Politico*, 21 July 2015, http://www.politico.com/story/2015/07/this-time-hillary-embraces-gender-card-120441.html?hp=t4_r

131 Hillary Clinton, testimony before the Senate Foreign Relations Committee, 23 January 2013.

132 Heilemann & Halperin, *Game Change*, pp 34–5.

133 Toni Morrison, 'Talk of the Town: Comment', *New Yorker*, 5 October 1998, p. 32.

134 Monmouth University National Poll, 15 July 2015. Available at http://www.monmouth.edu/assets/0/32212254770/32212254991/32212254992/32212254994/32212254995/30064771087/947b4d56-8c7b-4dd4-a2e3-d36b1c78d231.pdf

135 Public Policy Polling material available at http://www.publicpolicypolling.com/pdf/2015/PPP_Release_NH_82515.pdf

136 As occurred in the election of 2008 when President George W. Bush left office after two terms and his Vice-President, Dick Cheney, chose not to run.

137 Lauren Leatherby, 'Hillary Clinton Returns To A Very Different Arkansas', *NPR.com*, 18 July 2015. http://www.npr.org/sections/itsallpolitics/2015/07/18/423890622/hillary-clinton-returns-to-a-very-different-arkansas?utm_source=twitter.com&utm_campaign=politics&utm_medium=social&utm_term=nprnew

138 Unclassified US Department of State Case No. F-2014-20439 Doc. No. C05773O2, 'Happy New Year!', 3 January 2010. Released 31 August 2015.

139 Unclassified US Department of State Case No. F-2014-20439 Doc. No. C05777269, 'Confidential', 30 June 2010. Released 31 August 2015.

140 Unclassified US Department of State Case No. F-2014-20439 Doc. No. C05774155, 'Re: Masked 'Hillary Clinton' robs Va. Bank', 30 December 2010. Released 31 August 2015.

141 Hillary Clinton quoted in Warner, *Hillary Clinton*, p. 71.

142 Memo from Celinda Lake and Stan Greenberg to the Clinton Campaign, Re: Research on Hillary Clinton, 12 May 1992, Diane Blair Papers.

143 Sally Bedell Smith, *For Love of Politics: The Clintons in the White House* (London: Aurum Books, 2007), p. 10.

144 Unclassified US Department of State Case No. F-2014-20439 Doc. No. C05775464, 'Note for HRC from Bono and All', 26 October 2010. Released 31 August 2015.

145 Unclassified US Department of State Case No. F-2014-20439 Doc. No. C0577302, 'Happy New Year!', 3 January 2010. Released 31 August 2015.

146 Meredith L. Oakley, *On the Make: The Rise of Bill Clinton* (Washington, DC: Regnery Publishing, 1994), pp 92–3.

147 Unclassified US Department of State Case No. F-2014-20439 Doc. No. C05771759, 'From Harvey Weinstein', 20 August 2010. Released 31 August 2015.

148 Mickey Kantor quoted in Bedell Smith, *For Love of Politics*, p. 10.

149 Keach Hagey, 'Hillary Unveils Her Biggest Asset in Iowa', CBS, 3 July 2007. http://www.cbsnews.com/news/hillary-unveils-her-biggest-ally-in-iowa/

150 Memo from Celinda Lake and Stan Greenberg to the Clinton Campaign, Re: Research on Hillary Clinton, 12 May 1992, Diane Blair Papers.

151 Hillary Clinton, *Living History*, p. 446.

152 Maggie Haberman, 'Clinton Ally pens e-book: The Benghazi Hoax', *Politico*, http://www.politico.com/story/2013/10/clinton-ally-pens-e-book-the-benghazi-hoax-98563_Page2.html

INDEX